THE ROCKY MOUNTAIN REVOLUTION

STEWART HOLBROOK

Kenmore, WA

NORTH WEST CORNER BOOKS

Northwest Corner books, an imprint of Epicenter Press Inc., publishes reprints of out of print titles about the Pacific Northwest. For more information, visit www.EpicenterPress.com

Originally published by Owl Publications, Inc. in 1956
Published by arrangement with Epicenter Press, Inc.

Cover prepress and interior design by Aubrey White

© Stewart H. Holbrook, 1956, 2018

Cover image: Library of Congress Prints and Photographs Division Washington, D.C., LC-DIG-ds-10032.
Cover illustration for *The Masses*, a monthly magazine devoted to the interests of the working people, June 1914. Illustration shows mine worker firing a gun after his wife and children were killed in a massacre at their tent camp by the Colorado National Guard and Colorado Fuel & Iron Company camp guards.

ISBN: 978-1-941890-28-8
ISBN: 978-1-941890-29-5

Library of Congress Control Number: 2018958083

Produced in the United States of America

Contents

Introduction: A Dean of Prisoners ... vii
Part One: ... 1
   1. The Whole life of Albert Horsley ... 3
Part Two: ... 11
   2. Fear Was in the Canyon ... 13
   3. The Second Battle of Bunker Hill ... 22
   4. The Great Diaspora ... 33
   5. A Jolly Miner on the Lam ... 40
   6. Cripple Creek: Background ... 43
   7. Orchard, the High-Grader ... 56
Part Three: ... 65
   8. The Tearing of Things Loose ... 67
   9. On the Care of Goons ... 76
   10. Independence Depot ... 83
   11. "…Maketh Thunder & Ruin" ... 92
   12. Bill Haywood Considered ... 100
   13. A Package for Mr. Bradley ... 109
   14. Poor Merritt Walley ... 121
   15. The Wobblies Are Born ... 136
   16. Murder is a Lonely Job ... 144
   17. The Big One ... 153
   18. A Man Almost Unnerved ... 163

Part Four: 173
    19. Confession 175
    20. Orchard, the Witness 181
    21. Mr. Darrow & Mr. Borah 192
    22. The Enigma of Harvey Brown 200
Part Five 213
    23. A Ward of the State 215
    24. He Reads the Papers 220
    25. The Shadows Grow Longer 224
    26. A Goth Survives Them All 232
Acknowledgments 239
Bibliography 241
Index 245

Introduction

A Dean of Prisoners

Boise lay sweltering in the dry heat of August in the intermountain region. The piles of brick and stone and concrete which composed the Idaho penitentiary stood in a brief spot of green at the base of yellow-brown hills that looked stark and grim to eyes unaccustomed to sagebrush. I had come here to call on a once celebrated criminal who went by the name of Harry Orchard, a professional killer of considerable stature. His record had long been familiar to me. There was nothing of the Western Bad Man in it, no flavor of the Daltons, of Harry Tracy, of Billy the Kid. Yet from none of these perhaps had emanated such unease as Orchard brought to much of Western United States.

He was a new type of killer. What interested me more than his technique, however, was the fact that he had more than a little to do with making the reputations of William E. Borah, Clarence Darrow, and William Dudley Haywood. In addition to his influence on the careers of these men, Orchard's activities had a lasting effect on what had been the most powerful labor union in the West. Meanwhile, he outlived the men he helped to make famous. He outlived the Western Federation of Miners which he helped to wreck. He outlived his era. For nearly half a century he remained in prison, a slowly fading legend, to die at eighty-eight just the other day. By then he was virtually forgotten. To most Americans the obituaries in the newspapers might just as well have had to do with some obscure Gothic character of the Middle Ages. This was so because no dime novelist had sought to immortalize him, nor had a movie scenarist. Possibly his career was judged too improbable for pulp or fiction.

I had come, as I said, to see the greatest hatchet man of his time. A blistering sun beat down on the prison yard as the warden led me to a little shack next to the chicken and turkey pens inside the Big Wall. Not a breath was stirring. The blazing sunlight made everything sharp, life-size. It was Sunday. The prison quiet was intense. We went into the comparable gloom of the shack and were welcomed by Harry Orchard.

I saw a stocky, healthy man, actually seventy-four years old but looking and acting and talking like one of sixty or less. His florid and tanned face had a pleasant smile. His eyes were clear and blue, his hair sandy and thinning. He was about five feet seven inches. He had broad shoulders. There was no trace of prison softness about him. The number on the back of his overalls was 1406. Since he had acquired that number, in January 1906, almost six thousand other men and a few women had entered the establishment.

Warden P. C. Meridith had given me to understand that Orchard had long since refused to discuss his criminal past with reporters, or with anyone save "close religious friends." Among these, as I knew, were Mrs. Frank Steunenberg, Sr., widow of Orchard's last victim, and Elder Frank Steunenberg, Jr., of the Seventh-Day Adventist Church. The fact that I knew the Steunenbergs, even if slightly, was made known to Orchard by the warden, who saw fit also to mention the "rather astounding" fact that, although a newspaperman, I no longer drank liquor. Orchard fairly beamed, even after I hastily explained that my teetotal regime was in no manner due to religious convictions but to matters of health.

The old prisoner had been sitting in a rocker when we came, reading Adventist literature, and at first our talk turned to William Miller, the Vermont preacher generally credited with being the Prophet of that church and with whose history I had some knowledge. The warden soon left us, and a little later Orchard got out a pile of neat manuscript he kept under the pillow of his iron cot. I saw it was in autobiographical form. It was still in progress. He told me he hoped it would appear as a book under some title to indicate it was "a sequel to the confessions of Harry Orchard, after thirty-five years in prison." He said it would deal chiefly with the subject of reformation. "It goes pretty slow," he said. "My dislike and unfitness for writing make it uphill sledding. But I am determined to finish it in order to let the world know of the transforming power of Jesus Christ." He paused a moment, then added, "Had it not been for Him, nobody would ever have known my story."

On the wall of Orchard's little house was a homemade bookshelf. I noticed it held mostly religious books and what are known in the trade as inspirational works. There was *The Hope of the World*, *Prisons and Prayer*, *Education and the Will*, a biography of General William Booth, the Salvation Army man, and another entitled *Theodore Roosevelt, First American*.

Our talk turned at last away from religion. "I like chickens and turkeys," said Orchard. "I still hope to get outside this place for a few years before I die. I'd like to make some experiments with the cross-breeding of chickens which aren't possible here in prison." He said he hadn't given much thought to getting a parole or pardon until he became interested in poultry. He applied once, in 1921, for a pardon. It was not granted.

The conversation came finally to the specific crime that had brought him to prison, and also to some of the many other crimes he had committed but of which he had never been suspected, much less arrested. Indeed, during a busy decade of crime studded with wife desertion, bigamy, burglary, arson, assorted larceny, and some twenty-odd murders, he was arrested but once. I asked him many questions. Though answering them could have given him no joy, he remained serene and objective, speaking quite freely, using no euphemisms. Only once, I thought, did he reveal any emotion. When I mentioned Big Bill Haywood's name, Harry Orchard's blue eyes narrowed and glowed like live coals. "Haywood," he said, "was certainly no friend of the working class."

We sat and talked out the long hot afternoon, while the air of the prison yard was filled with the drone of August insects and an occasional baying from the penitentiary bloodhounds in their nearby kennels. I watched to see if the mournful voices of the dogs had an effect on Orchard, who, as I knew, had often smeared his shoes with turpentine, or used pepper, to preclude tracking. None was visible. Bemused at sitting by this man whom Mr. Darrow had told me had "ice water for blood and no nerves whatever," I took out a cigarette and lighted it. Orchard sat back in his chair and looked me in the eye. He was displeased. He clucked. "Young man," he said, both reproach and warning in his voice, "don't you know that those things lead to crime?" For a moment I thought it a mere pleasantry. But no, this killer of twenty-odd men was serious. To him tobacco was the weed of the Pit that hath no bottom. I was patently in danger.

I realized I had lost stature in Orchard's eyes, yet my slip did not put an end to our discussions. He continued to talk easily of things and people—the mine in the Coeur d' Alenes in which he once owned an interest; of Mr. Darrow, Mr. Borah, and Detective McParlan; of the hotel in Caldwell, Idaho, where "something caused me to lose my reasoning power."

The shadows in the prison yard grew longer. Twilight came on. I needed another smoke but abstained rather than risk giving further offense to a man who, after all, had treated me with courtesy and was doing his level best to tell me how it had been in the time when Harry Orchard and the Devil himself ranged together all over the West, leaving death and sorrow and horror in their wake.

Only by some effort of the imagination was I able to dissolve the picture of this commonplace figure, rocking comfortably in his homemade chair, and replace it with an image of Orchard the dynamite man. It wasn't that I was naive in regard to the appearance of criminals. I had seen a sufficient number of them to know there was nothing on the surface to distinguish a murderer from a thief or, for that matter, from a saint. Yet, Harry Orchard in his rocker all but obliterated the Destroying Angel of his legend.

When I first saw him, thirty-five years after his valedictory crime, Orchard was still a legend of dread in the hard-rock mining camps and in many other parts of Western United States. One saw him plainly in the legend of the Coeur d' Alenes, aboard a train running wild down Burke Canyon; one watched him packing a box of giant powder to the Bunker Hill & Sullivan concentrator; then on the lam ahead of posses and bloodhounds over the hump into Montana. He appears again in Colorado, in the Cripple Creek legend, high-grading rich lodes of ore between spells of blowing up mine bosses, shaft houses, railroad stations, and a whole shift of nonunion miners. One sees him again as Thomas S. Hogan, riding the steam cars to lethal jobs in Utah and Nevada, in California and Idaho, beside him on a seat in the smoker his black valise.

This valise is his professional bag. It has been packed with care. In it are his groceries, namely, a bottle of whisky, a can of cayenne pepper, and the equipment of his calling—a neat package of No. 1 Gelatin powder in sticks, a box of detonating caps, a vial of sulphuric acid, some plaster of Paris, an alarm clock, a few lengths of stout linen fish line, a roll of fine wire; together with miscellaneous small hardware including a jackknife, an awl, and screw eyes; perhaps a round drugstore-type box of strychnine crystals; and, for emergencies, a loaded revolver. Up in the baggage car ahead rides his trunk. In it are several suits and assorted work clothes; a repeating shotgun and ammunition to fit; and a twenty-five-pound bomb suitable for "heavy work," a sort of multipurpose job that can be activated manually, or by contact, or by means of an alarm clock.

Such, briefly, was the legendary Orchard. Few legends have so much real substance as those about him. Unlike most if not all Western Bad Men, Harry Orchard needed no embroidery. The record was clear. It could be verified by the admissions to morgues and undertaking parlors and hospitals. Unlike so many popular Bad Men, Orchard's career did not lend itself readily to the Robin Hood myth. He neither robbed the rich nor gave to the poor. He was strictly a professional, all business. As a lethal character, he possibly stood alone. He was beyond embroidery. Legend could add little or nothing to his career.

When I bade him good-bye that evening, I could not shake off the feeling that the man I had been with all day was not the Orchard responsible for so much violence. I could not resist believing for the moment there must have been two Orchards—I mean two different physical beings, separate entities, unrelated the one to the other. The feeling, of course, passed. It did not return later during a correspondence over a long period. Yet, as a personality, I still recall him long after, perfectly cast as the alert, genial, and kindly past-president of almost any of the lunch-and-talk groups generically known in the United States as service clubs.

Part One:

The Businessman

1.

The Whole life of Albert Horsley

"It takes a lot of patience," observed Harry Orchard, "to produce good cheese." He made this casual bucolic remark when late in life he turned to confront his past in an effort to explain to himself and to others what had brought him into the shadow of the gibbet. He was trying hard to get back to the very root of his troubles. He put no trust whatever in psychiatry or in little else save the Old Rugged Cross, yet his notion about the relationship of cheese and patience may have been, even if unwittingly, fairly close to the mark.

He was born Albert E. Horsley on March 18, 1866, in Northumberland County, Ontario, when that British province was known as Upper Canada. One of his grandfathers was an immigrant from England, the other from Ireland. Little is known about them, though both were, according to their grandson, somewhat given to strong drink. Albert's parents were farming people. His father was a harsh man to his two sons and six daughters. He was also an incompetent. One after the other, as the youngsters were put out "to work for wages," the old man showed up to collect the few dollars they had earned and which he needed, he said, to finance his farm. Had it not been for the devoted mother, Albert would have early in boyhood run away from home.

Albert's schooling comprised a few terms which, all together, brought him through the third grade. Church and Sunday school, however, were a regular thing until he was almost twenty-one and went to work in the bush. Working in the bush was logging. After some local experience with ax and cant dog, young Albert took off for Michigan, where wages were higher than in Ontario, and became an axman, or chopper, at a camp in the wonderfully great white pines along the Tittabawassee River which, with streams named Flint and Cass and Shiawassee, united to form the fabled Saginaw and flow into Lake Huron at Bay City.

Twelve miles upriver from the lake stood Saginaw City, the lumber-making colossus of the world. The sawmills clustered here, together with those which hemmed the river at Bay City, cut one billion feet of pine into lumber a season, and for good measure sawed three hundred millions of shingles. The logs from which to make this stupendous pile of lumber were harvested along the upper reaches of the four tributaries, then driven down to the waiting saws.

It was the hallowed custom of the loggers to break their winter's work with a brief visit at Christmas time to the fleshpots of Saginaw City, a town whose second industry was inadequately described as the supplying of fun, frolic, and fighting; and among the six or seven thousand men from the woods who came to holiday there, during the last week of 1888, was young Albert Horsley. "I never," he was to recall late in life, "I never in all my experience saw a rougher, tougher place than Saginaw City." Although the similar observations of lifelong lumberjacks became in time almost a cliché, this statement made in his age by a man who knew intimately such cities as Butte, Denver, and San Francisco in their heyday, and the far from genteel towns of Cripple Creek and Telluride, Colorado, and even little Burke Canyon, Idaho, is comment worthy the consideration of any historian of Michigan's old lumber capital.

The gaslights of Saginaw City must have brightened the eyes of Water Street girls and put a glint into the forty-rod sold along that lively thoroughfare. "I was captivated by it," the old man who had known it in '88 admitted, "and it was my first experience with immorality and wickedness. There for the first time I became intoxicated." The grog made him deathly sick, he remembered, and of course he thought he should never touch it again. He could not have caroused very long that season, however, for in the spring he had sufficient wages coming to return to Ontario and to marry "Florence, a Scotch lassie."

Now we come to the cheese business. The manufacture of cheese was the leading industry in Orchard's native part of Northumberland County. Florence was already an expert cheese maker. The newlyweds rented an old factory, which appears to have been a building of modest size, and started in. Florence took charge of the actual manufacture. Albert made the rounds of the farms, collecting milk, and attended to the marketing of the finished product.

All went well for a time, for Florence was a hard worker and also dedicated to her craft in a community that set and demanded high standards for its chief product. But Albert seems not to have understood the necessity of getting clean fresh milk, or the need of exactness in pressing the new cheese, or the niceties of the aging or ripening process. Making good cheese, so he gradually discovered, did call for a great deal of patience, more patience, indeed, than Albert Horsley thought it merited. Meanwhile, he had become something of a man of affairs, driving about the country in a fast rig, attending the cheese auctions, joining a couple of lodges, drinking moderately, and doing a little gambling with lodge brothers.

He also looked around for any short cuts that might bring a decent profit from cheese without the expenditure of so much time as his wife held necessary. He found them. He began systematically to short-weigh the milk he bought and to short weigh the cheese he sold. He made "deals" with the county cheese inspectors. He mixed in local politics, which seems to have included the cheese board of trade—a powerful body in any dairy district of Ontario of the time—and once went so far as to purchase votes for a member of the provincial parliament. Something or other slipped. Young Horsley was threatened with prosecution and saved himself only by fast and effective perjury.

The petty-larceny dealings at the factory did not pay off very well, and, when a competitor offered to buy the Horsley factory and business, Albert insisted that they sell. He and his wife then took over a factory owned by a cheese company, with some sort of arrangement to operate it on shares. Albert managed to borrow enough cash to start construction of still another factory, and sufficient credit to finish it. This new project was in Brighton, several miles from the other factory. While the building was going up, Albert boarded with a Brighton man and his wife identified as Mr. and Mrs. S. "I became infatuated with the woman," he confessed.

In order to "go West and start all over again," Horsley first insured his new factory. A few months later, "on a moonless night," he crept through the streets of Brighton, a can of kerosene in one hand, a bundle of excelsior in the other. He collected eight hundred dollars on this, his first job of arson.

Mrs. Horsley had given birth to a daughter. Albert moved wife and child to the home of relatives. Then he dropped out of sight so manifestly that neither his wife nor others in the community were to know what had become of him until years later. What he did was to take a train to Detroit. Mrs. S. also disappeared from her home and went to Detroit. The happy couple registered at a hotel as Mr. and Mrs. John Little.

The unhallowed honeymoon in the Michigan city lasted one week. By then the apple in the Garden had been tasted to surfeit, and the fruit was sour. Mr. and Mrs. Little admitted to one another they had made a mistake. Yet they were too deeply involved to return to Northumberland County, Ontario. They bought railroad tickets to Nelson, British Columbia.

Nelson, which liked to call itself the Queen City of the Kootenays, was the center of a booming mining district. The big Silver King was being operated by a British syndicate. Lesser lodes were being opened up. The town itself stood on the south shore of the west arm of Kootenay Lake, an immense body of water formed by the river of the same name and surrounded on all sides by the Rocky Mountains. Mr. and Mrs. Little did not care for the scenery. They found the snow-capped peaks grim and threatening. They longed for the sunny slopes of Lake Ontario.

Though he had been captivated by the immorality and all-around wickedness of Saginaw City, the new Mr. Little professed to find Nelson a dreary spot. It had saloons aplenty, dance halls, and other places of iniquity, yet he was now virtually a married man. Mrs. Little thought he should stay at home nights. They also had a living to make in a strange town. With money left over from the cheese-factory arson, they rented a vacant building and converted it into a restaurant. Mrs. Little did the cooking. Her husband waited on tables. She was a wonderful cook. Her table attracted, among many others, a sawmill operator from nearby Pilot Bay who suggested the Littles move there and run a company boardinghouse.

The boardinghouse did famously. The Littles hired a couple of girls to help in kitchen and dining room. Mr. Little took a contract to get out several hundred cords of wood. He engaged a small crew. Things were going well with both boardinghouse and wood job, even if rifts were becoming increasingly frequent in the common-law domesticity of the Littles, when one day a minister of the gospel from Nelson appeared without notice at the boardinghouse. He came, said he, at the request of Mrs. Little's mother in Ontario. Mr. Little was somewhat taken aback. How, he asked, did Mrs. Little's mother learn that her daughter was in British Columbia? That, the good man explained, was simple enough: Mrs. Little herself had written her.

Mrs. Little thereupon confessed that unknown to Mr. Little she had indeed written her mother, who had promptly sent a pleading and pitiful letter addressed simply to the minister of her religious denomination in Nelson. Here now he was, and he gently suggested it might be best all-around if Mrs. Little returned home to make her peace not only with her heartbroken mother but with her forsaken husband.

Possibly more relieved than shocked, Mr. Little lost no time. He bought a ticket for Mrs. Little and put her on a Canadian Pacific train for Ontario. He then tried but failed to get someone to take the wood contract off his hands but did manage to sell the boardinghouse business to a cook for a trifling sum. Then he too left Nelson. A day later he was in Spokane, Washington, circulating in the Skidroad district around West Trent Avenue, having an occasional beer and free lunch in Jimmy Durkin's saloon, a favorite with hard-rock miners and loggers, and making the rounds of the swarming slave markets to read the Help Wanted boards.

Sensing rightly that he was about to enter a wholly new field of activity, and perhaps also with a look over the shoulder toward his deserted family and the sheriff of Northumberland County, Ontario, the man who was born Albert Horsley and became John Little thought it well to place still another baffle between his nativity and the chance of arrest and extradition. Now, in a Spokane employment office, in the gentle April of 1897, he signed a job ticket as Harry Orchard and was soon on a train for Wallace, Idaho, where he was to drive a milk wagon for Markwell Brothers. This name was to stick. True, he was later to find need for other aliases on occasion, for brief periods, but for the next fifty-seven years he was generally to pass as Harry Orchard.

The Markwell Brothers turned out to be congenial employers. Their milk ranch, as dairies there were known, was two miles west of Wallace, population about two thousand, the trading center of the

Coeur d'Alene mining district. Orchard thought it a bit queer that the only thing the brothers asked was not who he was nor where he was from but whether or not he had ever "been mixed up in any labor troubles." He could truthfully say that he hadn't. He was still naive about mines and miners and seems to have had no idea the Coeur d'Alenes were as notorious in the West for labor wars as Pittsburgh, Pennsylvania, was in the East.

Orchard's milk delivery route spanned eight miles between the Markwells' ranch and Burke, the mine camp at the very end of the narrow canyon of the same name. He also left milk at camps along the way, but most of the product was for the miners and their families in Burke, a town, Orchard discovered, which seemed never to go to bed. Burke took the roving, sporting eye of the new milkman. This is how the place looked to him in the spring of 1897.

"The canyon," Orchard remembered, "was only about one hundred and fifty feet wide at the bottom, so it was hard work to squeeze in the town. There was one street. The railroad tracks ran up through the middle of it to the Tiger-Poorman mill. The stores sat on the south side and they had to be built out over the creek, which used a flume to pass through the town.

"On the north side they had to blast away the hills to make room for buildings. There were maybe a dozen stores, barbershops and so forth, six saloons, and the Tiger Hotel. Every saloon had one or more gambling layouts, including stud poker, blackjack, faro, and roulette. Beyond the stores and saloons came the sporting houses. There were usually about ten cribs in operation, plus a fairly large dance hall. Then came the residence section. The schoolhouse stood about one hundred feet from the red-light district. There was no church in town, nor a library, nor a theater." All of which was just about right for the young man who was less than sophisticated.

It was still the era when many, perhaps even a majority, of miners considered themselves as potential mine operators. The Horatio Alger legend was no stronger in the slums of New York City and on the tired stony farms of New England than in the mine camps of the West. Almost every mucker or driller who had worked on the Comstock in Nevada, at Butte in Montana, or in Colorado's Leadville and Cripple Creek knew at first or second hand some laborer like himself who had struck it rich. Right there in the Coeur d'Alenes the names of prospectors and mine workers who had become suddenly and wonderfully wealthy already marked the map with mines and towns like Wardner, Kellogg, Sullivan, and O'Rourke.

Mining was a gamble. Everybody knew that. Any common miner who possessed the least token of the gambling spirit was ready to chance a few hundred dollars in some hole or other. It was much the same with saloonkeepers, storekeepers, lawyers, and barbers who had come to follow their several trades and professions in the mine towns. They were ready to take a chance. Not even a lowly milkman was immune to the pervasive urge. While Harry Orchard was still driving his route up Burke Canyon, he bought a one-sixteenth interest in the Hercules mine, paying two hundred dollars down and agreeing to pay another three hundred in installments.

In 1897 the Hercules was little more than a "favorable" prospect in the side of a mountain that hemmed Burke in its canyon. Yet the satisfaction of owning a piece of its future gave Harry Orchard the urge to live nearer the Hercules. During Christmas week, 1897, he gave up his job with the Markwells and moved to Burke where, for a hundred and fifty dollars down, he bought the good will of a local wood and coal business.

Wages were good, cash circulated fast in Burke, and Orchard's fuel business thrived from the first. He paid the early installments on his mine investment promptly and watched with interest the development work at the Hercules. He also spent an increasing amount of time in the saloons which, as said, were also gambling houses. Although he drank perhaps more than was good for him, and visited the red-light cribs regularly, it was the faro bank, the roulette wheel, and the poker table that got most of the profits from Orchard's business. By the following spring he was so desperate for ready cash that he sold his interest in the Hercules chiefly to pay gambling debts. His habits, however, did not improve. By the summer of 1898 he was so hard pressed that he took in a partner, James McAlpin, a Scotsman to whom the saloons and faro banks and red lights offered nothing he could not well do without.

Years later McAlpin was to testify that Orchard's greatest weakness was gambling. Less than a year after McAlpin joined him in the fuel business, Orchard was glad to sell to the Scot his share of it for a hundred dollars. His career as a businessman was done. So were his days as a mine owner. When he had blown the last dollar McAlpin paid him, Orchard went to Lewis Strow, a shift boss at the Tiger-Poorman mine, Burke's largest producer, and asked him for a job.

"I can put you on as a mucker," the shift boss said, and told Orchard to go first to the Burke miners' union hall and join up. Orchard did so and became a member of the Western Federation of Miners, of which the Burke local was a part. Possibly no man ever joined a labor union more casually, or with less comprehension. Then, a union button on his cap, mucker Harry Orchard got into the cage of the night shift and went down into the deeps of the Tiger-Poorman, to shovel lead and silver ore.

Part Two:

The Wage Slave

2.

Fear Was in the Canyon

It is most unlikely that Harry Orchard was ever a union man by conviction, or that he even understood the necessity of organized labor. When he joined the Burke local, he was a down-and-out small businessman who was obliged to have a union card before he could go to work for wages. He remained at heart an individualist, basically what all good Marxians mean when they say Capitalist. Indoctrination by devoted and eloquent union men did not change him.

It seems also unlikely that few fresh and naive recruits to a labor union ever got more indoctrination in a short time than Harry Orchard. He got his card from the Burke local on the last day of March 1899. Twenty-nine days later the Burke local held an emergency meeting that blew the Western Federation of Miners across the front pages of newspapers the country over. The explosion was both figurative and literal. Into it went some six years of slowly accumulating fear and forty-five hundred pounds of actual dynamite.

It was little to wonder if the souls of many men in Burke Canyon were filled with dread in 1899. The violence into which the unwitting Orchard was about to stumble was the first major test of strength between the Western Federation of Miners and the Mine Owners Protective Association of Idaho.

It seemed to be Harry Orchard's destiny that both here and elsewhere in the mining regions he just happened to appear on a scene when fears and hates of long standing were about to explode into events of considerable importance. Volition had nothing to do with it; chance, everything. And because Orchard was to reach a certain kind of professional eminence in connection with the federation, if much to its sorrow, let us leave him for the moment as an acolyte of the Burke local union and hark back briefly to the Burke Canyon of seven years before, a period when Orchard was still Mr. Horsley, the cheese man of little patience in Ontario.

Both the Western Federation and the Idaho mine owners' group had their inception in what are still remembered locally as the "troubles of 1892," an affair that marked the end of the happy time of employee-employer relations which all mining communities were to enjoy, briefly enough, before the demands of industrialism did away with the Peaceable Kingdom.

The mining towns of the region lie deep in the narrow canyons of Shoshone County in the panhandle of Idaho. The first camp came into being because of placer gold discovered by Andrew J. Pritchard, surely one of the oddest prospectors of record. He was a fanatical Free Thinker. He called his first strike "The Evolution." He belonged to one or another of the several Liberal Leagues then active in the United States, and it was only to members of the League that he made known his discovery. His plan was that his comrade Free Thinkers would establish colonies along the gold-laden streams and use the fortunes, not for luxury or riotous living, but to "educate the Philistines" along the lines favored by the Liberal Leagues.

But some of the Liberal Leaguers to whom Pritchard wrote of his discovery were loose vessels indeed. They leaked the news, and, before Pritchard knew what was up, the region was swarming with prospectors, few of whom had yet heard of Charles Darwin or Evolution. The placer gold did not last very long, but before the rush was quite done a non-Liberal Leaguer, Noah Kellogg, uncovered what a local expert described as "outcroppings of the greatest blowout of argentiferous galena ever known." By which he meant lead and silver. Other silver-lead discoveries followed. Mine camps grew quickly up around them, and by the early nineties the Coeur d'Alene mining district had become one of the great lead and silver producers in North America.

The Northern Pacific entered from Montana by way of Mullan Pass over the Bitterroot Mountains and through the mining town of Mullan to Wallace, the chief trading center of the district, from which a branch line followed a wild creek up the deep canyon through Gem and Frisco to Burke. The Union Pacific came into the district from the west, passing through Kellogg and Wardner to Wallace and a connection with the Northern Pacific.

The region was as compact as it was mountainous. It extended east and west no more than thirty miles; north and south less than that. All of the towns, save in Burke Canyon, were built on varying levels to climb the hills to the mineheads. Burke Canyon was so steep and narrow that the several towns were strung out along and even over Canyon Creek; and in Burke town the railroad tunneled under and through the Tiger Hotel. In winter deep snow, accompanied by avalanches, often isolated the little towns one from the other. They could not, however, be isolated from the dynamic change that was overtaking so much of American industry.

The troubles that were to grip the Coeur d' Alene's were perhaps no more inevitable than those which split the Union in 1861. And surely no less inevitable. Seen in retrospect, the war between the North and South does not seem to have been inevitable. It is so with all wars, once they are done. Reasonable men of good will could have prevented them. Or that is the way hindsight has it. What hindsight cannot supply, however, is the climate of fear that prevailed at the time the shooting began.

History indicates nothing more surely than that reason cannot prevail against fear. The fear that prevailed in all the Coeur d'Alene mine towns was less the work of belligerent and cruel men than it was the result of a universal trend in American industry. Small outfits were disappearing into big corporations operated by absentee owners. Even as late as 1899 the trend had not done away with all purely local enterprises, as witness the Hercules property in Burke Canyon whose owners were still a locomotive engineer and his wife who ran a boarding house, a schoolteacher, a grocer, a barber, half a dozen common miners, and, until recently, the coal-and-wood man, Harry Orchard. But the Hercules and a few other small producers were exceptions. Mining in the Coeur d'Alenes was dominated by the huge Bunker Hill & Sullivan Mining and Concentrating Company, the Helena & Frisco, and the lesser yet large concerns operating at and near Mullan, and at Gem in Burke Canyon.

No matter their personal feelings, the resident managers of the big operators must do the bidding of the absentee owners who lived in Spokane, Portland, San Francisco, and New York City. Absentee owners were not of necessity heartless men. Their minds, however, tended to become calloused by absorption with balance sheets to the exclusion of consideration of conditions under which their employees lived and worked, or the wages paid. Always between them, the owners and the miners, was the wall of the resident manager.

It is not strange if labor relations suffered tensions that brought suspicion and fear, not alone to employees but to employers too. The miners became "arrogant." The mine owners turned "greedy." By the time these and worse adjectives became common in corporation offices and mining towns, it was a sign that the simple, free-wheeling era in the Coeur d'Alenes was passing. The Peaceable Kingdom was cracking. In pioneer times there had been but one class of men in the camps, and it was composed of miners who owned an interest in a mine property even while they swung a pick or wielded a shovel, and they expected, one day soon, to join the ranks of those described as magnates and to adopt the symbols of magnates, who wore square-cut plug hats, carried gold-headed canes, and smoked cigars that cost ten cents straight.

But that day had passed. By 1892 there were two classes in the mine towns, and, though it was possible still if unlikely to move from the lower to the upper, it was increasingly the belief of a majority of miners that their lives were henceforth dependent wholly on wages. The more bitter among them described their condition as that of slaves chained to the Wage System. These favored the organization of workers to take over the means of production and abolish the wage system. But the great majority of miners believed it best to organize for the purpose of demanding and getting the highest wages consistent with general economic conditions.

The first union of hard-rock miners was organized in 1863 at Virginia City, Nevada, by miners of the Comstock Lode. Six years later the Virginia City and nearby Gold Hill unions combined to bar the employment of Chinese within the limits of those towns. By then most of the Comstock mines were described as "strong union jobs" where no man could work longer than one month without joining. It is generally believed that the idea of unions among hard-rock miners in the newer camps at Butte, Leadville, and the Coeur d'Alenes was spread by foot-loose men who had worked on the Comstock. In any case, small local unions were formed in the eighties at Burke, Gem, Mullan, and Wardner, and in 1889 these groups banded together in a federation styled quaintly the Coeur d'Alene Executive Miners' Union, the first of its kind.

The first action of this new group had to do not with wages, but with a hospital, which was built in Wardner with thirty thousand dollars from the union's funds and put under the supervision of Sister Joseph, Mother Superior of the Order of Providence. The combined unions requested that the companies pay the hospital fees of one dollar a month, deducted from wages of the miners, to the hospital. All agreed to do so, except the Bunker Hill & Sullivan.

The second action of the Coeur d'Alene Executive Miners' Union had to do with technology, namely, the introduction of compressed-air drills, which reduced the number of skilled men, throwing them out of work or forcing them to take jobs as muckers. The union asked all mine companies to adopt a uniform scale for all underground men. All did so, though the "Bunker Hill & Sullivan acceded to the demand only after several days of obstinacy."

It was the operators who made the next move. They had seen the signs. The miners were becoming "arrogant." Late in 1891 the operators, among them the celebrated John Hays Hammond and the aggressive Frederick W. Bradley, whom we shall meet again, organized the Mine Owners Protective Association. They quietly secured from Pinkerton's National Detective Agency the services of an operative, or spy, Charles Siringo, who was selected for the dangerous job by James A. McParlan, superintendent of the Pinkerton's Western Division headquarters in Denver. Siringo promptly came to the district in the guise of a carefree and likable boomer, under the name of C. Leon Allison.

Siringo-Allison, who much later wrote a book which the Pinkertons forced the publisher to withdraw and revise, was described by an attorney for the mine owners as of medium height, agile and strong, and "courageous to the point of recklessness." It is perhaps significant of events that were soon to follow that he got a job as mucker in the mine at Gem and was presently elected secretary of the miners' local union there.

On the first day of 1892, the Mine Owners Protective Association announced a shutdown of all operations in the district. This action was necessary, said the association, in order to compel the railroads to reduce freight rates which, it appeared, were all out of reason. Down went the mines. A worse time for the miners could not have been chosen. Snow buried the little towns. There could be no hunting game for the table. Provisions at the stores grew scarce and climbed in price. The several unions went into action to obtain potatoes and other farm produce and opened commissaries.

It turned out to be a long, hard winter on sparse rations, a season the miners with families would not soon forget. In March the operators posted notices that the mines would open on April 1. They had meanwhile talked turkey and tough to the railroads and got a reduction of two dollars a ton in the freight rate. Reading as much in the papers, the miners had reason to believe that wages would be the same as paid before the shutdown. Not so. To clear up *that* matter, the Protective Association published a new wage scale, lower than before the shutdown.

When the combined unions protested, the operators intimated that the unions were trying "to run the whole country ... to terrorize everybody...by threats and intimidation," and declared, "it is about time to call a halt." No miners in the West, remarks Vernon H. Jensen,[1] "would have taken such direct, if not abusive language, and they didn't." They issued a public statement denying "that we are nothing but a band of anarchists," and stood fast by their wage demand.

Public opinion sided with the unions. The operators seemed ignorant of this fact, or perhaps did not care. In May they started to bring in men from outside the state. A few small groups of these imports, protected by armed guards, managed to arrive and were quartered behind newly built stockades before the miners were alerted by railroad men and local law officers, both of whom favored the union. The railroaders also acted of their own accord to harass the mine operators. When one consignment of eighty men from Grass Valley, California, arrived at Tekoa Junction, Washington, a trainman there told them they would have to ride in boxcars the rest of the way to the mines. They were thereupon herded into cars of a freight train headed for Pendleton, Oregon, and next morning found themselves in wheat and cattle country, more than two hundred miles off their target.

The mine owners were granted a federal court injunction restraining the unions from interfering with procurement of men. Governor Wiley of Idaho issued a proclamation calling upon the

---

1 In his authoritative Heritage of Conflict.

miners to cease interfering with the mine owners. Public opinion was still with the miners. Sheriff Cunningham of Shoshone County attempted to intercept a new trainload of nonunion men at Wallace but failed when the train ran on through the town and up the branch line to Frisco. By the time the sheriff got there, the new men were safely behind the barricade recently erected at the Helena & Frisco mill below the mine. Armed guards patrolled the barricade.

The news spread quickly that the Frisco was to resume just as soon as Idaho militia, which rumor had it were on their way, arrived. During the night more than a hundred miners from Burke walked into Gem. At least as many more walked in from Mullan. Some were armed. Others must have been given arms after they arrived.

At break of dawn, the possibly too-alert guards at the Frisco mill barricade saw a single miner walking up the road to Burke and opened fire. The miner ran back to Gem, less than half a mile from the mill, and the town, swarming with fearful and long idle and angry miners, went into action. One body of them marched in loose formation up the narrow canyon as if to attack the Frisco mill head on. The guards opened fire. The attackers were just beyond range. They kept their distance and began to work their way up the almost sheer canyon wall opposite the mill. Sporadic firing continued from both guards and union men.

While the attention of the guards was held to the front of the barricade, union men circled the hill and got above the mill. They loaded an ore car with dynamite, lighted the fuse, and sent it rolling down the track. It failed to explode. The miners next shut off the water in the flume that led to the mill. Into the dry flume they put case after case of powder to go sliding swiftly down the steep chute. From the final case streaked smoke from a burning fuse. The explosion shook the canyon.

Although the explosion blew a large part of Frisco mill to bits, no one was injured. The guards and nonunion men inside the barricade hoisted a white flag. The union men took possession, then started to escort some sixty prisoners down to the union hall in Gem. They discovered that the town of Gem had been turned into something of a shambles. Almost as soon as the attack had started on the Frisco mill, the guards behind breastworks at the Gem mine poured a volley of bullets into the town below. Gus Carlson, James Hennessy, and Harry

Cummings, union miners, were killed. Another round of blind firing brought down two more miners identified only as Bean and Stanley. Among the sixteen wounded during a third and a fourth spate of bullets from the Gem guards was an active union man, George A. Pettibone. It was he who had suggested the idea and helped to shut off the water from the Frisco flume and to send the dynamite scooting down the dry chute.

While the dead were being laid away and the wounded being cared for, a special train arrived from Wallace. In it were the sheriff and deputies, the district attorney, and several United States deputy marshals. A white flag appeared at the Gem mine breastworks. The Gem guards and nonunion miners surrendered their arms. Truce was declared in Gem.

That afternoon Van De Lashmutt, a recent mayor of Portland, Oregon, who had mining interests in the Coeur d' Alenes, was in Wallace, Idaho, and saw a melancholy procession. "It was the coroner," he said, "driving a wagon in which were five dead men from Gem. The wagon was followed by some two hundred strikers, about half of whom carried Winchesters, the others with side arms."

There was no trouble in Wallace. The two hundred strikers seemed to melt away. Unknown to the mine operators, they and two hundred more of their comrades from Mullan proceeded after dark to Wardner, twelve miles west, and during the night mined the concentrator of the Bunker Hill & Sullivan with boxes of dynamite. They apparently did this unsuspected. The more than three hundred armed guards had mistakenly been stationed at the mouth of the Bunker Hill & Sullivan mine.

With daylight, a committee of the strikers went to the mine company's office, informed the management of the arrangements they had made, and declared the concentrator buildings would be blown up if the nonunion men and guards were not discharged at once. C.U. Clement, resident manager agreed to the demand.

It now became known to the strikers that the Mine Owners Association had asked the governor of Idaho to declare martial law and to ask for federal troops. He had done so, and the soldiers, under Brigadier General William P. Carlin, were already on the way. The strikers' committee demanded of resident manager Clement that he stop the troops. If not, the concentrator would be blown up anyway.

Clement managed to reach General Carlin by wire at Cataldo, west of Wardner, explaining the critical situation and asking that the troops remain at Catalo until the next day.

While the troops waited just outside the district, the several hundred guards and nonunion miners from Gem, Frisco, and Wardner were put aboard a train and moved under union-miner guards to Old Mission, where a steamboat was to take them down the Coeur d'Alene River. Just what happened at the boat landing that night is obscured by conflicting reports. It seems certain, however, that several of the unarmed nonunion men were driven into the river by union miners led by one Poynton, reputedly a reckless and ruthless man from Butte, and shot and killed while they struggled in the water.

General Carlin and the troops moved in to Wardner. Union miners and sympathizers were arrested and kept in stockade enclosures called bull pens at Wardner and Wallace. Some five hundred indictments were returned by a federal grand jury. No miner was convicted of a crime. George Pettibone and three others were jailed for contempt, but later set free by court order. Four hundred and eighty of the indictments were quashed. Martial law continued until November.

The Coeur d'Alene unions had been badly damaged but not broken. Their influence continued strong at all operations save that of the Bunker Hill & Sullivan, which refused to hire known union men. The most important result of the strike was the organization at Butte, in May, following the end of the Coeur d'Alene troubles, of the Western Federation of Miners.

3.

The Second Battle of Bunker Hill

It became clear to Harry Orchard, during the four weeks he was to work as a mucker in the Tiger-Poorman at Burke, that the policies of the district unions were determined in large part by the Western Federation of Miners. This group was organized in May 1893, when representatives of fifteen locals widely scattered over Montana, Idaho, Colorado, Utah, and South Dakota met in Butte to discuss combining into a federation similar to the Coeur d'Alene Executive Miners', which had shown a notable united front in the recent troubles of 1892. The delegates were unanimous that only in one big federation would hard-rock miners be strong enough to wring from the organized mine owners "a fair compensation" and improved "protection against needless risk to life and health."

For the next three years, however, the Western Federation was little more than a paper organization. Then, at its fourth convention in 1896, the delegates elected Edward Boyce president. Boyce had worked in the Bunker Hill & Sullivan at Wardner. He had been a leader in forming the Coeur d'Alene Executive Miners' Union. He had been from the first a member of the Western Federation's executive board. Now he was president. Things began to happen. In the next six years, during Boyce's regime, the federation grew to have two hundred unions, to own five hospitals and maintain wards in twice as many more, to own and operate several co-operative stores, and to maintain reading rooms or libraries in most of its fifty-odd halls. Its influence was to be felt in varying degrees, yet always felt, throughout its jurisdiction, which extended over the Rockies and into the Far Western states and British Columbia.

Edward Boyce was a tall, energetic, and fearless man, of quick intelligence, who could talk to miners in their own language, who wrote even better than he spoke, and who was quite competent to deal with "capitalists" on their own ground. He leaned strongly toward socialism, yet he built the Western Federation into the most powerful labor group in Western United States by his insistence on high wages and the closed shop. He considered the American Federation of Labor to be "moribund," and told its leader, Sam Gompers, that "the laboring men of the West are one hundred years ahead of their brothers in the East." The usefulness of trade unions, he said, had passed.

When he joined the Burke local, Harry Orchard did not know the difference between a trades union and any other kind. But he learned fast. Now that he carried a card and attended union meetings, he began to hear a great deal about Ed Boyce, head of the Western Federation, who even then in April of 1899 was in the Coeur d'Alene district on "important business." The business, so Orchard gleaned from talk in the Burke miners' union hall, had to do with the Bunker Hill & Sullivan Mining and Concentrating Company. That hard-bitten outfit was the only nonunion operation in the district. It had consistently followed the policy of discharging union men as soon as they were identified by company spotters, who were said to be as numerous as they were efficient. The company was also paying lower wages than the operations in Mullan, Gem, Frisco, and Burke. The managers of these concerns—the way Orchard heard it—were putting pressure on Ed Boyce either to force Bunker Hill & Sullivan to raise wages to the union scale, or to permit the union mines to lower *their* wages.

So, on April 13, two weeks after Orchard became a miner, there was talk in the Burke union hall that the Wardner union had pasted notices at the Bunker Hill & Sullivan asking all employees of that company to join the Wardner local of the Western Federation of Miners. This was exciting stuff. A few days later Orchard learned that Ed Boyce himself and a committee had called upon Albert Burch, superintendent, to demand the Bunker Hill & Sullivan wage scale be raised to that of the unionized operations. Burch agreed—and at the same time discharged seventeen miners whose membership in the union had been discovered by spotters. This was notice that the Bunker Hill & Sullivan felt ready for whatever action the unions might take.

During the next three days "several hundred B.H.&S. employees quit" because union men had taken possession of the tramway by which many employees were carried to work. Orchard found the Burke union hall seething each night with loud talk, mostly by "short-stakers" or ten-day men, fellows who worked a few days, "then lay around the saloons a few days." They were hot to shoot scabs, blow things up, and "show the labor-hating Bunker Hill who's running things around here." The miners with families, however, had little to say. They were obviously worried. Many of them had gone through the "troubles of 1892," as the murderous affair at Frisco and Gem was still called. They went to bed that night, in their little houses along Canyon Creek, filled with boding. Harry Orchard felt no boding. He had a few drinks in a saloon next to the union hall, then went to his rooming house and so to bed. He was sleeping soundly when long after midnight two messengers from the union at Gem hove into Burke to rouse Paul Corcoran, secretary of the Burke local.

NEXT DAY WAS THE TWENTY-NINTH of April. Orchard arose at six o'clock as usual and put on the clothing he wore in the mine. On the way to the boardinghouse where he got his breakfast, however, a miner stopped him in the street to say there was to be no work that day. Not in the Tiger-Poorman or in any other mine in the canyon. Instead, there was to be an emergency union meeting right after breakfast. It was called for seven o'clock in the Burke hall. Orchard hastened to eat, then went to the hall. It was already filled to the doors.

What took place at this suddenly called meeting is not clear. As Harry Orchard recalled it, more than six years later, it was called to order by Secretary Corcoran, who explained that officers of the Coeur d'Alene Executive Miners' Union had met the previous night in Gem and decided that men from the several locals should go to Wardner and blow up the Bunker Hill & Sullivan property.

At this point Mike Devy, an official of the Burke union, came into the hall. He was quite angry and interrupted Corcoran, demanding to know why he had not been notified of the emergency meeting, and why it had been called anyway. Corcoran ignored Devy's first question, then explained again the reason for the meeting. Devy did not favor the proposed expedition to Wardner. He said that Burke miners should stay in Burke. Let the Wardner crowd do what they would. Corcoran took the floor from Devy and told the crowd that if their union comrades at

Wardner were not given support at once they would be forced to tear up their cards before they could get a job with Bunker Hill & Sullivan. Further, if Bunker Hill did not raise its wages, then the unionized companies at Burke, Frisco, Gem, and Mullan would be forced to cut their wage scales. This kind of talk made sense. The meeting voted, though by no great margin, to act on the recommendation of the central executive union. Corcoran issued orders.

Now the talking was done. It was time for action. The three hundred or more miners scattered quickly to their homes and rooming houses and the saloons. Less than half an hour later they swarmed to the railroad depot. Some were armed with revolvers; more had rifles. Orchard carried a revolver. All wore a small piece of white cloth, like a bandage, around the left arm. This was for ready identification of the Burke men who, at the meeting, had been told to take masks. As they gathered at the railroad station, perhaps half of the crowd were masked, bandit-style, with red or blue bandanna handkerchiefs.

Within a few minutes Orchard, standing with others on the depot platform, heard the whistle of the regular morning train corning up the canyon from Wallace. As it approached Burke, eight masked and armed men moved about in the waiting crowd warning them against shouting or any other demonstration. Orchard recognized several of these leaders. The train came in. It had no more than stopped when the eight men got aboard. They told the train crew what was up and directed them to add the half-dozen boxcars which stood in the Burke yards to the baggage car and two coaches of the regular train. This was soon done. The train crew seems to have made no protest, as yet. Whether or not they knew it, all telegraph wires out of the region had been cut during the night, but only after a code message had been sent to alert the secretary of the union at Mullan, seven miles distant on the Northern Pacific's line that entered the district from Montana.

Masked and unmasked, some four hundred men got aboard the train at Burke. Orchard had a seat in one of the coaches. Five or six of the masked and armed leaders rode in the locomotive. The first stop was at Frisco, where the engineer was told to halt the train so that boxcars would be spotted in front of the big powder magazine of the Helena & Frisco company. Orders were given. Willing hands broke open the magazine doors. Forty boxes of dynamite were loaded, along with a supply of caps. And the train moved on down the canyon to

Gem and stopped.

Discipline was still excellent. Under command of one of the masked leaders, a hundred or more men got off the train and went to the Gem union hall, where arms and ammunition were given them. They returned to the train. (Orchard learned later that the rifles distributed here had recently been shipped to Gem in a piano box from Denver, Colorado, by George Pettibone, the same who had been arrested at Gem in 1892 for his part in destroying the Frisco mill.)

Meanwhile, two hundred members of the Gem union, all of them armed and some masked, got aboard the train, making a passenger list of around six hundred men. Just as the engineer was told to proceed, somebody suggested that the forty boxes of powder were not sufficient to do a really good job on the property of the Bunker Hill & Sullivan. The concentrator itself was a huge, stoutly built plant; and there were also other buildings. Back up the canyon to Frisco went the train. Fifty more boxes of dynamite were put aboard, and the engineer was told to highball for Wallace.

Down the narrow canyon rolled what a railroad timecard would have described as a "mixed special." Within an hour more, the mixed special could have been considered a symbol—either of "anarchism" or of hard-pressed labor defending its right to a living wage. It is all in the point of view.

Down the canyon road that paralleled the track rode a single horseman in advance of the train. He tore into Wallace down Bank Street, halted in front of the office of the *Idaho Tribune*, official local paper of the Western Federation of Miners, and shouted: "They are coming!" Then he rode away in the direction of Wardner. This was notice to federation officials waiting anxiously in Wallace that the union boys up Burke Canyon had performed their duties successfully.

On the heels of the hard-riding horseman came the train. Peering from a coach window, Harry Orchard saw a vast crowd massed at the Wallace depot and lined along the tracks. In the forefront were nearly six hundred union members from the Mullan local. They had walked the seven miles from Mullan that morning, toting rifles which Orchard was told had been stolen months before from the hall where they had been stored since the militia company at Mullan was disbanded.

Back of the armed miners was a good part of the citizenry of Wallace, at least half and probably more of whom were sympathetic to the unions, even if their sympathy fell short of approval of the present expedition, the aims of which must by then have been fairly well known. Orchard saw Sheriff Jim Young of Shoshone County get aboard the train, Deputy Tom Heney with him, and was told by old miners that both men were strong supporters of the unions.

It took a little time for the Mullan six hundred to be loaded. The two passenger coaches and the baggage car were already filled, while in and on the boxcars were the men from the Gem-Frisco union. But the weather was fine, and the Mullan miners gladly took places on top of the boxcars, or sat on the floor inside, their legs dangling from the big doors.

The locomotive engineer was ordered to start for Wardner, fifteen miles west of Wallace. He balked. He pointed out that his was a Northern Pacific engine hauling Northern Pacific cars. The rails from Wallace to Wardner belonged to the Union Pacific. It was as unthinkable as it was dangerous to run a train over a "foreign" line without permission, he protested. Permission could not be had because the telegraph wires had been cut. And further, said the engineer, who could say they might not meet a train coming from the opposite direction on the single track?

The masked men with guns suggested to the engineer that he forget the rule book in an emergency, added that the engineer was right then in the midst of as big an emergency as he was likely to meet, and told him to get going. He blew a blast, the fireman rang the bell, and out of Wallace station moved the mixed special heading for Bunker Hill & Sullivan. A rousing cheer went up from the crowd around the tracks. The men on top of the cars yelled back. They were beginning to feel their oats. Some of them started to sing, and the train clacked over the frogs in the yard to the tune of "There'll Be a Hot Time in the Old Town Tonight."

"It all seemed," Orchard remembered, "like a gigantic picnic, or a Fourth of July celebration. I doubt that many of us that day thought we were breaking the law by stealing a train and forcing its crew to run us where we wanted to go, regardless of other trains. I had a loaded revolver in my pocket, like hundreds of others, but I never thought for a moment that we were doing anything except the proper and natural thing. Everybody was joking. It really seemed just like a big picnic, a clambake, a barbecue." Well, maybe to Harry Orchard, but not to old union heads and veteran miners who had fought bloody enough battles with company police on the Comstock, in Butte, and right there in the Coeur d'Alenes at Gem and Frisco. Men died in those battles. (But nobody ever won.)

On rolled the train down the wider canyon along the Coeur d'Alene River, carrying close to twelve hundred passengers and four thousand five hundred pounds of freight, all dynamite, heading for Wardner on a one-track line and with no knowledge of what other trains might be abroad and moving. The engineer kept the whistle cord down much of the time as they heaved around curves and pounded over long trestles. When the pine woods were not filled with the engine's moaning, they resounded to shouts in nearly every accent common to the United States and to much of Europe. Doubtless it all sounded like a monster lodge picnic, though it happened to be a full cargo of disaster.

THE MASKED LEADERS STILL HAD the crowd in control. As soon as the train stopped at Wardner depot, the men began to unload in good order and were formed into two lines along the track. Sheriff Jim Young and Deputy Tom Heney played their parts. They took their stand, with burlesque official manner, in front of the ranks of the armed miners, and the sheriff commanded them in a loud voice to disperse. Even the many miners with imperfect understanding of English knew this was merely a bluff—a make-believe show of authority—and laughed as heartily at the humor as anybody. The sheriff then conferred briefly with the masked leaders, advising them how to make the attack.

The eight leaders apparently agreed it was best to have one supreme commander for the attack on the concentrator. He was W. F. Davis, head of the Gem local, and now he outlined the plan of battle. The concentrator was in sight of and about one-half mile from the railroad station. It was the first objective. Before putting the main body of his troops in action, ten men armed with "long guns" (rifles) were deployed ahead to draw the fire of guards whom the attackers believed to be hidden in the structure and to number three or four hundred.

The advance detachment took off up the far side of the hill where the concentrator stood. Commander Davis then began to move his main troops forward according to the kind of weapons they carried. "All men with long guns this way," Orchard heard the command. They were to lead the attack. Behind the rifles were the men with revolvers. Orchard heard the call: "All men with side arms this way." Then the command was given to move forward, two by two, straight up the hill, head on for the frowning great wall of the concentrator.

Harry Orchard did not like the battle plan of Commander Davis. He told himself it was worse than foolish. If there really *were* any guards in the building, he reflected, they could mow down the attackers half a dozen at a time. Being strictly the non-martyr type, Orchard slipped quietly out of line and went into the depot restaurant. He was not alone. Several other miners were eating too. Pretty soon they heard gunfire. They quit the lunch counter to run out in time to witness the first tragedy of the day.

Though there were probably twelve hundred accounts, all different, of the battle of Bunker Hill & Sullivan, what set the actual shooting going was this: In the haste and excitement of preparing for action, not all of the main army learned about the scouting detachment sent ahead. When the scouts, who must have been as courageous as they were fanatical union men, found there were no guards at the concentrator, one of them fired his gun once. This was the agreed signal to Commander Davis that the way was clear. Let the main army come on.

In the main army, naturally, were numerous half-wits; and they, thinking their own scouts to be company guards, started to shoot at about three hundred yards. Watching the action from near the depot, Orchard saw spurts of dirt flying up all around the ten unfortunate scouts who were yelling desperately for their comrades to cease fire. But many of the men who had toted guns all the way from Mullan and Burke meant to do some shooting, and now the trigger-happy let go with army carbines, army rifles, hunting rifles, shotguns, and revolvers. The watching Orchard estimated that two hundred or more marksmen opened fire on the poor scouts. He saw one of the scouts throw up his arms, then fall on his face. By then Commander Davis and his lieutenants managed to halt the shooting. The dead man was Jack Smith, a veteran hard-rock man noted for winning top honors in championship drilling contests.

It was too bad, a good man gone. But this was not the time to mourn. Comrades toted Jack Smith to the railroad depot, laid him on the baggage-car floor, and covered the body with a quilt, while Commander Davis sent the powder men into action. There were ninety boxes of it in boxcars of the train.

The concentrator was half a mile from the track. Orchard and eighty-nine others each shouldered a case and started up the long hill.

As the dynamite detail was plodding along in orderly fashion, some of the rifle-and-revolver men were getting out of hand again. Show-offs among them were running all over the place, shouting for scabs to come out and fight, but the company's guards had fled the property when they saw the mixed special come in to Wardner station and start to unload twelve hundred passengers. The searchers for scabs, however, did flush Jim Cheyne, a young and unarmed company watchman, who had the temerity to stick by his post. Somebody shot him fatally. One other company employee, J. J. Rogers, described as a stenographer, was slightly wounded as he attempted to flee.

Commander Davis now appeared at the concentrator to take charge of mining the structure. He was an old experienced hand with powder, and now he had his men distribute the boxes of explosive where, as Orchard remarked, they would do the most good. "He had us place one charge," Orchard remembered, "beneath the ore bin where the ore comes into the mill. We then strung boxes of powder under the tables down the middle of the concentrator. Then, at the bottom of everything, down in the boiler room, we laid a charge such as miners call 'a lifter.' Fuses of different lengths were attached, so that the top charge at the bin would go first, then the one under the tables, and finally the one in the boiler room, which would finish the job from the ground up."

Harry Orchard, wholly unfamiliar with dynamite, was fascinated by this scientific distribution of powder in the Bunker Hill & Sullivan concentrator. It is significant, in view of his later career, that when Davis called for volunteers to set off the charges, Orchard was one of the first to step forward. Let him tell in his own words of his virgin experience as a dyno man. "So, I went down in the boiler room with another man," he said, "and after a while Davis came and put his head down through a trap door and called out to us to light our fuses. We lighted them and started to get out of there. We tried to get up the stairway, but the door was locked. The fuse was smoking good. We knew how soon it would be before it reached the cap. We also knew there were two charges above us with even shorter fuses burning. It was no place to be hanging around in on any count. The other fellow and I couldn't break the door at the top of the stairway. We hurried back down and found a window we could reach. We broke the glass and crawled through it. We ran as fast as we could down a side track." A moment or so later the first charge let go, then the second, then the big lifter. The immense building went up with a roar that was heard in Wallace, some fifteen miles distant, and shook windows and houses there.

It was now a little after half-past two in the afternoon. The fire, smoke, and noise of the explosion had reduced to rubble what was said to be one of the largest ore concentrators in the United States and also turned Commander Davis's army into an even wilder mob of twelve hundred men. Apparently without orders, and possibly in spite of them, they entered the huge and deserted boardinghouse, scattered kerosene throughout, then set it afire. Somebody shouted, "Get the boss's house, too!" and a gang, among them Orchard, kicked in the door of the imposing home of the Bunker Hill & Sullivan superintendent, and went inside. Orchard looked around at what to him was elegance— "furnished up fine," he thought—while the kerosene was being applied. While this was going on, other gangs were breaking windows and setting fire to lesser buildings and shooting guns indiscriminately. There was a great deal of yelling.

By this time, it must have been obvious to Davis that the comparative discipline his men had shown had been shattered as surely as the concentrator. The orders of himself and his lieutenants made no impression. He went down to the train and had the engineer blow a series of sharp blasts on the locomotive whistle. This did little to quiet the bedlam, but it did bring men running to the track. Davis held the train only long enough to let those who heeded the whistle get aboard, then ordered the engineer to start for Wallace, where the men from Mullan would get off and the train proceed up the canyon to Burke. The mixed special, its bell ringing, pulled out of desolated and flaming Wardner.

For the homeward journey Orchard took a seat on top of one of the boxcars. Quite a number of the boys had been hitting the bottle, and like any other drunks hated to see a dandy party come to an end. So, still in high holiday mood, they began shooting at the big wooden flume, alongside and high above the moving train, that still carried water to what was left of the concentrator. It made an amusing target. Every rifle ball that pierced its side brought a most satisfying squirt of water. The shooting continued until the train suddenly stopped.

Davis, who had been riding in the cab, got off and walked down beside the train and, like Colonel William Prescott on another long-ago and faraway Bunker Hill, admonished his men to conserve their powder. Davis spoke bluntly to his clownish marksmen, telling them that Federal troops might even then be leaving the Army post at Spokane for the Coeur d' Alenes. "Don't waste your ammunition," he warned. "We may have a fight on our hands."

This seemed to sober the crowd somewhat. At Wallace, when the train stopped to let off the men for Mullan, some of the boys tried to get into saloons near the depot. All were closed. The town seemed in a Sunday hush. The railroad station was overflowing with frightened women and crying children. They were the families of Wallace business and professional men, waiting for a train to take them to Spokane, or almost any other place away from a district where mobs could "steal railroad trains and destroy whole towns."

Leaving the Mullan men to get home as best they could, the mixed special started up Burke Canyon. There was no more shooting at targets. The drunks were drying out. Some were sleeping when the train reached Gem and had to be roused. It was early twilight when the train got to Burke. Harry Orchard ate a good solid meal, then went to his rooming house. He seemed to have no ill effects from his exertions on "the biggest day in Shoshone County history." Nor was he troubled with guilty feelings. "I went to bed that night as usual," he remembered, "without thinking much about it."

4.

The Great Diaspora

Work in the Tiger-Poorman mine at Burke was resumed on the morning following the Bunker Hill affair almost as if nothing more than a conventional holiday, such as the Fourth of July or Christmas, had intervened. But not quite. The day shift assembled at the main shaft was so depleted as to indicate something other than the average number of holiday hangovers. Many miners who had not been drinking at all on April 30 did not show up.

Harry Orchard was in the crew that went to work. During the day it became clear that a majority of the absentees were boomers, short-stakers, men without ties accustomed to move from job to job when they felt the urge to do so. Orchard had no ties, but here he was shoveling ore and hating it. There was a good deal of talk in the crew as to how much damage had been done to the Bunker Hill & Sullivan. Some estimated it to have been half a million dollars. Others placed it as low as a quarter of a million dollars. In any case it was agreed there had been one hell of a dynamite job.

Orchard shoveled away, ruminating still on how much like a picnic the affair had been, even though that had been a bad moment down in the Bunker Hill & Sullivan boiler room when he and the other fellow lighted the fuse, then found the door locked. Yet everything had turned out fine and dandy—that is, if you were as naive as Orchard. It was only when he heard a rumor, during the lunch hour, that Federal troops were coming "to arrest and shoot" the rioters that he gave some thought to his own safety. Much later he told a reporter: "It occurred to me that, after all, you can't steal railroad trains, dynamite mines, and burn villages without some reaction." He could hardly have made a truer observation.

Reaction had started to take form while the town of Wardner was still burning to ashes, when the resident manager of the Bunker Hill & Sullivan sent a wire from Fairfield, a hamlet in Washington State, to Governor Frank Steunenberg at Boise, the Idaho capitol, citing the lawlessness of the mining region. It seems to have been generally believed by union men that, in any difficulty with the mine owners, Governor Steunenberg would be on the side of labor. He had been elected by a fusion party of Democrats and Populists, which placed him in a most difficult position. If anyone "had the labor vote in Idaho," it was he. The experience of his predecessors in office also suggested that he ignore the "always troublous Coeur d'Alenes" and do nothing.

Steunenberg happened to be an American first, a politician second. He was ill and abed at home when the message came. He had no state troops. The Idaho National Guard was in the Philippines. He promptly wired President William McKinley for federal troops. On the same day, April 30, the War Department ordered Brigadier General H. C. Merriam, at Denver, to proceed immediately to Idaho. On May 1 the General and the Governor conferred at Glenns Ferry, near Boise, after which the General left for the mining region accompanied by Bartlett Sinclair as personal representative of the Governor, with all powers to act. On May 2 the General and Sinclair arrived at the scene, and after considering conditions General Merriam wired for troops to come from the nearest Army posts at Spokane, Walla Walla, and Boise. That same evening Bartlett Sinclair declared martial law. By next morning the troops began to arrive at Wallace and Wardner.

NEWS OF THESE EVENTS HAD gone swiftly up Burke Canyon almost as they occurred. Work in the Tiger-Poorman mine continued on May 1, as said, and the day shift, though much depleted, showed up again on the morning of the second, Orchard among them. By the third, the crew had shrunk still more, though Orchard was still present. Then, before noon, word passed through the mine that the troops actually were coming. Orchard and most of the others quit at noon and asked for their time. They were given time checks, not company checks that could be cashed at a bank.

Cash or no cash, Orchard was at last convinced that "some sort of reaction" to the Bunker Hill affair was taking place. After a hurried lunch he and many other miners climbed the high, sheer hill that hemmed Burke town on the north, where the midday sun had begun to melt the snow, there to wait to see what was going to happen. A businessman in Burke promised to let them know when, or perhaps if, it was safe to return.

Along in midafternoon the miners on the hill heard a locomotive whistle, and soon they could see a long train coming creeping up the canyon. When it reached Burke, its mission became clear to the watchers high above the town. Men in blue with rifles swarmed out of the passenger coaches and boxcars and went to work with the swift assurance of Federal troops. There seemed to be no fighting, no resistance. The soldiers, so Orchard noted, simply "rounded up the miners like a bunch of cattle and herded them into boxcars." Two hours later the train left Burke and started down the canyon, though not before a company of soldiers had been detailed to remain as guards. The unease of the refugees on the hill increased when they saw soldiers, rifles on shoulder, being posted, obviously as pickets, around the tight little town below them. Evening was coming on, with nothing in sight to eat.

Twilight came into the canyon. Orchard and some fifteen of his comrades prepared to shack up in a miner's cabin near their lookout on the hill. After dark two of the crowd were sent down to the town to find out what they could, and to get food. They discovered pickets on every corner but managed to pass and reach a street where married miners lived. From the womenfolk the spies learned that the troops "had arrested every man in the place, even to the postmaster." The spies rounded up some food and returned safely to their fellow refugees.

Much of the night in the miner's cabin was spent in discussion of what to do next. Orchard and a pal named Pat Dennison agreed to strike out in the morning over the mountains for Montana. The state boundary was only about four miles from Burke, but the nearest Montana town was more than twenty miles as the crow flies, and nearer forty by trail. The terrain was reputedly extremely rough, and snow was sure to be fairly deep near and at the summit of the Bitterroot Mountains.

At five o'clock next morning, Orchard and Pat Dennison started a trek which the former, at least, was never to forget. The snow was deep all right. At first it had a crust that held them. For an hour or so they made good time. By then the sun had come out, hot. The crust broke and they had to wallow. By afternoon they were trudging in deep slush. There was no trailside inn where they might stop. There was not even the cabin of a trapper. This was wilderness. The little food gave out. The slush seemed to deepen. The only thing that kept the two refugees from turning back was the fresh memory of the fast-working soldiers at Burke, and the still unknown fate of the miners who had been put into the boxcars. On they plodded on this, their anabasis, with no Xenophon to record either their suffering or their determination; and at last the snow gradually disappeared. By ten that night they saw the lights of Thompson Falls on the Oar Fork River and the Northern Pacific Railway.

Orchard and Dennison had themselves a big supper, a night's rest, and took a train for Missoula. Here they found other miners from the Coeur d'Alenes who had left the district on foot or freight trains by way of Mullan Pass. The reunion was brief. That very day the train from Wallace brought a detail of soldiers accompanied by what Orchard called "scab deputies." These deputies were old hands in the mining district and were for the purpose of identifying refugees. Missoula was no proper hiding place. Orchard, Dennison, and a few others left immediately. They went up the Bitterroot Valley looking for a man Orchard had known in his milk-wagon days at Wallace. They found him running a farm. Orchard talked the fellow into going over to the mining district to "get our trunks and what money we had coming." On return, he told the boys that things were sure hot in Wallace and Wardner. Several hundred miners were being held behind barbed wire in hull pens, and the troops were running down others daily and bringing them in.

With his trunk and wages, Orchard went to Butte and to the headquarters of the Western Federation of Miners, there to learn that the town was filled with refugees. He asked for a withdrawal card that would get him into a hard-rock union anywhere in the West, and had a talk with Ed Boyce, federation president. Boyce told Orchard and others that he blamed the Bunker Hill & Sullivan management alone for the Coeur d'Alene riots. "The same miners who blew up the concentrator at Wardner," he said, "would have waded in blood to their knees, if necessary, to protect the property of the Mullan or Burke Canyon operators. Bunker Hill did everything to aggravate union men."

Boyce added that "the trouble will soon blow over," and suggested that Orchard and the other miners stick around in Butte, or at least in Montana, until the Coeur d'Alene mines reopened. Orchard remained in Butte four weeks, yet the "trouble looked as though it had hardly begun," what with "five thousand Federal troops scattered over the district and more than a thousand miners in the bull pens." Or so he read in the papers. Orchard wanted no part of it. Hearing talk in the Butte miners' hall that there was plenty of work in Utah, he bought a ticket for Salt Lake City. He wasn't technically on the lam. True, he had lighted the fuse of the "lifter" charge that finished the Bunker Hill concentrator, but he was still unknown to the military, or even the scab deputies. No warrant was out for him. Retribution, however, was hanging like a cloud over the Coeur d'Alenes. Vengeance was going to be so thorough that miners who could not prove they were not in Wardner on April 30 were automatically suspects. For all practical purposes Harry Orchard was on the lam. We may leave him thus briefly.

GENERAL MERRIAM'S COMMAND NUMBERED LESS than seven hundred officers and soldiers. They proceeded to arrest miners indiscriminately in all the towns, took them in boxcars to Wardner, and put them into a big rambling storehouse for hay that had survived the arsonists. Two days after the arrests began this lockup was so dreadfully crowded that two hundred prisoners were removed and put in boxcars on a nearby siding and guarded by soldiers. Meanwhile, crews of imported carpenters were whacking up barracks like structures in Wallace and Wardner, around each an exercise yard fenced with barbed wire. These were the bull pens that old-timers like to talk about sixty years later. They were hastily built. The sanitary facilities were such as to cause much criticism. If a prisoner wanted bedding, he had to supply it himself. The state provided food. The prisoners did the cooking.

By mid-May General Merriam complained that the prisoners were most uncomfortably housed, that the sanitation was intolerable, and that he was dissatisfied with the slow progress being made by the state to improve conditions. At that time some seven hundred men had been taken into custody. By late May the number in confinement had been reduced to three hundred and thirty, nearly all of whom "readily admitted to taking part in the riot of April 29."

Bartlett Sinclair, representing Governor Steunenberg, proclaimed that until further notice no miners were to be hired without a permit from the State of Idaho. Permits could be procured from state agents in Wallace and Wardner. Parties applying for permits must be prepared: "First, to deny all participation in the riots ... and second, to deny or renounce membership in any society which has incited, encouraged, or approved said riots or other violation of public law."

The number of men held in the bull pens steadily grew less as the weeding-out process continued. Yet the freed miners were in no haste to ask for jobs under the permit system. General Merriam reported as much, adding that "there are large numbers of idle and sullen men in Mullan, Burke, and Wallace." Late in May Merriam believed that conditions no longer warranted his presence. He left Major Allen Smith in command.

To prosecute those miners who were identified as taking part in the rioting, Governor Steunenberg named James Forney, and to assist Forney he sent James H. Hawley and William E. Borah. None of the prosecutors believed anything would be gained through conviction of the common run of miners. They favored the freeing of all rank and file and worked to procure indictment of certain leaders of the unions. Among these was Paul Corcoran, secretary of the Burke local, described "as a man of some means and high standing in the community." (He was later tried and convicted of being an accessory in the killing of Jim Cheyne, the Bunker Hill & Sullivan watchman, and sentenced to seventeen years in the Idaho prison. After serving two years he was granted a full pardon.)

One by one the bull-pen prisoners were discharged, though not before they had attempted escape in the classic manner of prisoners of war. Unsuspected by guards, they had tunneled some two hundred feet when one of the diggers, seeking to ventilate the hole, pushed a stick upward and jabbed a soldier lying on the ground. When the men refused to dig out the tunnel and fill it, they were put on bread and water for eight days. The attempt to escape and the disciplinary measures created a big noise in the press, and the Secretary of War, who was Elihu Root, began an inquiry to see if the troops should not be removed from the district.

The troops were not removed until later, but the steadily mounting public protest against the "wanton brutalities of the bull pens" and "suspension of habeas corpus" brought immediate action by Congress, and the House appointed a special committee of members to investigate conditions in the mining district. The majority of the committee reported that the charges against the military of improper conduct could not be sustained. The minority found, however, that the actions of the military were "reprehensible," that the Governor of Idaho had pursued "a most tyrannical course of conduct," and charged "a conspiracy on the part of the officers of the Bunker Hill & Sullivan mine, and those who sympathize with them, to drive from Shoshone County all miners by the device of the ‹permit system' ... maintained by the use of United States soldiers."

The investigation brought out the fact that of the approximately fifteen hundred union miners in the district, only 528 had actually been put under arrest. Of these, 130 were married, 398 single. Three hundred thirty were citizens of the United States, 198 were aliens. Nativities were: 132 Americans, 99 Swedes, 63 Italians, 47 Finns, 43 Irish, and 144 of other countries. It is probably safe to assume that few of these five hundred miners resumed work under the permit system in the Coeur d'Alenes. They merely left the district. Perhaps as many more had gone away when the going was good, before arrival of troops and martial law.

The Bunker Hill & Sullivan affair of April 29, 1899 had two notable results. First, the power of the Western Federation in the Coeur d'Alenes was almost wholly destroyed. Second, as an Idaho historian observed jubilantly, "the leaders of the disturbance were compelled to scatter to different parts of the United States." He was right enough, too. He could have added that this nineteenth-century Diaspora of hundreds of miners, with bitterness in their hearts, bore seeds that were to flower with striking malevolence in hard-rock camps throughout the West.

5.

A Jolly Miner on the Lam

We left Harry Orchard on the lam, riding the steam cars out of Montana for Salt Lake City. Though he was one of the thousand or so union miners in the Diaspora from the Coeur d'Alenes, he carried little or no bitterness with him. True, the "inconvenience" of his leaving, what with the snow and slush in the Bitterroots and all, was "irritating"; yet he was as ready to charge this annoyance to the Western Federation of Miners as to the recalcitrance of the Bunker Hill & Sullivan Mining and Concentrating Company, even forgetting his own part in lighting the fuse of that "lifter" in the boiler room. He just wasn't a union man. He was a card holder.

And now that he was on the lam, he turned his casual flight into something like a *Wanderjahr* as carefree as it was instructive in the geography and customs of mining camps of the Western United States. He stopped only a few days in Salt Lake City, then went to Bingham Canyon, also in Utah, and to work in the nonunion mines there. There was a good deal about Bingham to remind him of Burke, Idaho. The town, much larger than Burke, lay along one narrow street at the bottom of a canyon, then mounted in layers halfway up the hills. Silver and lead still composed the ore, which was taken from deep mines, but the brilliant engineering of Daniel C. Jackling was about to turn Bingham into one of the big producers of copper from open-pit mines.

Orchard had no trouble getting a job. All the boss wanted to know boiled down to one thing: Are you from the Coeur d'Alenes? No, said Orchard, and he was given a shovel and put on the payroll. His shift boss told him that a blacklist prepared by the Mine Owners Protective Association of Idaho was being circulated in all hard-rock camps, and that it gave names of the men "who worked in the Coeur d'Alenes at the time the Bunker Hill was blown up and left there afterward." The list could not have been complete. Orchard was still Orchard. Neither in Bingham or elsewhere, so it turned out, was he obliged to use an alias, save the one he adopted when he fled Canada.

In the mine at Bingham, however, he met a number of miners he had known casually at Burke, or Frisco, or Gem. All had changed their names. They warned Orchard they had already discovered the worst thing a man could do was to admit he had ever worked in the Coeur d'Alenes. One said a Coeur d'Alene miner not only couldn't get a job anywhere but would be told to get out of town to boot.

Bingham Canyon's facilities for relaxation reminded Orchard of Burke, only more so. Thirty saloons were running day and night, with the Old Crow and the "16 to 1" among the favorites. The gambling houses also operated on two shifts. There was a red-light section, too. Orchard felt at home in them all. It was the gaming that took more of his money than red lights and red liquor combined. "I'd be in a place," he recalled, "and a poker game would be on. I would stand around a while, just looking on. Then, as soon as a seat was open, I would sit in."

Sometime in July he quit the mines at Bingham and went to Cottonwood Canyon to work for contractors who were sinking a shaft. It was here he first operated a drill, which paid much better than mucking. After two months he got in on the contract and stayed until Christmas, then returned to Bingham Canyon to go on a mine payroll as a driller. He remained in Bingham for almost a year.

Late in 1900 the fancy took him to see California. He spent a few days in San Francisco, then went to sparsely populated Lake County and "remained all winter." He seems to have left no record of what he was doing there. Come spring, he was away to visit southern California, then to Salt Lake City again, where he drove a milk wagon for the Keystone Dairy. Wherever he went, he "tested fully the fascination and folly of gambling." He left the milk route to spend the winter working in an unnamed mine in Arizona, jumped Nevada to work in another unnamed mine, then joined a few miners on a prospecting trip into southern Idaho. This may also have been the time he visited the Sumpter Valley mining region in the Blue Mountains of eastern Oregon.

Orchard's period of booming occupied almost three years, much of the time at good wages. Because he was still basically a businessman at heart, he was always making resolutions to stop wandering, save his wages, then settle down to "some little business for myself." Time and again he would find himself with several hundred dollars that might have served to get him out of the wage-slave class, only to lose it all when he sat down at a faro bank or took a hand at poker.

Occasionally he tried beating his way on freight trains by bribing the shack with a dollar, but this was for novelty. He did not enjoy hoboing. He much preferred to ride the cushions. He dressed well and lived well. When his life as Albert Horsley came to mind, and the abandoned wife and child arose to haunt him, which was not too often, he might drink more than was good for him, but these reflective moods troubled him less than his inability to keep away from games of chance. Now and then there came upon him the age-old excuse of the ne'er-do-well—that he was merely a creature of circumstances. Psychiatry had not then made this notion both scientific and respectable, yet it gave him comfort to think that life had conspired to make him into a wanderer.

These black moods, however, came seldom. Orchard was a jolly, lighthearted fellow who made friends readily and seemed, when in company, to have not a care in the world. He *looked* jolly, too, a ruddy face set off with bright blue eyes that kindled easily into a smile. His stocky figure was becoming a deep rounded barrel of a body, set on short sturdy legs. He possessed what, in an Irishman, would have been considered the gift of Blarney. Quite often, in fact, he was hailed as a "mick" or a "harp."

Now, in July of 1902, Orchard had come again to Salt Lake City after his abortive prospecting trip into southern Idaho. He had a little money left but must go to work soon. He could have returned to Bingham Canyon and his old job in the mines there, but he wanted to see Colorado and the gold camps. Cripple Creek was said to be booming. It was reputed to be a strong Western Federation union district. Orchard heard that many of the black-listed miners of the Coeur d'Alenes had gone to work there without troubling to change their names. This fact made no difference to Orchard. He had a proper withdrawal card from the Western Federation of Miners. He was still a man on the ramble, out to see the world. In Salt Lake City he bought a railroad ticket that would take him to Cripple Creek, the "highest gold camp on earth."

6.

Cripple Creek: Background

In the summer of 1902, when Harry Orchard arrived in Colorado, Cripple Creek meant three things—a stream, a city, and a mining district. The stream wasn't much, yet twenty-five thousand people lived in Cripple Creek city along its banks. Another twenty thousand lived in the several smaller towns nearby. And in that year the district produced seventeen million dollars in gold, bringing the total for a decade to $111,361,633. It was then and for a few years to come one of the biggest gold camps on earth.

Like most mining camps, Cripple Creek was set in a somewhat appalling region. It lay in the first range of the Rockies twenty miles west of Colorado Springs and eighty-five miles south and a little west of Denver. The altitude ranged from nine to twelve thousand feet. The miners who worked in the Buena Vista lived in "the highest incorporated town in North America." This was Altman, 10,620 feet above the sea.

Volcanoes had piled up the hills. Steaming hot waters from deep in the earth percolated to the surface, bearing gold telluride in solution, with quartz. The whole area presented a rough, gaunt aspect of barren rocky ridges, almost arid, with sudden valleys marked by scrub trees and in season with a wealth of alpine flowers. These brief patches of brilliance, however, did little to soften the feeling that here one was in a grim and bitter country. It was not, as one observer remarked, a place to invite human habitation. Yet, in 1902 fifty thousand human beings made it their home.

This was the region where the still unsuspected talents of Harry Orchard were to have their first flowering. It was mere chance that had made him a miner just in time to take part in the violent events in the Coeur d'Alenes. Now, three years later, it was his fate to arrive in Cripple Creek only a little before that district, too, was ready to explode. The opposing forces were the same here as in Idaho. They had been gathering strength in Cripple Creek for almost as long. The conflict here was to be more sanguinary. It was to involve more men. Perhaps it was worthy of the name much of the national press called it, which was "revolution."

Orchard, one should keep in mind, was no longer the naive scissorbill who got a union card only because he needed a job, then went to mucking halfheartedly in a mine. Three years on the ramble had turned him into a skilled miner, a drill operator. They had made him a fairly typical boomer of the hard-rock camps—a here today, gone tomorrow boy, out to see the world. He did not like mining. He was no dedicated miner like many of the old veterans who had started work in Cornwall, the Cousin Jacks whose fathers and grandfathers had been miners before them. To them mining was more than a job. It was a way of life, comparable to farming or going to sea.

No few of these Cornishmen seemed to find some sort of beauty in their hard, murky lives. One can believe that these underground men had a feeling for the dark stopes; that blinking, bobbing candles seen down a long drift were a kind of poetry to them; that the dripping of water from the fissures in some remote cave served them as a rippling brook has served other men above ground, as a kind of music. They could thrill to the power of a blast that made the metallic walls tremble, then fall apart. They were at least working in the very midst of nature. And when they came up to look at the sun, the sun may have seemed more wonderful to them than to those who are never long where they miss it.

Harry Orchard was none of these. Working in a mine was to him a hellish job. He was even less a union man than a miner. If three years as a wage slave gave him a new viewpoint in regard to labor organizations, he never indicated as much. His attitude remained unchanged. It was that of a businessman waiting for an "opening," an "opportunity." The Western Federation card in his pocket was merely a permit to perform as a working stiff until something, as the phrase has it, turned up.

Something good was to turn up right here in Cripple Creek. But if one is to understand how and why it turned up just when it did, then a little knowledge of background is needed. Otherwise Orchard's exploits here might appear to have been the work of a man bereft of reason. Yet he was not mad. He was sane to the point of bleakness. Conditions were simply approaching the proper ripeness when he arrived. He recognized the opportunity, for he had long since become sophisticated in regard to relations between the unions of miners and the associations of mine owners. Had he not with his own hands set off the lifter charge in the Bunker Hill & Sullivan's boiler room? Things like that tended to give a man confidence. And perhaps ideas.

IT HAD TAKEN CRIPPLE CREEK a full decade to ripen and present an opportunity that was to lift Harry Orchard out of the ranks of the wage slaves and open for him not exactly a business career, but a professional one. There had been no mining or much of any other activity in the area until 1891. In that year Bob Womack, a cowhand on the Bennett & Myers ranch along the Creek, was spending his spare time prospecting for silver. Among other efforts he dug a hole forty feet deep into the side of Mount Pisgah, a small volcanic cone west of Pikes Peak, and came up with some likely-looking ore. He toted a sack of it to an assayer in Colorado Springs. It panned out at around a hundred and forty dollars a ton, in gold. Whereupon Womack performed in the manner expected of lucky prospectors. He got good and drunk, and on recovery found he had sold his claim outright for five hundred dollars.

A rush got under way immediately, and in it was Winfield Scott Stratton, a kindly, sad-eyed carpenter who so much preferred prospecting to his trade than when he left home *this* time, to head for Cripple Creek, his wife divorced him for nonsupport. Mrs. Stratton's action, though understandable, was for her tragically premature. Stratton staked out a couple of claims near Womack's discovery. When he died ten years later he left a fortune of twenty million dollars, which lawyers had to defend against the claims of an even dozen women, all of whom said they were Stratton's widow. Incidentally, Stratton was only one of the twenty-eight authentic millionaires of the Cripple Creek mining district.

Less than two years after the original strike, Cripple Creek city had a population of five thousand. The adjacent towns of Victor, Altman, Independence, Anaconda, Goldfield, Arequa, and Elkton were coming or already had come into being. One hundred and fifty actual mines were being worked. Another five hundred or so had their substance as lithographs on handsomely printed stock certificates. The Colorado & Midland railroad was building a line in from Divide on the north. The Florence & Cripple Creek was coming in from the south. In their first full year of operating, these roads carried out more than six million dollars' of gold-bearing ore, little more than a sample of what was to come.

Then came the nationwide money panic of 1893. The price of silver sagged, closing mines all over the West. Banks and factories closed too. There was wage cuts and strikes. Bread lines appeared in most cities. Not so in Cripple Creek, whose gold mines continued to run full blast.

In 1894 there were violent strikes at Pullman, Illinois, and in the Eastern coal fields. State and federal troops were called, and a Socialist, Eugene Debs, was put in jail for "fomenting a revolution." Meanwhile, the news got around that the Cripple Creek district was booming. Plenty of jobs. Good pay. No strikes. The backwash of foot-loose men began to flood prosperous Cripple Creek. Every freight brought the jobless and the destitute. They had either to be fed at public expense or run out of town. Several hundred of them soon took off to join the "Commonwealth Army" organized by "General" Jacob Coxey, a Populist, to march on Washington and to demand that the government do something to "relieve social distress." But many others remained in Cripple Creek. To some of the astute mine operators it seemed a propitious time to get more work for the same pay.

Presently all the mines in the district posted notice that on February 1, 1894, the working shift would be ten instead of the usual eight or nine hours. The daily wage was not raised. The workday was merely lengthened. The miners were understandingly alarmed but not surprised. They had expected something of the sort, and the more intelligent of them had already taken steps. At Altman they organized Free Coinage Union No. 19 and affiliated with the brand-new Western Federation of Miners, with headquarters in Butte, Montana. Other unions in the Cripple Creek district were formed at Cripple Creek city, Victor, and Anaconda. These were included in the Altman charter from the Federation.

Elected president of the Cripple Creek union district was John Calderwood, a Scot born at Kilmarnock, who had gone to work in the coal mines at nine, come to the United States at seventeen, and attended the McKeesport School of Mines, from which he was graduated in 1876. Before coming to Cripple Creek, he had headed the local miners' union at Aspen. He was a grave, cool, and courteous man. He also was convinced that miners' unions were an absolute necessity. A week after the mine operators posted their notice, Free Coinage Union issued a demand that the working shift of all mines in the district be made eight hours. The lines were set.

One who knew the Cripple Creek miners of this era observed that they were not the mining population familiar to the Eastern coal fields. Few were foreign-born. They were "neither ignorant nor easily cowed," but were "of the characteristic frontiersman type." They had come to Cripple Creek "not so much to find work as to seek fortune." They were rough, ready, used to shifting for themselves. They were reckless, ready to cast everything on a single die. And they had "small respect for authority."

The same observer said the mine operators were as much frontiersmen as the working stiffs. Most of them had played in luck and knew it.

With such forces arrayed against each other, it was not astonishing that nothing came of the few attempts made in January to find a basis for settlement. On February 1 the mines went to the ten-hour shift. On the seventh parties of union men circulated throughout the district, calling out the men. By noon every mine was closed save the Portland, Pikes Peak, Gold Dollar, and a few smaller outfits, all of which had promptly agreed to the demand for an eight-hour shift.

Now there followed an uneasy quiet. All union miners working were assessed fifteen dollars a month for a strikers' relief fund. The Butte union sent eight hundred dollars, and seven hundred dollars came from miners in the San Juan district. In Cripple Creek city the Green Bee grocery offered credit to the strikers. Soup kitchens were set up in all the towns.

By the end of February all smelters in Colorado were either closed or running part time. In early March the operators' front crumbled some more when the Gold King and Granite mines resumed work on an eight-hour shift. On March 14 the ten-hour operators got the district court to enjoin miners against interfering with operation of the Cripple Creek ten-hour mines. Sheriff Frank Bowers went around posting the injunction notices. Though his training for the job had been mostly as bouncer in a saloon, with a brief term as a night town marshal, he was a bighearted fellow with a yearning to be loved by everybody. Being sheriff of El Paso County in 1894 was no occupation for him.

A few of the mines attempted to open with ten-hour shifts. But the nonunion help was "quickly discouraged." Then Charles Keith, superintendent of the Victor, phoned Sheriff Bowers to say that a gang of Altman miners were coming to destroy his mine. Bowers sent six deputies. As soon as they reached Altman they were seized by Altman town officers and a posse of miners claiming to be the Altman police force, who turned the invaders around and ordered them to leave. They did.

Sheriff Bowers phoned Governor Davis H. Waite, possibly enlarging somewhat on conditions and making out that Cripple Creek was virtually in chaos. In 1892 Waite had been the Populist candidate for governor of Colorado and was elected by a good majority. He was sixty-seven years old and has been described as a Moses with a flowing white beard and a voice like Rocky Mountain thunder. He had not long since horrified all conservatives by declaiming publicly that, rather than see "the money power" gain the upper hand, it was infinitely better "that blood should flow to the horses' bridles." Otherwise, said he, "our national liberties would be destroyed."

The Governor ordered out the militia to the number of three hundred soldiers, who went by train to Midland, then made an all-night march overland to arrive at Cripple Creek in the morning. After conferring with Sheriff Bowers, the militia commander refused to take his men up the hill to Altman. President Calderwood had assured the militia officer that neither he nor any member of the union would resist arrest. The soldiers were recalled at once.

Bowers now went ahead to arrest Calderwood, Mayor Dean and Town Marshal Daly of Altman, and eighteen miners, who were taken to Colorado Springs, tried on various charges, and acquitted. Except with the mining interests, President Calderwood and union members were gaining sympathy throughout the state. Their discipline had been perfect. But the excitements during March had advertised the strike widely through newspapers and attracted the usual crew of hoodlums and professional criminals. It is significant that a local commentator wrote that "a particularly turbulent element" came into the district from the Coeur d'Alene country of Idaho.

What had been an uneasy peace during much of April was dented by bits of violence. Stores and warehouses were broken into and arms and ammunition stolen. Several nonunion men were beaten up. A deputy sheriff was wounded. At a secret meeting in Colorado Springs of the mine operators, Sheriff Bowers was called into consultation: Could he furnish protection for a large force of strikebreakers? No, said he, he couldn't. The county was financially unable to engage and equip the army that such a move would require. The operators said that they would pay the bill. Bowers then agreed to muster the required army of deputies.

Though the operators had meant their meeting to be secret, news of it leaked, and the officers of Free Coinage Union at Altman prepared for the worst. President Calderwood had been asked by the Western Federation of Miners to tour Colorado's other mining camps on behalf of the Cripple Creek strike. Before leaving he asked an old friend, Junius J. Johnson, to take charge of union affairs. A former West Pointer, Johnson set about establishing a military camp and headquarters on Bull Hill, the high steep bluff that commanded the town of Altman.

Johnson was a calm and excellent commander. The camp quickly took form, and men were drilled and detailed to certain duties or responsibilities. A breastworks went up. A commissary was stocked. The first order of the day, any day, was strict discipline.

Commander Johnson's chief troubles stemmed from a gang of toughs who had mistakenly been admitted to union membership. Several of these were of that "turbulent" Coeur d'Alene element. Others were ex-convicts. Their leader was "General" Jack Smith whom, to keep peace, Johnson had to accept as his lieutenant. Smith's first act was to capture a couple of alleged spies of the mine operators and beat them nigh to death.

One evening late in May Commander Johnson received word that a small army of gunmen were on their way to the Cripple Creek district. Though they were officially described as "El Paso County deputy sheriffs," they were really ex-policemen and ex-firemen, all from Denver, who were being paid by the mine operators as agreed upon with Sheriff Bowers. A second message to Johnson reported that the first objective of the coming army was to be the strikers' camp on Bull Hill. Commander Johnson told his men that these mercenaries from Denver must not be permitted on Bull Hill; then he sent out details to make certain arrangements he believed might deter the gunmen without a formal battle.

At about nine o'clock on the morning of May 25—it was still 1894—two flatcars loaded with a hundred and twenty-five of the Denver gunmen rolled along the Florence & Cripple Creek railroad in full view of Bull Hill. The train stopped; the deputies got off and started to establish their base camp before marching up to attack the strikers at Altman. Just then, said a witness, "the whole sky over and around Victor town seemed to explode," and the shaft house at the Strong mine was wafted three hundred feet into the air, then disintegrated, by a blast that was felt even on Bull Hill, where wild cheering blended with the echoes.

A moment later a second blast ripped the Strong's steam boiler loose and sent it skyward; and down came a shower of timbers, hunks of iron, pieces of cable, and iron wheels of assorted sizes. The deputies, tough men though they might be, were appalled at such a welcome. They clambered back on the flatcars and the train backed out of sight of Bull Hill.

While the dismayed deputies reconsidered matters, the whole Cripple Creek area seemed to explode with excitement. Yelling mobs broke into liquor warehouses and emerged with cases, jugs, and kegs of whisky, and whole barrels of the same. This just happened to be also the day that the F.&C.C. railroad paid off its grading crew of two hundred men. Almost automatically they headed for the nearest saloons. By early afternoon the half-dozen towns in the Cripple Creek district were so many bedlams of drunken men.

This was the kind of chaos much appreciated by "the Coeur d'Alene element." That night a mob of union men loaded a flatcar with capped dynamite, then started it coasting downgrade in the hope it would collide with another car still on the track near the Denver gunmen's camp. Instead, it left the rails on a curve and exploded, killing a cow.

"General" Jack Smith collected his crew of drunken hoodlums and loaded two wagons with dynamite. He was, he said, going to blow up every mine shaft and every mine superintendent's house in the district. Commander Johnson prevented this worse than idiotic expedition from leaving camp. He ordered Smith to sober up, and then, if he felt like doing something for the cause, to take his gang and chase the retreating Denver army out of the district.

Smith sobered up—a little—then led his mob to Victor town. There, about midnight, they stole a work train, fired up the locomotive, then tore out of town southward with a miner at the throttle. Somewhere in the night out of Victor they caught up with the Denver gang and fought a bloody battle among the boulders. One deputy was killed, and one striker. Five more miners were captured by the Denverites.[2]

During the night Union President Calderwood returned from his organizing tour and moved quickly to prevent further bloodshed. He locked up "General" Jack Smith and asked saloonkeepers to close their doors. Quiet was restored, briefly, while more violence was being prepared. At a so-called Law and Order meeting in Colorado Springs, the mine operators' stronghold, Sheriff Bowers was authorized to engage twelve hundred additional deputies. They were recruited in all parts of the state, then sent to a camp established on the Colorado & Midland railroad at Divide. Governor Waite issued a double-headed proclamation: He called on the strikers to desist from their unlawful assembly on Bull Hill. He declared the big force of deputies to be illegal and ordered it to be disbanded. Then he ordered the militia to be alerted.

Neither the Bull Hill army nor Bowers's mob of deputies made any attempt to disband. Each remained in camp while an honest effort of arbitration was made by President Calderwood, mine owners Dave Moffat and J. J. Hagerman, various civic leaders, and Governor Waite himself. The meeting was held in a hall on Colorado College campus. It was forced to break up when a vast mob of howling citizens gathered at the college. They were bent on lynching Calderwood and Governor Waite, both of whom were blamed for the Cripple Creek disorders.[3] Judge Horace Gray Lunt stepped out on the porch to address the mob and hold their attention, and the governor of Colorado and John

---

[2] "In retaliation, says David Lavender, the union incarcerated three officials of the Strong mine who were caught in the shaft-house explosion; and "eventually all eight captives were released through a formal prisoner-of-war exchange unprecedented in United States labor strife." See his *The Big Divide*.

[3] See Benjamin McKie Rastall's account in *Bulletin of the University of Wisconsin*, No. 198 (Feb. 1908).

Calderwood slipped out a rear door, got into a cab that was waiting for them, and were taken to board the Governor's special train, and so to Denver. The incident is an illuminating commentary on the state of law and order in the Colorado Athens of 1894.

The determined arbitrators resumed their conference in Denver. Two days later the mine owners and the Free Coinage Union signed an agreement: eight hours' work for three dollars; no discrimination against union or nonunion men. It was a notable victory for the union.

But the business was far from finished. The army of deputies was still in camp at Divide. Bull Hill was still in the possession of the Free Coinage Union army. Governor Waite now turned out the Colorado militia and sent them to Cripple Creek. The Governor, whose support of the union never wavered, meant that the militia should prevent Sheriff Bowers's deputies from attacking the union stronghold. If calm could be maintained, then all would be well. Union miners were ready to return to work; the mine operators were anxious to have them.

But nothing even approaching calm could be maintained. By the time the militia arrived, in command of General E. J. Brooks, the army of deputies had broken up, cut telephone and telegraph wires, held newspaper reporters under guard, and advanced toward Bull Hill. At daybreak they ran into pickets. There was some shooting, though nobody was hit. The deputies paused to hold a council of war.

At this juncture the militia arrived. While the troops were unloading, General Brooks conferred with Sheriff Bowers and County Commissioner W. S. Boynton. Friction quickly developed as to which of the two armies should have command of the situation. Nor did it help to clarify matters that Bowers did not want the deputies to attack Bull Hill, while Boynton was determined they should. The bickering went on. Meanwhile, the Bull Hill army was busy with additional defensive measures.

Under West Pointer Junius Johnson, men had mined the hill with dynamite charges connected with electric wires to explode at press of a button. Every miner had a rifle and a cartridge belt. Every miner had in a vest pocket five dynamite cartridges the size of pencils, fitted with percussion caps. The Free Coinage Union artillery was a possibly unique combination of medieval and modern arms: a tremendous bow gun capable of throwing missiles a quarter of a mile with fine accuracy; the missiles were beer bottles filled with explosive and capped to go off on impact. These things, plus a grade steeper than that which faced the British troops at Bunker Hill, presented obvious hazards to any head-on attack.

The efficient and resolute preparations on Bull Hill were in contrast to the muddled complications that had stalled the Colorado militia and the army of deputies. Exactly who ordered whom to do what was never clear; but after a while the twelve hundred deputies started to move on the enemy. The enemy was ready. Just as the deputies began to march, the whistle at the Victor mine let go a long wail of warning. The hillside immediately took on the look of an anthill; from far below the deputies could see hundreds of men swarming to their posts.

General Brooks decided he must act. Bugles sounded, and the militia went forward at the double-quick. They intercepted the deputies before a shot was fired. In the name of the State of Colorado, General Brooks ordered them back to their camp, then led his own troops up the hill. The miners offered no resistance but permitted the militia to occupy their fort and Altman town.

The army of deputies, however, was bound to have some action. Instead of dispersing, they marched into Cripple Creek town, where they arrested many persons, clubbed a few more, and made themselves fairly objectionable. General Brooks speedily moved militia into the town and took charge. The deputies were put aboard a train for Colorado Springs.

The mines of the Cripple Creek district resumed work with an eight-hour shift. John Calderwood and some three hundred miners peacefully submitted to arrest on various charges ranging from disorderly conduct to attempted homicide. Only four were convicted, and all were pardoned long before expiration of their sentences.

Free Coinage Union No. 19, Western Federation of Miners, gained enormous prestige in labor circles in the United States, and with many people who had no connection with unions. By winning the strike it also gave a powerful impetus to the new and still weak federation just when it was needed.

The new sense of power prompted federation officials to send organizers to Leadville where the silver-poor mine operators were content to pay workers two and a half dollars a day. A union was formed and demanded a three-dollar wage. The operators brought in strikebreakers, many of whom were beaten up and run out of town by the union "regulators." Whereupon the owners of the Coronado and Emmet mines built a high board fence around their surface workings. One night soon the Coronado fence was dynamited, buildings set afire, and one town fireman shot and killed when trying to stem the fire. Then the union regulators attacked in force, to be met with gunfire from strikebreakers within the stockade. Three union men died. The attackers moved up a homemade cannon contrived from a length of steam pipe. It worked pretty well, too. One round served to blow a wide hole through the fence. In went the attackers, only to lose still another man. That ended the battle, but not the trouble. Militia were called in, and for a long period Leadville was virtually under military rule. The strikers eventually returned to work at the operators' terms.

A little later the federation won a partial victory at Telluride, where strikers closed the Smuggler-Union mine and ambushed an armed night shift of strikebreakers, killing three, wounding five more. They then chased the scabs into their stockade and besieged them. When their ammunition gave out, the scabs surrendered on condition they not be molested. The strikers agreed, then brutally beat their enemies. One died. Next, they marched the strikebreakers out of camp and over thirteen-thousand-foot Imogene Pass, and ordered them to keep moving.

A settlement was reached later by which the federation won its demands. So-called settlements often leave a few matters not quite settled. A year after settlement of the Telluride strike, an unknown gunman shot and killed Arthur Collins, manager of the Smuggler-Union mine, as he sat reading at his fireside. At Cripple Creek, more than three years after settlement of that strike, the homes of four men were invaded by thugs and the victims mercilessly beaten. At Altman, "General" Jack Smith was shot to death. Truces could be signed. They could not wipe out bitter memories.

One defeat, two victories. The Western Federation of Miners could feel it had done pretty well in Colorado. Except for the Coeur d'Alenes, it had made good progress elsewhere. When it staged the first Cripple Creek strike in 1894, the federation was hardly more than a name. By 1903, more than two hundred active unions were enrolled under its banner.

Edward Boyce, as related, was the dynamic leader who had done so much to get the federation away to a good start. In 1902 he resigned,

Cripple Creek: Background

and Charles H. Moyer was elected president. The new secretary-treasurer was William Dudley Haywood. Then, there was George A. Pettibone, no longer a miner but a man of parts so far as Western Federation affairs were concerned. It was he who back in 1892 at Gem-Frisco thought up the clever idea of sending dynamite down a dry flume to blow up the mill and was arrested for his pains. Many of the rifles used by miners in the Coeur d'Alene troubles of 1899 had been shipped in from Denver in piano boxes. This, too, had been Pettibone's work. Now in 1902 he operated a small store in Denver, an occupation that permitted him to devote considerable time and no little energy to his avocation, which was that of an unofficial adviser to the executive board of the Western Federation of Miners; and also, to his hobby, which was chemistry in its relation to explosives. Moyer and Haywood held him in high regard.

It is improbable that any of these three men ever had heard of Harry Orchard when he arrived in Colorado in the summer of 1902 and applied for membership in Free Coinage Union No. 19 of the Western Federation of Miners, whose hall was at Altman, high on Bull Hill. He was still just another hard-rock hobo, a nondescript boomer, out on a tour of drinking, wenching, gambling, and, of course, mining. It was Haywood, Moyer, and Pettibone who were to give direction and meaning to what up to now had been Orchard's commonplace and rudderless life.

7.

Orchard, the High-Grader

Orchard's first twelve months in the Cripple Creek district were to be fairly interesting, though not exciting, and quite prosperous. He got a job almost at once in the Trachyte mine, running a machine drill at four dollars a day. On his first payday he joined Free Coinage Union No. 19 at Altman, of which W. F. Davis was then president. Orchard knew Davis. He had been one of the leading figures of the Coeur d'Alene unions when the boys blew up the Bunker Hill & Sullivan mine back in 1899. Orchard was also fortunate in finding a genial boardinghouse in a saloon operated in Independence by Johnnie Neville, old-time miner who had been injured in a mine accident before he went into the liquor business.

Orchard had worked in mine towns in Idaho, Nevada, and Utah, but had never seen anything like the Cripple Creek district. A trolley-car system ran all over the region; and between the larger towns, such as Cripple Creek and Victor, the cars ran every half hour. The steam railroads also ran suburban trains. There were plenty of saloons to quench the thirst of a hard-drinking population, honky-tonks and plain and fancy bawdyhouses to satisfy the needs of the large number of single males. There were good hotels. Both Victor and Cripple Creek had an opera house for road shows and an occasional season of stock. Orchard thought the district more like an extensive city than a mining camp. He was glad, too, that there were "hardly any foreigners."

There seemed to be plenty of jobs for everybody. After a few weeks he quit his job at the Trachyte, got another in the Hull City, tired of that, and moved over to Vindicator No. 1, near the top of Bull Hill. Here he stayed, having noted at once that the miners in this fantastically rich and deep hole in the ground had raised high-grading to an art.

High-grading was stealing ore and could be done with profit only where the quartz was of extraordinary richness. A good deal of the Vindicator ore ran to three dollars a pound. The boys called it "picture rock," or "glomings." It was said to be "something good for the vest pocket." Orchard learned to keep an eye peeled for pieces of sylvanite, which was almost pure gold. It was the custom for drillers to work in pairs. Orchard and his partner first joined the racket by secreting small hunks of the richest ore in their dinner buckets, then progressed to dropping high-grade screenings down between their underdrawers and pants legs, which were tucked into the shoes. Greed naturally increased with every successful theft, and one night at quitting time Orchard was so heavily loaded that his partner feared they had gone too far. "If you stumble," he told Orchard, "you won't be able to stand up again without being helped." But they made it without trouble, and, later that night in a phony assayer's office, the load tipped the scales at something over fifty pounds.

The racket could not have been carried on except for the many crooked assayers near every mine in the district. Orchard did business with four, all in the little town of Independence, and there were said to be thirty-odd such offices in Cripple Creek city. The accepted method was for the miner to deliver the ore to the assayer, who would crush it then and there, extract the gold, weigh it, and give the miner one half. Fifty per cent was the standard fee "for taking the risk."

It *was* a risk, too, and one night no less than eight so-called assaying offices were blown up by explosions in Cripple Creek, Victor, and Independence, scattering instruments, scales, and other equipment all over the street. It was generally believed the mine owners were responsible, though no one was arrested or even charged with the disorder. High-grading was generally condoned in the district, anyway. Merchants and saloonkeepers liked the flow of extra money. It was "easy money" and likely to be spent the same way. Even if arrested with his pockets filled with rich ore, no miner would be convicted by a Cripple Creek jury, and a local judge was said to have ruled that stealing ore was not larceny because "mineral is real estate."

The dynamiting of the assay offices was something of a sensation, and Cripple Creek dearly loved sensations; but it was ineffective. High-grading continued, and competition increased. The more energetic assayers started regular collection routes. An agent would go to a miner's room or house right after he had come off shift and collect the ore; or the miner might leave his ore in a stipulated saloon or cigar store to be picked up. In time, several assayers provided miners with neat canvas belts lined with flannel and containing pockets for ore.

Though Orchard figured that the phony assayers stole from the miner about half of his stolen ore, he discovered it did no good to complain. When he started shopping around, he found they were all alike. The returns were always the same. Yet, for many months, Orchard's picture rock brought him more money than his four-dollar-a-day wages. He felt fairly wealthy, and soon found he was spending far too much in genial Johnnie Neville's saloon. He had started keeping company with the widow of a miner who had been killed in an accident. She had her own home. Orchard found it pleasant, and came to believe, briefly, that he would be more content as a homebody than as one of the boys whose social life centered in Neville's grog-shop. He did not trouble to tell the widow he had a wife and daughter, or even his true name. They were married in June 1903. The new Mrs. Orchard appears to have been an honest, decent, God-fearing woman. It is possible, too, that Orchard himself believed he had settled down to the quiet life of a hard-working and high-grading citizen.

Then, on August 8, and to the alarmed surprise of every working miner in the district, the Western Federation ordered its thirty-five hundred members to quit work in fifty Cripple Creek mines. The strike call was a stunner. A cardinal rule of the Western Federation of Miners stipulated that a strike must be voted by the miners concerned. Cripple Creek miners had not been asked to vote.

Harry Orchard and many others were dismayed. Cripple Creek wages were good. Working conditions were as good as those anywhere. When the strike call came, hundreds of miners crowded the union halls demanding to know what had happened, and how. The call was official enough. The surprise was due to the fact that the rank-and-file union members had never taken the trouble to read the proceedings of the last convention of their federation. At that meeting the delegates had been inspired by the hellfire urging of their new general secretary, William D. Haywood, to pass a resolution granting the federation's executive board the right to call a strike when it seemed best to do so, and never mind voting by the rank and file.

Now, in their several union halls, the Cripple Creek miners were informed of what had happened: The strike was to support the federation's failing attempt to organize the workers in the smelters of Colorado City. Specifically, it was called because of the refusal of Charles MacNeill, manager of the Colorado Reduction & Refining Company, to rehire nine union men he had fired. The federation then requested the mine operators to cease sending Cripple Creek ore to the Colorado City smelters. They refused. So, out of the Cripple Creek mines walked thirty-five hundred men, Harry Orchard among them.

Though much blood was to be shed, there was really little genuine enthusiasm for the strike on the part of the miners. They felt that they were being used to club the mine owners into clubbing the smelter operators into recognition of the federation at Colorado City. This would not have been so bad if the smelter stiffs had shown marked desire to join the union. But they hadn't. And now a total of nine smeltermen were responsible for thirty-five hundred miners going on a strike they had neither voted nor wanted.

The Cripple Creek mine owners, however, presented an almost solid front. They felt keenly about it. There were no grievances to adjust, nor any apparent method of settlement save to join hands with the Western Federation. They determined to break the strike without compromise of any sort. President Moyer and Secretary Haywood of the federation were just as determined to win recognition for the union throughout Colorado. Orchard's old pal from the Coeur d'Alenes, W. F. Davis, told him that the federation officials were ready to make Colorado "a slaughter ground" if necessary. Davis was now president of Free Coinage Union, which Orchard had joined, and whose members were often called the "Bull Hill dynamiters" from the reputation they had won during the strike of 1894.

Except for the big Portland mine, which the union permitted to run to supply its own mill at Colorado City, the Cripple Creek mines were all closed by August 10. Many merchants announced that they would not give credit during the strike. The unions opened stores for members in Cripple Creek, Victor, and Anaconda, selling groceries at cost. The Western Federation's treasury was believed to be in fine condition to support a long strike.

Along with the others, the Vindicator mine was closed. Orchard thought he saw an opportunity to "keep off the union's bread line" and also make a few dishonest dollars while the mines were down. He proposed to his working partner, a Joe Schultz, that they see what they could do in the way of high-grading at night. Schultz was agreeable.

It was neither an easy nor a particularly safe occupation. The shaft house of the Vindicator was brightly lighted and guarded by mine detectives. Within a hundred feet of the shaft house was an old unused shaft. One night Orchard and Schultz entered this opening unobserved, then began a precarious descent that took them down a thousand feet, mostly by old ladders that were broken in many places, and rotten in others. They had to be careful about lights, too, lest they meet guards patrolling the many levels. From the shaft, the two men made their way some two thousand feet along a drift until they came across some rich ore. With picks they dug out a load of forty pounds, packed it back down the slope, then up those dubious ladders to the opening. It was still night above ground, and they got away unsuspected. The assayer rated the ore at a dollar a pound, charged a twenty-dollar fee, and left the two men ten dollars each for the night's work.

This was pretty good, if a man didn't mind crawling down and up two thousand feet of ladder rungs, wondering which was sound and which wasn't, and taking chances with mine guards who were notoriously trigger-happy during a strike. Orchard and Schultz made several more expeditions during the first four weeks after the mines closed, bringing up from forty to eighty pounds of ore each trip. The stuff panned out from fifty cents to a dollar a pound.

The strike meanwhile began to develop the characteristics common to American labor disputes. One week after the strike call, the mine owners announced they would open. First was the El Paso. A crew built a ten-foot fence around the shaft house. Seventeen armed guards were put on duty. The Golden Cycle was next. When men came to erect a fence, an armed picket attempted to stop them. He was arrested and put in jail. Up went the fence.

After dark the next day, Thomas M. Stewart, an old man who had been in the crew of carpenters putting up the Golden Cycle fence, was taken from his home by five masked men, cruelly beaten, shot in the back, and left for dead. He managed to crawl to the Victor trolley line and was taken to the hospital. Then, a gang set upon John T. Hawkins, a justice of the peace at Altman, and beat him up.

The mine operators declared that Cripple Creek was in a reign of terror, then asked Governor J. H. Peabody to send troops. He sent a commission to investigate, then acting on its recommendation ordered seven hundred National Guardsmen, under Adjutant-General Sherman M. Bell, to Cripple Creek. In the troops were units of infantry, calvary, and artillery. Headquarters was set up near Goldfield, with subsidiary camps on Bull Hill near Altman, at the El Paso and Golden Cycle mines, at Elkton town, and in Cripple Creek itself.

Guards were stationed at all the mines. There were sentinels on the highways. Telegraph lines of the Western Union and Postal companies connected headquarters with Denver and with the subsidiary troop camps. And, when night fell, people all over the district could see the beams of an enormous portable searchlight that stabbed the dark and swept the stark hills, the shaft houses, miners' homes, and union halls.

At about the same time the troops arrived there came also what certainly was an organized influx of hard-looking characters, several of whom were recognized as ex-convicts. These men were immediately made deputy sheriffs. Orchard knew at least two of them who had been sent to the penitentiary for crimes committed in Cripple Creek. He figured they had been pardoned from the pen with the understanding they would serve as deputies during the strike. It was a reasonable assumption.

Orchard did not like the look of things, especially when his friend Davis of the Free Coinage Union told him that it had been the Bull Hill dynamiters who had beaten up Hawkins and Stewart. Orchard's memories of 1899 in the Coeur d'Alenes now prompted him to take steps. He was a member of the union, but he was not what could be described as a strong union man. He told his wife he was going on a fishing trip with his friend Johnnie Neville. And that was what he did. The two men went to distant Routt County, up on the Wyoming border, and spent the next four weeks fishing and drinking.

Orchard had thought that the strike might be settled while he and Neville were whipping the streams of Routt County. But, when they returned to Steamboat Springs to take the railroad for Cripple Creek and saw their first newspapers in a month, it was clear the troubles were far from over. The press was filled with date-lined stories from Victor, Goldfield, and Cripple Creek. But Johnnie Neville still owned a saloon in Independence; Harry Orchard not only had a wife there but also, some few hundred dollars in the bank at Victor.

The fishermen arrived home to find that the strike was being rapidly lost. From the first the military leaders had obviously been in closest sympathy with the mine owners. Indeed, General Bell had expressed himself clearly on this point. "I came here," he stated for the press, "to do up this damned anarchistic Federation of Miners." When criticized by the *Victor Record*, a morning paper and organ of the miners' union, a detail of forty-five guardsmen arrested Editor George E. Kiner and four employees and put them in a sort of bull pen that had been hastily erected around the Goldfield jail. When Mrs. Emma Langdon, linotype operator, heard of the arrests, she went to the office, barred it, and got out the paper with a leading story headed, "Somewhat Disfigured but Still in the Ring." The *Record*'s force was kept in the stockade one day, then turned over to the civil authorities charged with criminal libel.

Friction between citizens and soldiers increased daily. A few strikebreakers and mine guards were beaten up. When habeas corpus proceedings resulted in a court order to free several prisoners from the stockade, a company of infantry plus a troop of cavalry delivered the ten miners to the courthouse, and a Gatling gun was set up directly in front of the building, while a detail of sharpshooters took positions on the roof of the National Hotel across the street. None but court officers and members of the bar were permitted to enter the courthouse. Martial law had not yet been declared, though it might as well have been. It was obvious, wrote an observer who had nothing to gain either way, that the troops "were devoted not so much to the simple preservation of order as to the crushing of the unions' activity."

Six days after arrival of the guardsmen, the Golden Cycle resumed operations with an almost complete crew of strikebreakers that were shipped into the district. Then came reopening of the Findlay, Strong, Elkton, Tornado, Ajax, and Thompson mines. On September 17 a carload of seventy strike-breakers arrived under military guard and were escorted to the mine heads. Next day came more strikebreakers.

By then the mine owners' association was carrying advertisements in papers as distant as Duluth, offering three dollars a day for common labor and free transportation to all who stayed one month. They were not always careful to state that a strike was on. Emil Peterson told the strikers what happened to him: At Gilbert's Employment Office, 5 South Avenue, Duluth, Minnesota, so he related, he signed for a job firing a boiler at five dollars a day, the fare of eighteen dollars to Cripple Creek advanced. Another seventy-five men left with Peterson in charge of a burly agent. They picked up some sixty more at St. Paul, and the whole gang were taken to Colorado Springs before they learned that strike conditions prevailed in the Cripple Creek district. The men grew restless, but were kept in hand overnight, then put aboard a train for the mines. The train stopped somewhere near Victor. The guards ordered the men to get off and line up. At this point, Emil Peterson related, he shouted, "Don't go to work," and started to run. A guard drew his revolver and shot several times but missed. Peterson made his way to the Victor union hall and told his story. He didn't know what happened to the other imported men.

When Johnnie Neville and Harry Orchard arrived in Independence, they found a town in the grip of suspicion and fear that is a characteristic climate of the dead calm that so often precedes the shooting.

Part Three:

The Professional Man

8.

The Tearing of Things Loose

The surface calm of the district fooled nobody. Orchard felt the tension immediately in the now quiet streets where people walked but no longer laughed or shouted. They spoke in hushed tones, after looking around to see who was near. It was present in the saloons, which were still open but were as hushed as they used to be filled with tumult. The quiet pervaded even the hall of Free Coinage Union at Altman, where Orchard went to get the news, to hear what the boys were talking about.

It was obvious that the mass of miners was becoming discouraged as one after another the mines opened with nonunion crews. Not only that, but only too many former union members were slinking back to their old jobs. The National Guard was resented. These troops contained many men who should never have been given uniforms or guns. Some of the junior officers quickly developed a maddening officiousness. Many of the privates should have been in school, possibly reform school. Orchard saw them peddling whole hams they had stolen from the commissary to anyone who would buy, then heading for the nearest saloon.

The uneasy calm was rippled during November's first week by two attempts to wreck the Florence & Cripple Creek railroad's night train that carried strikebreakers from the mines to the rooming houses in Cripple Creek town. Railroad detectives arrested H. H. McKinney, a member of Free Coinage Union, who confessed and implicated Orchard's old friend, W. F. Davis, and six other union men. All except McKinney were released on bail.

Like almost everyone else, Orchard grew nervous and restless in the tense quiet. Perhaps he could manage a little more high-grading in the Vindicator. He could use the cash. So, could his partner, Joe Schultz. Joe was agreeable. It would not be so simple now that the mine was running, but they knew all the backways. It was worth exploring anyhow.

The two men got into and out of the mine without meeting anyone, though they heard work going on and thought it too risky to start digging for picture rock. During their tour, Orchard happened to notice about a carload of dynamite that had been stored in a crosscut on the eighth level of the mine. It gave him an idea.

Next day, in the union hall, Orchard talked to Davis, just released on high bail from the charge of attempted train wrecking. Davis seemed desperate. More strikebreakers were coming into the district daily, he said, and several mines were working with full crews. "If we can't do something to scare the scabs from entering the district," he said, "and scare our own men to keep them in line, we're going to lose this strike."

Orchard broached his idea. "There's a whole carload of powder in one place in the Vindicator," he said. "If the boys want to do something, they could go down and set it off. It would blow up the whole mine. Kill everybody down there." Davis seemed interested. He asked a number of questions and said something to the effect that he would think it over. Two days later he looked Orchard up and without more ado asked him if he could get into the Vindicator and set off the load of dynamite when one or the other of the two shifts was at work.

They talked a while. Orchard professed that he had suggested more as a joke than anything else. Davis was not a joker. As the head man of the most radical union in the district, he knew that the executive board of the Western Federation would hold him largely responsible for failure of the strike. It was now failing fast. He made a business proposition: if Orchard would set off the powder, he should have two hundred dollars direct from Western Federation headquarters. What was more, Davis would have Slim Campbell help Orchard. Campbell was one of the Bull Hill dynamiters gang. He, too, was then out on bail, like Davis, in connection with the futile train-wrecking job. Orchard told Davis he had rather go alone than with Campbell and agreed for two hundred dollars to set off the big charge in the Vindicator. Davis said he would have the money as soon as the mine was blown up.

Orchard went to see Joe Schultz. Yes, he would go. That very night, toting fuse and caps, they entered the Vindicator by their usual route and went to the eighth level. The stock of powder was right where it had been, near the main-shaft station, which was bright with electric lights. The two men had planned to do their work as soon as the shift went to the surface for lunch at midnight. Now they waited for ten minutes or so in a dark stope to make sure all hands had gone up. They would have to work fast; the crew would be back in half an hour.

At ten minutes past midnight, Schultz and Orchard went to the brightly lighted station, which they had reason to believe was now deserted. It wasn't. A cage was there waiting, the cager in it, and alert. "Hurry up, boys," he called. "This is the last cage." He thought the two men were miners of the leg-dragging sort, always a little late, and he was irritated. "Hurry up," he repeated.

Orchard and Schultz were too astonished to say anything. They simply started to back down into the dark of a drift. The cager was suspicious. Possibly he was an undercover man as well as a cager. He lighted his lamp and started to follow the two strangers. He was gaining rapidly when Orchard pulled out his revolver and shot twice in his direction. The cager turned and ran back.

It was now up to Orchard and Schultz to get out of the Vindicator as fast as they could, and never mind the powder. The fugitives had first to go up a hundred feet in a stope, then down a drift for perhaps a quarter of a mile, then down through an old stope on the timbers, and to crawl on their bellies through a narrow passage they had dug in their high-grading days. Then, the way was up—a good nine hundred feet on the same ancient ladders they had used before. By the time they approached the surface opening, according to Orchard's watch, a half hour had passed. He figured the mine was by then being searched by guards and told himself it would be a wonder if the entrance they were heading for was not guarded too. He stuck his gun into the front of his belt, thinking it wiser to shoot his way out than to remain in the mine and be run down later.

The Vindicator's captain of guards, however, did not know the mine so well as Orchard and Schultz did. It turned out he had posted an armed guard at every entrance except the one by which the two fugitives now made their exit. When they were clear of the mine, Orchard remarked to Schultz that never before had the world outside looked so large or so good to him. Many years later he told an acquaintance that in seventy-five years he had never been quite so scared as on the night that he and his partner crawled and climbed from the bowels of the Vindicator mine to breathe the fresh rarefied air of Bull Hill and see the clear great stars of a November night in Colorado.

The affair of the two mysterious strangers shooting at the cager in the Vindicator was the talk of the district next day; all entrances to the mine were still being watched; the entire workings were being searched by armed detectives; the gunmen were thought to be still hiding within the mine. The effect on the strike was not very strong. A few nonunion miners quit the Vindicator, but the ranks were quickly filled with newer imported strikebreakers.

Orchard scarcely had the nerve to demand the two hundred dollars from Davis for an explosion that never went off. But he did ask for thirty-five dollars, and this went to pay taxes on property owned in South Park by Mrs. Orchard. He also asked Sherman Parker, secretary of Free Coinage Union, for money. Parker told him there wouldn't be any money unless "something was pulled off." He said that if Orchard had killed the cager, or almost anyone else in the Vindicator, it would have been easy to raise money from federation headquarters. "But you got to tear something loose," Parker said.

Orchard felt aggrieved. Thirty-five dollars for the hazards he had gone through. Bad luck had prevented setting off a disaster that would have frightened every scab out of every mine in the district. But you couldn't collect anything on the plea of misfortune. He was cheered presently when Davis and Secretary Parker came to him with another offer. If he could rig up some sort of a trap so that when the cage came down with a load of scabs it would set off an explosion, it would be worth exactly five hundred dollars to him.

Orchard pointed out that this might well not work, because the cage was often run down the shaft empty, in which case the blast would not kill anybody. But he had a surer plan. For five hundred dollars he would rig an infernal machine that would certainly kill a few men and so scare the others they would ask for their time and go away forever from Cripple Creek. All right, said Davis, go show us what you can do, and you shall have five hundred dollars by the time the mine is cleared of smoke and bodies.

Joe Schultz wanted no part of the plan. He told Orchard it didn't sound good to him; and anyway, he and a few others of the union boys were working free-lance in a leased hole in the ground they hoped might become a paying property. Orchard thereupon looked up a couple of characters of whom little or nothing is known. Billy Aikman said he was not afraid of a little blood and would be glad to help, and Billy Gaffney was agreeable.

Orchard went out and rustled twenty pounds of dynamite, which he did not think was enough for the job. He was always a heavy-loader when it came to powder, anyway, and he asked Gaffney if he could locate some more powder. Gaffney came back with at least thirty pounds. Every stick was frozen solid, but Gaffney had been a powderman in his day, and he thawed the stuff over the stove in his house, which was handy to the Vindicator.

The conspirators planned in this fashion: Orchard and Aikman were to pack the powder into the mine and set the trap; Gaffney was to remain just inside the mouth of the shaft as lookout. At half-past two one cold morning in mid-November, the three men left Gaffney's house for the mine. Gaffney took post inside the shaft. The other two, each carrying some twenty-five pounds of powder, went down an unused and unguarded shaft to the fourth level, then across a long drift to shaft No. 1. Here they climbed down to what they thought was the seventh level—but was actually the sixth—and set the trap at the main-shaft station where miners left or took the cage, coming down or going up.

Orchard's scab exterminator was a fairly complicated and ingenious device. He and Aikman first buried the powder in dirt and rubble on the mine floor close to the shaft. Then they fastened Orchard's revolver to a timber directly above the powder and placed a box of fulminate caps a few inches from the gun's muzzle. They strung a slim wire from the gun's trigger to the guard rail of the shaft. Then Orchard cocked the revolver. The two men stopped briefly to admire the arrangement, then left.

They were somewhat put out to find Gaffney the lookout man was not at his post, and apparently nowhere else around the mine. But nobody else was in sight either, and the two men got away without incident. Orchard just happened to have a bottle of turpentine in his pocket. He scattered it in their tracks as they walked away from the Vindicator. When they found Gaffney later, he told them he had "got to coughing" and thought he had better leave. He was obviously no man to have along on an affair of this sort.

Before Orchard was up next morning, W. F. Davis was at his house to inquire about matters. He had expected to hear there had been an explosion that had torn the Vindicator into chips; but the day shift had gone to work, and nothing had happened. Orchard replied that the trap had been set and was merely waiting for somebody to lift the guard rail to get out of the cage at the seventh level. He had planted it on the seventh level, for that was the place where the scab miners were working. None of the other levels, he said, was being worked at present.

Davis remarked it was sure queer, and after Davis had gone Orchard got to feeling a little queer, too. If the scabs had gone to work, as Davis said, then they must have gone to a level other than the seventh. Orchard went down the hill to where Billy Aikman lived. No, Billy had heard nothing. He and Orchard went back up Bull Hill to watch the Vindicator's shaft house. Nothing happened that day, nor the next, nor the next. Orchard pumped everybody he dared to, trying to learn if there had been any changes in the levels being worked. The answer was always the same: the scabs were still on the seventh level. It was baffling. Worse was the no-explosion, no pay-deal with Davis and Parker.

On November 21 the mystery cleared. On that morning Charles H. McCormick, superintendent of the Vindicator, and Melvin Beck, shift boss, were blown to bits when they stopped their cage at the sixth-level station, lifted the guard rail, and started to get off. The bungling Orchard and Aikman had mistaken the level and had set up their device on the sixth where no work was being done. For six days, as luck would have it, no cage had stopped at this station. But, next day, two well-liked mine bosses had come to the sixth to see about starting some drilling. They got it. The sixth level and the shaft were turned into a shambles by the explosion. But no scab was so much as scratched.

Orchard may well have felt mortified, if nothing more, to have made a mess of trying to kill scabs. But only briefly. If the union leaders had really wanted things torn loose, then the explosion in the Vindicator had more than done it. Up to now nothing had had so powerful an effect on the Cripple Creek district. Governor Peabody immediately declared Teller County to be in a state of insurrection and rebellion. He cited the Vindicator incident as need for martial law. Within a couple of hours, a major and a detail of fifty cavalrymen rode through Victor,

Goldfield, Independence, and Altman, stopping at each to read the Governor's proclamation.

The local police were deposed. National Guardsmen were set to patrolling all the towns. Citizens were ordered to bring in their arms and turn them over to the military commander. The Western Federation hurriedly got out a handbill and distributed it throughout the district. It was a message from Federation President Moyer: "I strongly advise every (union) member to provide himself with the latest improved rifle. so that in two years we can hear the inspiring music of the martial tread of 25,000 armed men in the ranks of labor." As a piece of inanity it matched General Bell's statement about "doing up the damned anarchistic federation."

John M. Glover, a lawyer in Cripple Creek town, openly defied the Governor's order to turn in shooting weapons. The militia came to arrest him in his office. Glover took a revolver from his desk and opened fire, blindly, from behind his locked door. The troopers fired back, wounding Glover. Then they broke in the door and took him off to jail.

Arrests of union men were generally resumed. They were put in a bull pen at Goldfield. When a member of the Western Federation's executive board, James A. Baker, arrived from Rossland, British Columbia, to open a union store for the strikers, National Guard officers advised him to leave the district at once, or be arrested. The militia grew arrogant and exercised what a disinterested observer described as "petty tyranny on every possible occasion. It became a question whether one could go along the street without being molested." He reported that drunken militiamen were a common sight, and that sentries near the Cripple Creek High School "sought to flirt with students through the open windows, throwing notes into the building."

The mine owners issued a statement to the effect that their association was determined to drive the disturbing and dangerous element of the Western Federation of Miners from the district "and from the state if possible." They put into effect a new hiring-card system that prevented any members of the union from getting work.

From the Western Federation headquarters in Denver now came hundreds of copies of a protest poster which union members promptly tacked up in all the Cripple Creek towns, in Colorado City, Telluride, and other places. Done in full color, in the likeness of the American flag, each of the stripes carried a legend: Martial Law Declared in Colorado, Habeas Corpus Suspended, Free Press Throttled, Free Speech Denied, and so forth. Under the flag was a photograph of union member Henry Maki apparently chained to the flagstaff with handcuffs, and a caption saying that the strikers were struggling to break "not only the chains of Henry Maki, but the chains that bind all the workers."

This lurid and effective piece of propaganda was the work of Bill Haywood, secretary-treasurer of the federation, who always liked to stress the idea of workers chained to the wage system, and in any case was seldom short of ideas.

When General Bell was shown the poster, he called the press to say, "Habeas corpus be damned! We'll give 'em post-mortems!" This, too, made considerable noise.

In Denver Haywood and Moyer got into a street fight with deputy sheriffs. Moyer was felled by a man wearing brass knuckles. Haywood knocked the deputy to the sidewalk. Another deputy clubbed Haywood with a gun, forcing him to his knees. Haywood drew a revolver and shot the fellow three times. Police, ambulance, and a patrol wagon arrived to take Moyer and Haywood to jail. Moyer was patched up and released, Haywood booked on the charge of an assault to commit murder. Before the deputy had fully recovered from his wounds, Haywood was released, apparently without bail. Both he and Moyer were soon arrested again, this time on an indictment at Telluride charging the two men with "desecration of the flag." Haywood was beaten up again, and his right ear nearly severed. But both he and Moyer were found not guilty on the desecration charge and released.

Despite the excitements due to the flag poster, the Cripple Creek area after several weeks of martial law remained quiet and orderly. The troops were being gradually withdrawn. By mid-January 1904, only a hundred and seventy men remained on duty as a sort of token. On April 11, all guardsmen left the district. Although many mines were still hampered by a lack of men, all mines were operating, either with imported nonunion miners or with local miners who had signed the new employment cards and thus disavowed union membership. The strike, even to the rank and file of miners, appeared to be at an end. The mine owners were feeling pretty good. The mines were producing sufficient ore to keep the Colorado City smelters busy with one shift. The recruiting and importation of non-union miners from outside the district was going ahead with less difficulty than before.

It was now June. For more than six months, or since the Vindicator explosion and subsequent martial law, there had been no outbreaks of violence in the Cripple Creek district.

9.

On the Care of Goons

It would be a grave error to assume there is no pride, or jealousy, or artistic temperament in the ranks of professional hatchet men, or goons. During the period of comparative quiet after the explosion in the Vindicator, Harry Orchard got to brooding on the lack of appreciation of his efforts. For one thing, he had not been paid his fee. To be sure, he had bungled the job somewhat by killing the wrong men, yet he certainly had "torn things loose," which was what President Davis of the Altman union had wanted. The explosion had certainly revived interest in the strike. It was common talk among strikers that Western Federation headquarters was wallowing in cash contributions from unions in Utah, Oregon, Idaho, Nevada, Montana, and British Colombia.

For another thing, now that he had occasion to reflect upon it, Orchard had not been asked to help with the "easy" job of wrecking the trains carrying the night shift to Cripple Creek mines. That they had been abortive, that not a car had left the rails, was beside the matter. Compared to the dangers Orchard had taken to set the charge in the Vindicator, the attempts at wrecking trains were a picnic, or so they seemed to him. That he, Orchard, was not even suspected of the Vindicator job, while H. H. McKinney was in jail in connection with the railroad affair, was nothing more than proof of Orchard's superior talents.

With nothing much to do, Orchard took to drinking heavily and a great bitterness fastened upon his sodden mind. Again, he asked Davis for money. Davis put him off with promises. Orchard now began to refine his resentment. Had he not been obliged to rustle the dynamite himself? Was it not his own revolver, bought with his own money, that he had used to explode the charge in the Vindicator? Now he was dead broke, but Davis would not "give me a pleasant look, or a few dollars."

Any treatise on the employment of goons should begin with the hard-and-fast rule that they should be both praised and fed. "I felt pretty sore," Orchard recalled, "and made up my mind to notify the railroad authorities." That is exactly what he did. He went to the office of D. C. Scott in the Cripple Creek depot and "told him everything" about the attempted derailments. Scott was employed by the railroads as a sort of secret-service agent. He worked closely with K. C. Sterling, head detective for the mine owners' association.

The "everything" that Orchard told Scott did not include a word about the Vindicator explosion. Orchard intimated that none of the strikers, unless possibly union officials, knew who pulled that job. But he could and did give the railroad detective details of the train-wrecking attempts. These were merely the accounts Orchard had picked up secondhand, but they impressed the railroad detective. He gave Orchard twenty dollars on the spot, and said he could have one hundred dollars a month if he would work for Scott. Orchard protested that he "was a union man at heart," but promised he would inform Scott of "anything of importance."

A little later Orchard received a letter from Scott asking him to call. He did so. Scott suggested that he go to Denver and make a visit to Western Federation headquarters where he might learn something or other about plans for carrying on the strike. He gave Orchard a railroad pass, and some money.

Orchard walked quietly into the federation offices, which had just been moved from the Mining Exchange Building to the Pioneer Building. It was the first time he had met Charles H. Moyer, federation president, and William D. Haywood, secretary-treasurer. Orchard introduced himself and was much pleased that these men recognized him as the courageous perpetrator of the Vindicator job. The ebullient Haywood slapped him on the back and praised him mightily, saying that Orchard had "got two of the kind we like to get," that one mine boss was "worth a carload of scabs." A few more jobs like that, Haywood declared, and "we would have everything our own way."

This was the kind of appreciation Orchard had long believed was his due. Haywood went on to tell him he should spend a few days in Denver enjoying himself, then go back to Cripple Creek and tear something loose. He added that nothing Orchard could do would be "too fierce" to suit the federation. He remarked that none of the tin soldiers, as he termed the National Guard, had yet been hurt, and that he wished an example would be made of them.

Bill Haywood knew just how to inspire a goon to greater efforts, and he also knew that goons should be kept in food and liquor. He gave Orchard three hundred dollars, merely telling him to be careful not to make any show with the money. When they parted, Haywood said that if Orchard would "only keep up the night work," he could have more money any time he wanted.

Back in Cripple Creek again, with money in his pocket and Haywood's praise in his ears, Orchard seems to have had no more dealings with Scott the railroad detective. At least there is no record of it. Orchard felt he had now taken on some importance and was determined to show the boys at headquarters he was just the man to do the tearing loose that would revive interest in the strike. His next attempt, however, amounted to little. He got some roofing pitch which he melted. He took a dozen sticks of dynamite, wrapped them in burlap, put them into a pail, then ran the melted pitch around the bundle. When it had cooled he hacked it up to look like a large chunk of coal. Into this he bored a hole. Into the hole he inserted a black-powder fuse filled with giant detonating caps. He sealed up the hole.

With this sinister piece of sculpture under his coat, Orchard one night looked up an aged miner named Dempsey, who, because he was old and believed harmless, was permitted by guards and soldiers to wander around as he would and asked him to heave it the first good chance he got into the coal bunkers of the Vindicator mine. Later that night Dempsey called Orchard on the telephone to say that he "had delivered the goods." Dempsey was obviously drunk when he called. Possibly he did heave the bomb, although neither they nor later, so far as Orchard ever knew, did the thing explode.

Yet Harry Orchard was on the way to a busy and highly successful career as a professional terrorist. On a second visit to federation headquarters he was introduced to George A. Pettibone, once a miner, as related, but now the genial and witty operator of a store in Denver. Orchard was given to understand that, though Pettibone had no official connection with the Western Federation, he was a close friend of Haywood and Moyer and was often consulted by them on union matters. Moyer humorously referred to Pettibone as the Devil because of the latter's abiding interest in dynamite and other explosive or inflammable materials.

Orchard like most people took an immediate liking to Pettibone, a man of medium stature with the eyes of a ferret, yet filled with good nature and cynical humor that belied his sharp and darting glance. As an old union man from way back, he had a fund of amusing stories and graphic comment. He recalled for Orchard how he had sent the cases of dynamite down the Frisco flume. "The whole mill," he said, "went up like an umbrella."

Now in Denver, Chemist Pettibone took Harry Orchard in hand and taught him some of the mysteries, among which was how to prepare what he called Greek fire. This concoction was made of stick phosphorus, bisulfide of carbon, benzene, alcohol, and turpentine.[4] The two men stirred up a batch and tested it. Orchard thought it worked fine; the more water you poured on, the faster it burned. Moyer and Haywood suggested that Orchard take the ingredients for a good big mess of it back to the mining district with him and use it where it would do the most good. Pettibone warned that it would be dangerous to buy all the stuff needed at one store. You had to have bottles with glass stoppers, too. He and several friends shopped around Denver, and, when Orchard took the train that afternoon for Cripple Creek, he had in his valise sufficient chemicals to mix several gallons of the weapon. As the train rolled along into the mountains, Orchard's mind conjured up ways in which he might use the Greek fire most effectively. It would do, he thought, to heave a few bottles through the car windows of the trains carrying nonunion miners to work the night shift. And perhaps one could get near enough to drop a gallon jug of it down a mine shaft.

Orchard got the stuff home without incident and stored it in the kitchen. But it stank to heaven, and after a bit he went out and dug a hole in his backyard and there buried it. Next day he hunted up Steve Adams, a member of Free Coinage Union who seldom worked

---

4 The classic Greek fire, used by the Byzantine Greeks in ancient warfare, which was said to have started to burn with wetting, was vomited through long copper tubes at the enemy or was hurled in pots and barrels. Scholars report that naphtha, sulphur, and niter went into its composition.

in a mine but always seemed to have money. He had given Orchard to understand that he was one of the Bull Hill dynamiters. Orchard approached Adams and told him about the Greek fire and indicated they might pick up a few dollars by using it on scab labor and in scab mines, of which the district already had far too many. Steve was game for anything. He also said that he already knew how to mix the stuff Orchard had brought. But before they could prepare the hell brew Moyer suddenly appeared at Orchard's house. For some reason or other he had changed his mind about Greek fire. He told Orchard that, if used, "people might have an idea where it came from." His fears possibly came from something that McKinney, the train wrecker now in jail, had confessed. In any case, Moyer was positive; Greek fire was not to be used.

Orchard was a bit disappointed. He had seen with his own eyes the wondrous fire that burned so hot and so mysteriously, no matter how you doused it with water. He was also beginning to think of himself as a scientific terrorist, perhaps a sort of savant devising arcane methods of destruction. But orders were orders—or at least they were when Orchard chose to obey them.

But there could be no harm in testing the new material in an experiment that had nothing to do with the strike. Orchard's old friend, Johnnie Neville, came to mind. His saloon had been doing badly. Johnnie was too trusting to be a good saloonkeeper. During the many months of strike and violence, many a miner had come to him for a few drinks, or even bottles, promising to pay when work was resumed. Johnnie could not say no, if he liked a man, and he liked most men. Thus, his business was in such shape that he told Orchard he might as well shut down and go fishing.

The stuff buried in his backyard gave Orchard an idea. Long ago he himself had insured a cheese factory, set it afire, and got the insurance. He went now to Johnnie Neville. "Don't shut up your saloon," he said. "Go get some insurance on it, then I'll burn it up for you." Neville got the insurance, and, after a decent interval, he and Orchard and Steve Adams worked half a night carrying out good whisky in kegs and bottles and burying them in a safe place.

Orchard and Adams proceeded to mix up a batch of the hell-fire. Orchard took five bottles of the stuff and emptied them in the upper rooms of Neville's place, shut the doors, and went away. Within a short time, the whole structure was burning fiercely, and it continued so when firemen played their hoses on it. The saloon was completely destroyed. Johnnie Neville got his money. It was that easy. He was most appreciative of the efforts of Orchard and Adams.

At about this time preparations were being made for the annual convention of the Western Federation of Miners, to be held in Denver. Delegates from unions from all over the West were coming. The executive board thought something should be torn loose at convention time to impress the delegates that headquarters was right on the job, fighting the battle for unionism. Various suggestions were made and discussed. The most popular was to "do something big" about the horde of scab miners now working in the Cripple Creek district. This very subject was still being planned when Pettibone interrupted a meeting of the executive board.

Lyte Gregory, he said, had just arrived in Denver. He was a notorious all-around fink, who had been a mine company detective at Idaho Springs, Colorado, and in a strike in the coal fields of southern Colorado had been a leader of deputies and company gunmen. He was known as a particularly hard character who enjoyed beating up miners and reputedly had once helped to mutilate a striker. The Western Federation's board knew enough about Gregory to tell Pettibone that yes, there should be something done about him.

Harry Orchard and Steve Adams apparently just happened to be in Denver. Pettibone hastened to recruit them for the work in hand, then led them to a saloon on Curtis Street where Lyte Gregory, the marked man, was having a drink with Foster Milburn, a trustworthy union man from Idaho Springs, who had agreed to act as a sort of decoy, to shepherd Gregory into range of the hatchet men. Pettibone now left the scene. Adams and Orchard got a good look at Gregory in the saloon.

Gregory tossed off another drink, then went out and got aboard a streetcar. Adams and Orchard took the same car. When Gregory got off on Santa Fe, near Tenth Street South, he went into a saloon. Milburn followed on the next car.

Leaving Adams and Milburn to watch Gregory, Orchard went to his hotel room to get a sawed-off shotgun he had brought from Cripple Creek. He broke it down—that is, made it into two pieces, barrel and stock—put them under his overcoat, and returned by car to the saloon.

Gregory was still inside, playing cards.

A little after midnight Gregory emerged from the saloon and started down Santa Fe Street alone, the three men following on the opposite side of the street. While walking, Orchard got out his shotgun, assembled it, and the three started across the street to reach Gregory. There was little or no light, and the hunters failed to see wires that were stretched along the sidewalk to protect the grass of the parking strip. They were moving fairly rapidly to get on with the kill when they hit the obstruction. Whether or not they fell, they made sufficient noise to warn Gregory. With the instinct of a veteran gun fighter, Gregory reached for his gun and began backing to a fence along the sidewalk. Just then Orchard let him have it. At close range he shot the man three times.

Lyte Gregory fell dead before he could get his gun from its holster. The three men ran down an alley, then separated. By the time police got to the scene, all three men were safe in their rooms. Orchard felt quite satisfied with the night's work. He had removed him whom Haywood had described as "a filthy hyena of the barbarous mine barons."

10.

Independence Depot

When the federation's executive board resumed sessions next day, Haywood saw to it that the members were supplied with copies of newspapers which told of the mysterious murder of Lyte Gregory. It was generally agreed that delegates to the convention would be impressed; and, in view of Gregory's notorious reputation as a professional enemy of Labor, few could have any doubt that his removal had been arranged by the Western Federation.

Haywood also used the murder as an inducement to James Murphy, board member from Butte, to sign a Western Federation document permitting expenditures from the union's emergency fund. The matter had come up the day before, and Murphy had refused to sign it. Now that Murphy had read the news, Haywood tossed the emergency bill to the table in front of the Butte member and blandly suggested that he sign it. He did so. Later that day, Haywood congratulated Orchard on the night's work, adding that the rubbing out of Gregory had had a good effect on Murphy.

Steve Adams promptly went on a drunk. Friends took him in charge, bought him a ticket, and shipped him back to Cripple Creek. Orchard attended the opening meeting of the Western Federation's convention. Only a few of the executive board members knew who had killed the mine detective, but Orchard got no little satisfaction from hearing the unknown killer discussed and praised for his fine work.

Pettibone and W. F. Davis and Sherman Parker of the Altman union took Orchard aside and suggested that now was the time for him to return to Cripple Creek and "blow up something." Pettibone said Moyer and Murphy were organizing a faction in the Western

Federation to oust Haywood. Pettibone and the Altman union men, along with many others, were sure to favor Haywood if the matter came to a showdown; but, said Pettibone, the affair might well bring on a split causing some of the districts to withdraw. What was needed right now was some incident that would unite all factions. Cripple Creek was the logical place for such an incident to happen. It was near enough to assure good coverage by the Denver newspapers. The more he thought of it, the more enthusiastic Pettibone grew. Why, said he, if something were torn loose now when all the union leaders were *out* of the Cripple Creek district, the mine operators would hardly know whom to charge with the crime.

Orchard may have reflected that if none of the union leaders were in the district, then investigation of any new outrage must be devoted to known rank-and-file union men who were. This, of course, took in Orchard himself. But, if he gave it any thought, it did not deter him. "I don't think," he told Pettibone, "it would be much trouble to blow up the railroad depot at Independence."

At this point in the discussion Haywood joined the group. When the subject was explained, Haywood said it sounded like a good idea, and remarked that "anything goes with me." He gave Orchard some money, warned him to use care, and departed. Orchard left the hall for the Denver depot, pausing only to step into a store and buy an alarm clock. He arrived that evening in Cripple Creek.

The often devious but occasionally direct mind of Harry Orchard had suggested the depot at Independence for attention for logical reasons. If killing a batch of scabs was the goal desired, then this was the place to catch them when the early night shift quit the mines and gathered on the depot platform to take the 2:15 A.M. train to their homes or rooming houses. Orchard knew the terrain around about. He knew the depot and had thought that its architecture presented certain possibilities. The alarm clock was an afterthought that had occurred when Pettibone mentioned that "all of the union leaders were out of the district." Well, a device might be timed to go off after Harry Orchard himself had left the district. It was worth consideration, anyhow.

WHILE THE CONVENTION DELEGATES IN Denver debated and quarreled, Harry Orchard went methodically about his business. He first looked over the lay of the land. The town of Independence lay in a deep valley, just below Altman and half a mile from Victor. The depot of the Florence & Cripple Creek railroad stood high up on a hillside. The typical mountain roughness of the entire district was more than usually marked here by broken contours. Dumps from the several mines formed an enormous disorder, over which the railroad ran, and through which it occasionally had to tunnel.

The place where the depot stood was, moreover, poorly lighted, a gloomy spot, full of pitfalls, abounding in chances for secret work and concealment—things which Orchard had not overlooked. He had chosen well on all counts. Somewhat later a man familiar with the region remarked that the town of Independence was "the heart of the Cripple Creek mining industry" and that its railroad station was "in a spot peculiarly suited to the perpetration of crime and deeds of darkness."

As a partner in the job, Orchard first sought out Billy Aikman; that experienced goon, however, had bought a half interest in an Independence saloon and thought he should tend to business. But Steve Adams, who had sobered up, said he was ready for any old thing. Now for the explosive. Orchard rightly sensed that getting a supply of powder such as he wanted should be done with care. The old free-and-easy days of dynamite had passed. Mine stocks were carefully guarded now. Storekeepers were chary about selling the stuff. Orchard went to see an acquaintance, Floyd Miller, who was working on a lease and had a legitimate use for blasting powder, and said he'd like to get two boxes of giant caps and a hundred pounds of dynamite. Miller thought he could buy it without question. Orchard gave him the money.

That night Adams and Orchard went to Miller's home, got the powder, and carried it to a small and unused cellar behind a deserted cabin not far from the depot. Adams had a key to the cabin. It was now Thursday evening. Orchard told Adams to meet him at the cabin Saturday night. They would then prepare the charge and set it off when the two-fifteen train arrived Sunday morning. Orchard had decided against using the alarm clock to detonate the caps. He did not place complete faith in machinery, and he was determined that this job must come off perfectly. Killing Lyre Gregory had more than obliterated Orchard's bungled efforts in the Vindicator mine. It had shown him to be certain death. He could not afford to have anything go wrong with the depot job.

Orchard had also cooked up a scheme which he believed would be a workable, perhaps an airtight alibi in case he should be suspected. He had proposed to Johnnie Neville that the two of them go on a fishing trip. Johnnie was delighted. He no longer had a failing whisky business on his hands. Good old Harry Orchard had removed that with his patent Greek fire, and Neville had the insurance money. It so happened that Joe Adams, a brother of Steve, had a team of horses and a wagon for sale. The two men bought it, and Orchard—still thinking ahead—also purchased a secondhand saddle which he put in the wagon, remarking that it might come in handy.

Arrangements for the fishing expedition occupied Orchard much of Friday and Saturday. He was too busy to check up on Steve Adams, but hoped for the best, trusting that Steve would keep away from the bottle.

It was now Saturday evening. Neville and Orchard loaded their gear and provisions into the wagon, along with Charlie, the ex-saloonkeeper's young son, and jolted at work-horse pace out of Independence, taking the road that led toward Colorado Springs. Neville showed a mild interest in the saddle Orchard had bought. Orchard told him merely that he planned to take one of the horses that evening and ride back to Independence, where he had a little work to attend to. Neville was wise to the ways of the mining district. He said no more about the saddle, nor asked what sort of work his friend had to attend to.

Some six miles out of Independence the fishermen made camp for the night. Orchard saddled one of the horses. He called Neville aside and remarked that, no matter what happened, he, Orchard, was supposed to be there all night, right there in the roadside camp with Johnnie and little Charlie. Neville said he understood. Orchard started back for Independence.

When he had come within a mile or so of the railroad station, Orchard tethered his horse in the bushes, and walked on to the cabin. Steve Adams was already there, and sober. It was ten o'clock. From the powder cache in the cellar Orchard took a small wooden box. The two men went into the deserted cabin. Steve lighted a candle and watched while a master of explosives went about the making of an infernal machine. Orchard was one of the pioneers in the technique of the booby trap or set bomb. Terrorists in both Europe and the United

States were still throwing their bombs at their victims, often sacrificing their own lives in the same explosion, or at best being caught while running away. Though his was no soaring imagination, Harry Orchard considered such methods worse than silly. When one of his jobs let go, he meant to be in the clear.

His original plan for the railroad depot called for a time bomb. With this in mind he had bought the alarm clock, but on reflection decided against it. Experiments with it showed the alarm mechanism to vary as much as a full minute from the time set. Sixty seconds one way or the other could mean disaster—disaster in that even a brief delay could permit escape of the quarry. No, a time arrangement would not do. The risk of failure was too great.

While Steve held the flickering candle, Orchard went to work with a deftness that belied stubby fingers. He first made a tiny wooden windlass. To this he fastened, with strips of leather, two little empty vials. With his finger he spun the windlass. It turned perfectly. He explained to Adams that a slow steady pull on a wire would turn the windlass and spill the acid he would put into the vials on a pile of giant caps resting on the dynamite.

It had taken close to an hour to construct the main works of the machine designed to blow up scab miners. Adams and Orchard went outside to scout the neighborhood. It was past eleven o'clock. Most of the small houses climbing the hills were dark. Independence had gone to bed. The night was unusually chilly for June. But the sky was lowering. No sign of moon showed. Each man picked up a box of dynamite and went over to the depot. It, too, was dark. The night agent and telegraph operator had gone home.

A long platform stretched across the front of the depot and extended beyond on both sides. The two men carried the dynamite as far as they could under the platform; then Orchard got down on his belly to crawl a bit farther; he wanted the charge to be set as near as possible to what would soon be the center of activity. Adams passed the powder forward. Orchard scooped a hole in the debris beneath the planks, and into it pushed the two boxes. On top of the boxes he placed the giant caps. Now to set up the windlass and fill the vials.

"This," he recalled, "was ticklish business. It was very dark in there, under the platform, and I had to fill the little bottles without seeing them." (But his nerves were good—that is, if Orchard had any nerves.)

"I got out the bottle of sulphuric acid from my pocket. I put a piece of cardboard on top of the caps and powder, lest I spill some of the acid. Then I filled the two vials, bearing in mind that a single drop of the acid would set the whole thing off. To make everything doubly certain, I had sprinkled a mixture of sugar and potash on top of the caps. I knew the acid would set this on fire in an instant. It was ticklish business."

Orchard now attached one end of a long length of light wire to the windlass, then backed out from under the platform. He and Adams payed out the wire as they moved slowly away from the depot along a spur track to where stood an old ore house. Here Orchard took a few turns with the wire around a broken chair rung. The two men sat down to wait. Orchard produced a bottle of turpentine, and he and Adams gave their boots a good smearing.

It was a little past midnight, two hours until train time. One wonders how this pair of savages whiled away the laggard minutes. What did they talk about? Did they have a bottle? Steve had just recovered from a notable bout with barleycorn. It is more than possible he was in a condition that called for stimulant. Yet, Orchard had, up to this point in his career, remained stone-cold sober when there was work to do, and he was quick to criticize men who got drunk on such occasions. Perhaps they had no liquor that night. They must have talked about something. Orchard was a gregarious man. Adams was a dedicated chatterbox. Here they sat on a rusty spur track by a tumble-down ore house, two hunters waiting at a salt lick for the game to come. Scarcely more than a stone's throw up the hill their game was still swinging picks and shovels, holding drills deep in the Findley and Shurtloff mines.

A little before two o'clock the night began to lighten. The clouds blew away. A pale moon came out. Orchard complained it was a hell of a time for a moon. But soon they heard the wail of a locomotive echo against the high cliffs above. The Florence & Cripple Creek's two-fifteen was going to roll in on time. Orchard stood up, then picked the chair rung from the ground and motioned to Adams to take hold of one end of the stick. This was to be strictly a co-operative affair. The whistle was still echoing when the waiting men heard the miners—the scabs—come tearing down from the Findley shaft house. In another two minutes, just as the train was putting on brakes for the depot, Orchard and Adams applied tension by pulling slowly on the chair rung. An instant later the charge went up with a fearful roar. A good part of the little sleeping town lit up as if by a flash of lightning.

It had been Orchard's intention to haul in all the wire as a precaution against leaving evidence to indicate how the dynamite had been set off, but he forgot all about wire in the rain of rocks and planks and other debris, including pieces and shreds of human beings, that beat down on and around him and Adams. The two men simply ran away from there as fast as they could. They followed the railroad track to a spot near the old Victor mine on the north side of Bull Hill, then separated. Adams continued on around to Midway, where he lived. Orchard found his horse, mounted, and took off down the road toward Colorado Springs.

THOUGH ORCHARD'S ANIMAL WAS MORE used to working in double harness than as a saddle horse, he made good time. He had got cold standing so long. The road was all downgrade. Orchard let him gallop, reining him in only a couple of times when they were approaching spots where houses stood close to the road. He did not want the occupants to hear a horse running. He was still thinking about an alibi. At a little after three o'clock he got to the wagon camp. Both Johnnie and little Charlie were awake. Orchard lay down to catch a little sleep.

They breakfasted early and continued on the road to Colorado Springs. Neville was showing some interest in what had happened in Independence, remarking that during the early morning the ground had shook where he lay in the wagon. Orchard gave an evasive reply. Neville was not to be put off so easily. Was it the Findley mine, he asked? Orchard grew irritated, and his answer was short. "I wasn't there, and I don't know," he said. But by late afternoon, as they approached Colorado Springs, they met a fellow on the road who asked if they had come from Cripple Creek. They said they had, and the man told them there had been a big explosion at Independence, that "sixty people had been killed and many more injured." The railroad depot had been blown to bits. It must have been a mighty charge, the man said, for it was reported that people living close by the depot had been thrown from their beds.

Johnnie Neville was startled and worried. His home was less than three hundred feet from the depot and his wife and other children were in it. He demanded to know of Orchard exactly what had happened.

Orchard admitted that a blast had indeed occurred but added that he himself had been close by when it happened, and he was certain nobody but scabs on the station platform had been killed, or even hurt.

That night the fishermen, camped some four miles beyond Colorado Springs, managed to buy a newspaper. The disaster was of course all over the front page, and, though the report indicated a belief that the explosion was doubtless chargeable to "lawless union elements" and said that "a lengthy piece of wire with wood handle on one end" had been found by detectives, nobody was mentioned as under suspicion. This was good news to Orchard, and so was the admission, quoted in the story, that "police are at a loss to explain the method used."

But Neville's eye caught an item that set him to walking up and down. It reported that the explosion had blown a piece of plank through the roof of the home of Mr. John Neville, that a sliver of it had struck Mrs. Neville where she lay in bed. Despite the story's assurance that "Mrs. Neville was not seriously injured," Johnnie and little Charlie were much worried.

Orchard was becoming a little uneasy himself. It was most unfortunate that his old friend's wife had been hurt. But the paper said it was only a slight injury. Yet here was Johnnie making a fuss about it. Orchard thought this might be a proper time to recall to Johnnie that his saloon had been burned without injury to anybody. This crime, as Orchard was well aware, lay heavily on Neville's mind, and the man who set the fire meant that the memory of it should not fade. Again, he impressed Johnnie of the need that he, Harry Orchard, was "sound asleep in the wagon" at the very moment the Independence depot was dynamited.

Next day they camped on the outskirts of Denver. Leaving Johnnie and Charlie with the wagon, Orchard went downtown to Western Federation headquarters. He found Haywood, Pettibone, and the others greatly pleased with his recent piece of work. They told him that it was "the only thing that saved the federation from splitting up," that there had been "no more kicking," and that the "Murphy-Moyer faction" had been demolished. All the old hands had been re-elected to their offices. The federation's internal politics had been settled for a long time to come, or so it seemed.

While Orchard was at headquarters, Steve Adams came in. He said that, on the day after the explosion, friends had come to his home at Midway (some four miles from Independence) and advised him to get out of the district at once. He had no idea, he said, what had caused him to be suspected; but he took his friends at their word and Monday after dark had started walking to South Park, caught a train there, and came to Denver. His leaving had not been too soon. Later that same night, according to reports from the district, some men came looking for him at his house. Their intentions had not been stated, but the report said they were "looking for Adams because he was a dynamiter."

Bill Haywood asked Adams and Orchard what they intended to do. Adams said he was going to send for his wife to come to Denver and would then make up his mind what was best. Orchard said that he and Neville were already on their way to Cheyenne, Wyoming, and planned to stay away from Cripple Creek for a while. It was to be what Orchard termed "a pleasure trip." He and Johnnie would do some fishing, and prospecting. Pettibone, who appears to have been a sort of pay-off man, in addition to his other and wholly unofficial duties, gave two hundred dollars to Adams and three hundred to Orchard. What Steve Adams did next is not clear, but he was to show up again. Orchard returned to his wagon camp. He and Neville bought a tent and other items for an extended camping trip, and drove north out of Denver, heading for Cheyenne, little Charlie still with them.

11.

"...Maketh Thunder & Ruin"

The light from the rocking head lamp of the two-fifteen was already flooding Independence depot when the explosion came. Almost automatically the locomotive engineer applied his air, the brakes went tight, and the little train slid up to the platform on locked wheels, while a dreadful rain of earth, rocks, timbers, and parts of men beat down on the roofs of the coaches.

Phil Chandler, a miner, was lounging at the far end of the platform, and started walking toward the train, when there was a blot of flame accompanied by "a sharp noise, more like a whistle than an explosion," and he was blown "rapidly through the air," to fall on his thigh. Both legs were broken. He was lucky, for when he sat up to look around, the first man he saw was John Police, an Austrian, who had "gathered his footless legs in his arms and sat by the track, silently writhing."

Inside the cars the men for the graveyard shift of the Findley mine were sprayed and cut by shattered glass from the windows. They piled out of the coaches to find a great yawning hole where the platform had been. By the light of the same waning moon that Harry Orchard had cursed only a few moments before, they could see indistinct forms scattered along the track. Some were still and quiet. Others cried, or merely moaned.

The train backed away until the headlamp could light the scene, and the unharmed shift of miners went to work to separate the dead from the mangled but still living of their comrades of the early night shift. The two rows grew swiftly longer in the bright glare—thirteen dead, twenty-four badly injured. All these had come from the Findley. The men from the Shurtloff escaped by being a couple of minutes late;

they were running for the depot when Orchard and Adams pulled on the chair rung.

Somebody in Independence had the presence of mind to telephone Bert Carlton in Cripple Creek town. Chief owner of the Findley, and of other mine properties, Carlton roused James Murphy, the Findley manager, and Sheriff Henry Robertson. They called doctors and nurses, and by 3:00 A.M. the entire group was aboard a switch engine rolling up the track to Independence. More help, including deputies and mine officials, and additional nurses and physicians, arrived before daylight on a special train.

While the dead were being removed, and the injured taken to hospitals (six amputations were necessary), the space around the depot was roped off, and the ground searched. A possible clue was seen in "about 200 feet of wire running to a nearby stump where its end was attached to a chair rung." Bloodhounds were brought and put to work. The dogs might well have been confused in such a shambles, but in any case, Orchard had brought along his bottle of turpentine.

In going over the scene of disaster, everyone was impressed by the force of the explosion. One mine boss judged that enough dynamite had been used to "blow up the town of Independence and wreck the city of Victor to boot." The charge had been obviously aimed at the depot platform. Nothing at all remained of its beams and planks. The depot itself still stood, but one could look right through it, and parts of the heavy roof had been torn away. Four hours after help arrived, searchers with sacks and tin pails were still picking up bits of flesh and bone. One dismembered body was found a hundred and fifty feet on the hillside above the depot.

True to the spirit and tradition of mine towns of the era, more violence was brewing. Everyone who had lived in the district for any length of time knew as much. Even the children. The first aftereffect of the tragedy was a vast boding of evil that fell, as though it were a shadow seen, over all the area, pervading homes, saloons, stores, and schools. Nobody went to work. People spoke in hushed voices, and long lines of them stood and moved slowly to view the dead in the morgues or to visit their mangled husbands or fathers or friends in the hospitals. Bows of black crape, with long ends that hung down nearly to thresholds, appeared on the doors of modest homes here and there. Some melancholy priest or sexton tolled the bell in the spire of the

Catholic church in Victor town.

Before noon the commissioners of Teller County held an emergency meeting in Victor. By common consent, wrote a reporter, the explosion was attributed to the Western Federation of Miners. All sorts of wild rumors were going the rounds; every union man was to be driven from the district; union officers were to be burned at the stake.

The mine owners' association and a group of business and professional men, called the Citizens' Alliance, announced that they were "prepared to keep order." Because Sheriff Robertson was believed to be a union sympathizer, he was ordered to resign. When he started to argue, he was told to think better of it, lest he be hanged for his pains. A resignation was put in front of him. He signed it and left the district. The county commissioners promptly appointed Edward Bell sheriff. He in turn appointed a large number of deputies "of the mine owners' choosing." The mine owners announced that a mass meeting of citizens would be held in Victor at three o'clock that afternoon, when speakers would address townspeople on the subject of law and order. The place of meeting was to be a vacant lot across the street from the Victor miners' union hall. It is doubtful if better arrangements for a continuance of violence could have been made.

In the city of Victor, a community of more than twelve thousand population, and almost in the heart of its business district, was the fateful vacant lot. A steep bluff, topped by the Gold Coin shaft house, rose sheer on one side. Buildings of considerable size formed two more sides, and the whole was a sort of amphitheater. Across the street, as said, was the union hall. Near it was the miners' union store.

By two o'clock people were gathering from all parts of the Cripple Creek district. An hour later the lot and the area round about was packed with humanity. The crowd was mostly men, though there was a scattering of women and many boys. A majority of the men were nonunion miners—but not all. It turned out that a good many, union and nonunion, were packing guns.

One hesitates to say that this meeting was "called to order" at precisely three o'clock as advertised. But at that hour Clarence Hamlin, attorney and secretary of the mine owners' association, mounted an empty wagon near the center of the lot and began his address. Hamlin was well, or rather widely, known in the district. It was part of his job to issue work permits to such miners as would quit the Western

Federation, and to import nonunion miners.

Hamlin's speech, wrote a nonminer who was there, was "from the first violent and unrestrained, with all judgment and caution thrown to the winds." Hamlin had plenty of courage. He could not but have known that he stood exposed in the midst of more than two thousand people whose passions were already deeply stirred; or that in this crowd were men who hated and feared one another with the same fanatical hate and fear that in olden times had moved mobs to butcher Protestants, hang Catholics, and burn witches.

Hamlin talked on, either unknowing in ignorance, or knowing only too well in venality that in his audience were men who had been Molly Maguires, other men who had seen the flash of the Haymarket bomb, still other men who carried scars from Homestead, Pennsylvania, and bitter memories of bloody times in the moody Coeur d'Alenes.

Either he knew, or didn't know, and in any case, he talked on. He denounced union miners as a gang of cutthroats. He shouted that membership in the Western Federation was a badge of murder and arson. Some man in the crowd shouted an angry question at the speaker. Another man struck the questioner in the face. Still another man drew a revolver and belted the head of the man who struck the questioner who asked the question of Speaker Hamlin.

All was ready. A single shot was fired. Then came a fusillade—and cries, shouts, oaths, all the noises that two thousand people make in anger and in fear. The mob stampeded, stumbling, falling, trying to get somewhere, anywhere, away from this dusty piece of ground on which now lay five men, oozing blood. It was something of a miracle that, when the lot had cleared, only five men were down and only two, Roscoe McGee and John Davis, were dead.

Somebody now recalled that one of the highlights of Hamlin's law-and-order speech was his invitation to "chase these Western Federation scoundrels out of the district. Chase them so far they will never come back," and that "the time has now come for every man to take this matter in his own hands."

It was an appeal for anarchy, and anarchy followed, though it first took the guise of law and order. The local National Guard companies were called out. A picket line of soldiers was stationed around the Victor union hall from the windows of which, many believed, had come gunfire during the riot. Riflemen were placed on top of adjacent buildings. The new sheriff, Bell, walked into the hall, which was filled with miners, and ordered them to disperse. They refused. The sheriff went out. Who gave the command is not clear, but, once Bell was out of range, the militia opened up with rifles, firing several volleys into the hall. By the time four miners had been wounded, a white handkerchief waved from a window. Sheriff Bell and a company of soldiers entered the hall, arrested all present, and escorted them to the Victor jail.

The union hall was no sooner cleared than a mob rushed in to wreck the furniture, rip curtains, destroy membership ledgers, and smash everything that was smashable.

The first shades of evening found mobs gathering in Cripple Creek town, in Independence, Altman, Goldfield. The police seemed to have disappeared. The guardsmen appeared not to notice. As darkness fell, the mobs went into action. The union hall in Cripple Creek town was invaded and utterly wrecked. The union store there was broken into, its stocks tossed into the streets, and crude oil and kerosene poured over the edibles. Other attacks were made on the union stores in all the towns.

When the stores and meeting halls of the union had been cared for, the mobs turned to beating up stray union men on the streets, then holding them for arrest by guardsmen. More than two hundred union men soon crowded the jails, and others were put in hastily prepared bull pens. At Goldfield, the military put all the town officers under arrest, and appointed a new crew from the ranks of the Citizens' Alliance.

Next day, in the absence of Governor Peabody, Lieutenant Governor Baggott declared Teller County to be again in a state of rebellion. General Sherman Bell and militia troops were sent to the area. Bell's first act was to dispatch soldiers to Danville, a new mining camp some twelve miles from Victor, but in Fremont County. During a clash here, one man was killed, and fourteen miners were brought prisoners to Victor for incarceration.

Under style of the Military Commission, General Bell set up offices in the mine owners' association headquarters, and appointed a court of seven to try the more than fifteen hundred miners who were being held under arrest, and to recommend deportation for those who refused to denounce the Western Federation. Deportation, General Bell declared, was permitted under a law for dispersal of a mob. On the first day of the "examinations," twenty-five union members were allowed to say good-bye to their families before being loaded under guard on an F.&C.C. train and sent out of the district. On the second day, seventy-two were deported. These were eventually put on board the M.-K.-T. and Santa Fe Lines and taken to a desolate spot two hundred miles east of Cripple Creek, then marched across the state line into Kansas, and there abandoned. A day or so later an even larger group was taken south to the New Mexico state line and dumped in a cedar-and-pinion wasteland.

The deportation court worked without a hitch. It examined 1,569 miners, recommended 238 for banishment in the Siberias of Kansas and New Mexico, held 42 for trial by criminal courts, and released the remainder. It was known that an even larger number than were deported had simply scattered into the mountains of central Colorado.

In the meantime, the wrecking of the union stores, plus expulsion of so many breadwinners, had left several hundred families virtually destitute. The Western Federation had started to issue food and other supplies, but Colonel Verdeckberg of the militia forbade any direct aid to miners' families and ordered that all supplies should be turned over to the military to be issued. The poverty of the stricken families would have been worse than it was had it not been for many sympathetic citizens who refused to respect the military order.

Martial law did not protect the Victor *Record*. On the night of June 8, this organ of the minors' union was entered by a mob armed with sledge hammers. They proceeded to demolish the press and linotype, then scattered type and destroyed subscription and advertising records. When the editor of the Victor *Star* offered the *Record* use of his office and press, the *Star* editor was visited by members of the Citizens' Alliance and threatened with boycott.

On June 21 the great Portland mine opened with full crews, all nonunion; and other properties resumed, also with nonunion men. By July 26, with all mines running, the National Guard was sent home, and Governor Peabody declared Teller County to have recovered from its state of rebellion.

Yet, there were union miners who, in the face of everything that had happened to them, still persisted in the Cripple Creek district. Five such who had been deported and had returned to their homes in Victor were promptly taken by groups of masked men, escorted out of town, robbed of their watches, cruelly flogged, and warned it would be worse if they returned. Another, A. L. Leduc, was waylaid, robbed, beaten with the handles of whips, and run down the Canon City road by unmasked vigilantes.

G. R. Hooten, former manager of a union store, was taken from his home and beaten. When union store managers at Cripple Creek and Victor, T. H. Parfet and John Harper, returned to settle the affairs of the wrecked concerns, Parfet was assaulted and Harper beaten so badly as to require hospitalization.

In desperation, the Western Federation sold the union stores to the Interstate Mercantile Company. The Cripple Creek unit was opened for business early in August. Within twenty-four hours it was attacked by a mob of several hundred men who tossed out the manager and clerks without allowing them either to close the safe or to remove the books. Windows, counters, and fixtures were demolished. Tons of goods were thrown into the street, where they were stolen or left to the dogs and the traffic.

The Western Federation refused to call off the Cripple Creek strike. It never was called off. By August of 1904, however, it had been wholly lost. Years later local unions were reestablished, but the federation never recovered its former influence in the district or, for that matter, in the opinion of its historian, Vernon H. Jensen, its influence in Colorado.

Due in no small part to Bill Haywood, the Cripple Creek unions had sowed the class consciousness which he believed in time would make union labor the dominant force in the United States. Instead, class consciousness had sprung up and destroyed them. Control passed from one class to another. In Cripple Creek class rule was supreme, or nothing. A gentle clergyman of Victor town, sympathetic to the common run of miners, noted that passion joined with power "maketh thunder & ruin," and reflected sadly with Hosea of old about the bitter fruits of sowing the wind.

When the shooting was over, and the smoke had cleared, Benjamin McKie Rastall, who knew the region well, remarked that though the violence and bitterness which had developed were probably due mostly to the isolation of a district centered in one industry, he thought that something else entered into it too. "The psychologist," he wrote, "will wish to trace the great altitude, well above 10,000 feet, as it works to make men more irritable and easily excited." The rarefied atmosphere, he thought, tended to "make sudden and extreme bursts of passion." Possibly it did. Yet it was neither passion nor irritability that designed and carried out the tragedy at Independence depot. It was the dedicated ambition of Harry Orchard, a psychopathic nonentity who wanted to be a somebody.

12.

Bill Haywood Considered

Approximately six weeks were required for Cripple Creek to pass through the new violences prompted by the Independence depot explosion. The mines meanwhile began to resume operation with full crews of nonunion men. Harry Orchard was still absent. He and Johnnie Neville, little Charlie with them, were wandering aimlessly through Wyoming with their two-horse rig and camping outfit. Charlie was fourteen years old. He was having a wonderful time, what with Indians to be seen, and cowboys, and the astonishing big sky all around. In the minds of the two men, however, certain fears were developing. We shall return to them a little later. It is time to look now at William D. Haywood.

It will be recalled that the depot tragedy occurred when the Western Federation of Miners convention was being held in Denver. As the delegates gathered on the morning of June 6, Haywood noticed "the horror-stricken look upon the faces of them all." They had just read the news. When the meeting opened, Haywood suggested that the explosion be made a special order of federation business. This took the form of offering a reward of five thousand dollars for the arrest and conviction of those responsible for the outrage. It was also voted to send a committee of union miners to Cripple Creek to "investigate the matter."

If the mass murder at the depot actually did solidify the rank and file of the federation, as Haywood believed, it had no such effect on members of the executive board. Haywood was already sneering at Moyer, belittling Moyer's "martyrdom" in the Telluride jail, and ready to criticize almost anything Moyer did or suggested.[5] It was perhaps Haywood's greatest misfortune to be a natural leader who was wholly incapable of working in anything like harmony with an executive board, or committee, or anybody on the same level of authority as himself. In a different field, Ethan Allen comes readily to mind. Allen and Haywood both were superb leaders, even when they led to disaster. Neither could follow.

AT THE TIME OF THE Cripple Creek strike Haywood was thirty-five years old, a mighty figure of a man well over six feet, big-shouldered, big-headed, big-necked, big-handed, every line of his body proclaiming enormous strength. A pair of cold blue eyes, one of them sightless, were shaded by a mop of brownish hair and supported by a hard jaw, the kind described in a prizefighter as granite. By 1904 his character was permanently molded. He was hard, tough, immensely resistant, and warped by the life he had led in the mines, the things he had seen. There was no little of the dreamer in him, enough to be touched by the utopian vista which socialism seemed to promise. Given this ideal, and his abilities, and there you had a character who could bend men to his will. He had little patience with either obstacles or men. He was neither farsighted nor politic. It was probably not in him, said an acquaintance, to withhold a blow when he had the power to inflict it. It certainly never occurred to him to be choosy of means.

He was born February 4, 1869, in Salt Lake City, of a Scottish-Irish mother from South Africa. His father was of old American stock, so thoroughly American—Haywood liked to say—that the line doubtless ran back to "the Puritan bigots and the Cavalier pirates." The boy was not quite four when his father died. Four years later his mother married a miner, and they went to live in Ophir City, a mining camp in Utah's Oquirrh Range. He attended school there. He also began his education in the manners of mine towns. On the way to school one morning, he

---

5 This statement is not made on the strength of *Bill Haywood's Book* (1929), an alleged autobiography but largely ghost-written by a Communist hack to meet the current party line. That Moyer and Haywood disliked each other and were often not on speaking terms was common knowledge to intimates and acquaintances in both the Western Federation and the Industrial Workers of the World.

saw a local worthy named Slippery Dick shoot and kill another man in the street and noted the casualness of it all. Slippery Dick blew into the barrel of his revolver to clear the smoke that was still curling from it, put the gun into his pocket, and strolled to a nearby saloon. Another time he saw three men dead on the ground, following an argument. Guns were not the only weapon. One night Duke's Hotel blew up from a charge of dynamite, and next day Vigilantes gathered and ran a pimp and his woman, both suspects, down the canyon. These and other scenes of violence were accepted by the youthful Haywood as a natural part of life. His sightless eye was due to an accident, not in a mine as generally supposed, but which happened when the boy was cutting a limb of scrub oak to make a slingshot.

The family returned to live a while in Salt Lake City, where young Bill was sent to an academy operated by nuns of the Sacred Heart order. He worked in a store during vacation and did other jobs.

One of the favorite sights of youngsters was the aged figure of Porter Rockwell walking down the street. Mormon boys whispered to Gentile boys about the terrible deeds that Rockwell was supposed to have committed when he was a Danite or Destroying Angel of the church. These rumors made the old man an appealing figure of mystery, and Haywood, along with others, would run to see him, with his long gray beard, gray shawl, gray hat, and gray hair falling down over his shoulders, and what Haywood remembered as "a not unkindly face."

Young Haywood continued in school until he was fifteen, then went to Eagle Valley, Nevada, to work in a mine of which his stepfather was superintendent. Old-timers in the crew were members of the Knights of Labor. From them he learned about the function of unions. From them, too, he got a different interpretation than the newspapers gave of the significance of the current tragedy in Chicago, where a bomb had exploded in the Haymarket, killing many policemen and several casual bystanders.

Tiring of the mines, Haywood married Nevada Jane Minor, and filed on a homestead. It was too slow. He worked a short time as a ranch hand. He boomed around, briefly holding jobs as a teamster and a miner, then started a professional poker game in a new mining camp. The game flourished from the start. For the first time in his life, Haywood had a thousand dollars. He thought to double it at faro and was cleaned out in a night. He still owned a horse. News from Idaho had it that the old camp of Silver City, dating from the sixties, was in a new boom. Haywood started overland out of Winnemucca, Nevada.

The way to Silver City, he recalled years later, was rugged, bleak, and gray. But the town really was booming. Haywood couldn't get a room in any of the small hotels, and spent his first night on the floor of an old shaft house. He readily got a job, then sent for his wife to come on. This was the place where Haywood was to begin his spectacular rise to prominence. He seems to have identified himself with Silver City more than with any other spot in the United States.

A thousand miners lived in the town that lay in a canyon between two towering peaks in southwestern Idaho. The gulch was lined with boulders and mine tailings. There were two streets, one occupied by "yellow, red, black, and white prostitutes." On the other were seventeen saloons, several small hotels, assorted business houses, a Masonic temple, and the printing shop of the *Owyhee Daily Avalanche*. The newspaper's name was no fantasy. Snow fell enormously deep here. Haywood recalled that the cabins and small houses of the miners were covered to the roofs for months on end, presenting a picture of smoking stovepipes rearing up through the white blanket.

Mining accidents continued to kill or maim large numbers of men every year. Haywood himself was badly injured in a Silver City mine. This camp was the place where the young man first heard of one way to stop accidents: organize. Organize in the Western Federation of Miners. Haywood heard as much and a great deal more, in the summer of 1896, when Ed Boyce came to speak at Silver City.

In the magnetic Boyce Haywood saw "new hope for the working class." Tall and slender, with a fine head, Boyce also spoke with a quiet assurance that was loaded with implications of a better day coming—if miners had enough brains to do "as the owning class did," which was to organize. Now, in Silver City, Boyce told the boys how the Western Federation had come into being right after the troubles in the Coeur d'Alenes, as related earlier; and of the union's efforts in Cripple Creek in 1894. When Boyce was done talking, several hundred miners, including Haywood, became charter members of Silver City Miners Union No. 66 of the Western Federation. Haywood was elected a member of the finance committee. This minor office did nothing to prevent him from following his natural bent. Within a year, no matter what office he held, Haywood was in fact running Union No. 66 with a firm hand. Due largely to him, nearly all of the thousand miners in Silver City had signed union cards. Two years after he himself joined, Haywood was on his way to Salt Lake City, a delegate to the Western Federation's convention.

Things now began to move swiftly for the big young man with the big snarling voice, the quick mind, a plenty of sardonic wit, who did not know fear. He was elected to the federation's executive board and was sent on a tour of all Western mining districts. He was appalled at the desolation around Butte and at "the copper soul" of that town, which then had the largest union in the United States. At Burke, Idaho, and the other nearby mine towns, he talked with the kin of union members killed during the recent strike, with the wounded, and with others still in the bull pens.

When he returned to Silver City, to work briefly again as a miner, his head was filled with ideas. Digging gold out of rocks was among the many things he wanted no longer to do. One day when operating a drill four thousand feet down in Silver City's Blaine mine, he stopped the machine, picked up an empty powder box, and on one side of it wrote "a resolution condemning Governor Steunenberg" for his actions during the 1899 strike in Idaho. That night he took the boxside home, copied the resolution on paper, and at the next meeting introduced it to Union No. 66. It was adopted and ordered to be printed in the *Miner's Magazine*.

Soon after this, Haywood worked his last shift in a mine, then went to Denver for the Western Federation convention. He was elected general secretary-treasurer. He moved his family to Denver and rented a house within easy walking distance of the Mining Exchange Building in which the Western Federation had established headquarters after moving from Butte.

To most men, being a secretary-treasurer of anything is an office job. It wasn't to be such for Haywood. Bookkeeping was not one of his strong points, then or ever.[6] His so-called office hours were erratic. In the early days he was usually at what was termed "the point of production." During his first weeks on the job in Denver, he spent

---

6   Ralph Chaplin, author of *Wobbly* (1948), who long before that was a prominent member of the I.W.W., told me that Haywood's idea of keeping books was to make a few notes on scratch paper and old envelopes, which he kept, even while wearing it, in his derby hat

evenings in organizing men employed in the Globe, Argo, and Grant smelters.

Boyce soon made it known that he did not want to serve again as federation president. He was succeeded by Charles H. Moyer, who had been a smelter man in South Dakota.

Eugene V. Debs came to address the Western Federation's 1901 convention. Bill Haywood liked the lanky, baldheaded Socialist, who had been in Colorado before to organize and speak during the 1896 strike at Leadville. Debs was genial, talkative, and already somewhat given to the bottle. Haywood had just joined the Socialist Party, and now he and Debs discussed a plan for a bureau of education to explain to the miners how the Utopia of Socialism could be achieved.

The rift between Haywood and Moyer doubtless took shape soon after both men were elected to office in the Western Federation. In the summer of 1903 it widened when Haywood was determined that the smelter workers of Colorado should be organized. In July, previous to a meeting at Globeville, he sent a telegram to Moyer, then in Butte, to say there was a growing demand for a strike. Moyer replied that Haywood should postpone action until he returned. Haywood wanted no postponement. He said nothing about the wire from the president of the federation. He harangued the meeting, and at midnight, when Fourth of July cannons boomed, anvils exploded, and whistles blew, the meeting voted unanimously, so Haywood reported, to strike.

By the time Moyer returned to headquarters, the smelter-men's strike was on. It has been related earlier that Haywood had got the convention to pass a resolution permitting the federation's executive board to call a strike without sanction by individual unions. Urged by Haywood, the board, on August 8, issued a strike call to miners in the Cripple Creek district. Almost ten months later came the explosion at Independence depot, and Orchard, Neville, and young Charlie rolled out of Colorado on their fishing trip.

THERE WAS AS YET NO feeling of urgency in Harry Orchard to get beyond the state's borders. He was not a man fleeing. He had boldly entered Denver when excitement was at its height, collected his fee, then he and his two companions continued north, heading for Cheyenne, Wyoming, a little more than a hundred miles. The two-horse wagon jolted leisurely across the hot, windy plateau, passing through the town named for Horace Greeley, averaging twenty-five miles a day.

Arrived on the outskirts of Cheyenne, the fishermen made camp on Crow Creek, then went into the city and to the saloon operated by Pat Moran, a good friend of Pettibone, who had told Orchard that Moran was "all right." When they made themselves known, the saloon man handed them a copy of the Denver *Post*, and they read a little item which said authorities wanted to query both Orchard and Neville "in connection with the Independence explosion." Orchard's smugness thinned a little as he read on to find fairly accurate descriptions of himself and Neville; to read that they were said to have "a good supply of provisions and are heavily armed." The item stated also that the fugitives were believed to be either in Wyoming or New Mexico.

If all this ruffed Orchard somewhat, it frightened Neville horribly. He excitedly demanded that he and Orchard go to the Cheyenne paper and ask them to print a piece saying the wanted men were innocent of any crime and were in Cheyenne, ready to return if wanted. Orchard showed no excitement. He told his friend menacingly that they had better wait a while and think it over before telling anyone where they were. That same night W. F. Davis of the Altman Free Coinage Union and another man showed up at Moran's saloon. They had just come from Denver. Davis reported in so many words that they were "making a getaway." The entire mining district was under rule of the "Vigilantes," he said. Miners were being arrested "in wholesale lots."

Orchard was not a man who scared easily. He remained calm enough to see in his present situation a fair opportunity to tap headquarters for more money. In Moran's saloon he sat down and composed a letter which he sent off to Pettibone in Denver, suggesting that he could use five hundred dollars to good advantage. He did not send this letter through the mail. He gave it to Moran, along with a round-trip ticket and a ten-dollar bill "for the trouble." Within twenty-four hours Moran came back and handed Orchard a package containing five hundred dollars in bills. Orchard suggested to Neville that they resume their fishing trip.

The two-horse wagon, with the animals refreshed from several days of rest, covered the sixty miles to Laramie in two days. The wanderers bought some provisions. Orchard and Neville visited a barbershop, and young Charlie, used only to mining towns, saw lots of cattle and some more cowboys. Neville was worrying because he had not heard from his family. If Orchard worried about anything, it was what to do about Johnny Neville, a thoroughly frightened man who was now a suspect in a crime of some size.

After a couple of days in Laramie, the expedition took to the road again, working north and west through dry barrens, to arrive on July 10 at Thermopolis on the Bighorn River. Though there was then no railroad within one hundred and thirty miles, the travelers found people "from all parts of the United States" in Thermopolis taking baths in the hot springs there. The observant Orchard noticed scores of small piles of stones scattered around the several springs, and on inquiry was told these were monuments erected by grateful people who "had come to the springs as a last resort and had been cured." Neville, who was suffering some sort of skin eruption on his face, wanted to try the hot baths. Orchard didn't mind. There was nothing much the matter with *him*, but he too took the baths.

By this time the two men were talking about buying a saloon somewhere and settling down for a while. They had heard that the town of Cody, on the Shoshone River in the Yellowstone country, was growing. Orchard thought Cody worth a visit. But Neville believed the Thermopolis baths were doing him good; he wanted to stay and take them a while longer. Orchard was agreeable, for he was beginning to think he would be safer alone than in Neville's company. He urged his partner to remain and continue the baths. He, Orchard, would take one of the horses and ride on to Cody, look over the situation, then return. That is what he told Neville.

So, Orchard got out the saddle he had thoughtfully bought, in order to make his night ride away from Independence depot and said good-bye to Neville and Charlie. He rode fifty miles or so to the Greybull River and stopped overnight in what turned out to be a lively little town named Meeteetse. He could get a stage from here on to Cody. Orchard turned the horse and saddle over to the stage company, asking that they be returned to Neville at Thermopolis, and he himself continued on to Cody.

Waiting for him in the Cody post office was a letter postmarked Denver. It was from Pettibone. It told Orchard that police were "hot on your trail and you had better take to the tall timber." Here was something worth consideration. Orchard put faith in Pettibone. The older man had taught him the mysteries of nihilist chemistry. He was jovial company. He also seemed to be the man who paid off. If Pettibone thought Orchard should be careful of his movements, then Orchard would do as much.

Cody was a railroad town on the Burlington Route. Cody also had a long-distance-telephone exchange. Orchard called Neville, still taking the baths at Thermopolis, to say that Cody looked like a pretty good saloon town and he thought Johnnie might well come on there, when he had finished his treatments; but that he, Orchard, was taking a train into Montana and would write as soon as he settled somewhere.

With nothing much on his mind, Orchard got into a Cody poker game, and left the table a winner by some two hundred dollars. Next day, when the game resumed, however, he soon discovered the boys were ganging up to clean him. He quit and went to another saloon to tackle the blackjack table. Within a few minutes he lost the rest of his roll.

Being broke was nothing to cast down a man like Orchard. In the free and easy manner of the time, he went to the operator of the gambling place, a Mr. Hall. He jovially remarked he was dead broke, and just as jovially asked Mr. Hall to lend him fifty dollars. He had already let it be known that he planned to buy a saloon in Cody. Mr. Hall let him have the money. "This will get me to Denver," Orchard said, after thanking his benefactor warmly, and added that he would be back within a few days. Then he went to the Cody depot of the Chicago, Burlington & Quincy railroad, and purchased a ticket for Denver. He never returned to Cody, nor did Johnnie Neville and Charlie ever get there.

13.

A Package for Mr. Bradley

After his return to Denver, Orchard spent a good deal of time with Haywood and Pettibone. The three men met often in Pettibone's home and store or talked in the yard. Most of the conferences, as Orchard remembered them, had to do with a decision as to which enemy of the Western Federation should be the next to get it.

Haywood reported that they had put a fellow named Art Baston "to work on Governor Peabody" but that he seemed terribly slow. Baston was a married man. "They don't seem to work so good after they get married," Haywood observed. (Orchard was married only part of the time.) Another candidate for attention was Andy Mayberry, superintendent of the Highland Boy mine at Bingham, Utah. Mayberry, it seemed, had fired a hundred and fifty miners because they had taken part in a labor demonstration. This sort of thing should be discouraged, Haywood said, or federation men would come to think their union gave them no protection.

Orchard spoke up brightly to say that he was well acquainted in Bingham, having once worked there as a miner, and also knew Andy Mayberry. "Well, then," Haywood said, "that's no place for *you* to go." Pettibone remarked that they had already sent Steve Adams to Wardner, Idaho, where he was "to help Jack Simpkins get rid of some claim jumpers." When that job was finished, Adams was to go to Caldwell, in the same state, "to get ex-Governor Steunenberg." This apparently was the first time Orchard learned that the former chief executive of Idaho was actually on the list of persons marked for removal.

Steunenberg and those claim jumpers, however, were not the only errands Steve Adams was to carry out on his trip. Bill Haywood had the wild idea, characteristic of his boundless imagination, of hiring a gang of professional criminals to kidnap Charles MacNeill, of Colorado Springs, a power in the Colorado Mine Owners Association. On his way to Idaho, Steve was to stop off at Granger, Wyoming, and to get in touch with the notorious Hole in the Wall gang, bank and train robbers, which had been led by the rollicking if deadly Butch Cassidy. Like the earlier James Boys, Cassidy's crew of thugs had somehow or other grown into the old Robinhood legend of robbing the rich to give to the poor. For all his hardness, or perhaps because of it, Bill Haywood had succumbed to this pleasant myth, and figured Cassidy's gang would welcome the chance to abduct mine owner MacNeill and hold him for a ransom big enough not only to pay the outlaws for their trouble but also, said Haywood happily, "pay the federation. for the cost of the strike it had staged on behalf of MacNeill's smeltermen." Rob the rich operator, pay the poor miners.

It looked like a wonderful idea to Haywood and possibly also to Pettibone. though the latter seldom permitted himself flights of fancy. What was wrong with it was that the gang had long since been broken up. A couple of them had been shot and killed. Two more were in prison, and Butch himself and one other were in South America. So, when Steve Adams looked up the man Haywood had told him to see in Granger, Wyoming, he learned he was late. "The birds has all flown South," he reported to Haywood in a letter, then continued on to northern Idaho to take care of those claim jumpers, an affair that was later to bring Clarence Darrow into the Coeur d'Alene country.

The interesting conferences of Haywood, Pettibone, and Orchard continued in Denver. The next likely prospect discussed was Frederick W. Bradley, of the Bunker Hill & Sullivan Mining and Concentrating Company. He had been manager of that operation in 1899 when the mill was dynamited; and now, in 1904, though still an official of the Bunker Hill concern, was also head of the mine operators' associations of Idaho and California.

Orchard knew well enough that Bradley was the only mine operator in the Coeur d'Alene district with whom the federation had been able to do nothing. All of the other operators in that region had come to recognize, at least to some degree, the unions. Not so Mr. Bradley. He was adamant in opposition to organized labor. It was long past time, so Haywood said, that he was made an example.

Sitting around in Pettibone's back yard, on a quiet Sunday in Denver, Haywood told Orchard that an attempt had already been made to do away with Bradley. Steve Adams and another hatchet man named Ed Minster had been sent to San Francisco, where Bradley lived, with orders to get him one way or another. Exactly how the two thugs went about the business is not clear. In any case, they failed. This time, Haywood swore, there must be no failure. Bradley, he said, was busy raising an immense fund from mine owners and planned to use it to drive federation men out of California and Idaho. At last Haywood asked Orchard if he could handle the job. Orchard said sure, he could handle the job. Who, after all, had blown the Cripple Creek region apart?

On Monday Pettibone bought a ticket to San Francisco for Orchard, and gave him money for the trip. Before leaving Denver, Orchard went out to do some shopping. He bought a nice new black valise, packed ten sticks of dynamite in it, just in case it turned out to be that kind of a job, and got aboard a Union Pacific train for San Francisco. For the time being he was John Dempsey.

Registering at the Golden West Hotel as Dempsey, Orchard consulted the San Francisco "telephone guide," then called Fred Bradley's office to check his quarry. Mr. Bradley, he was informed, was out of town. He had gone to Alaska on a business trip. He was expected to return "in about three months."

Here was another example of lack of planning on the part of the Western Federation's command. Steve Adams had been delayed a week or more, while on his way to Idaho, to "get in touch with Butch Cassidy," a man who had long since left Wyoming for South America. Now Orchard had arrived in San Francisco, his new valise filled with dynamite, only to face many weeks of inactivity. Reflecting smugly, as is the case with most hired hands, that he himself would have taken steps to learn where the quarry was before traveling halfway across the continent to blow him up, Orchard settled down to wait Bradley's return.

The first thing, of course, was to get some more money from headquarters, and to that end Orchard wrote Pettibone asking that one hundred dollars have sent him at once. Though he reported that Bradley was out of town, it is improbable Orchard mentioned he faced a delay of three months. Headquarters might have recalled him. The money came from Denver, and Orchard, like any other man of leisure, took off for Caliente Springs.

Refreshed by four pleasant weeks of rest, drinking, and a little gambling in the summer resort, Orchard returned to San Francisco, engaged a room in the Presidio district, and sat down to read a batch of Denver newspapers to see what had been going on back in Colorado. The news was a little disquieting. Johnnie Neville had been arrested in Wyoming, extradited, and taken to Cripple Creek, where he was being held without recourse to bail. Orchard noted also that several other men whom he knew had been arrested in connection with Cripple Creek violences. What made him uneasy was the possibility that Neville would break down under confinement and questioning and tell what he knew about the dynamiting of the Independence railroad depot.

Well, that was the risk one had to take in this business. Orchard wrote Pettibone for another advance, and got it by Postal Telegraph, indicating that conditions at headquarters were still good. September passed, while Orchard strolled the streets of the Bay City, drank moderately, and read the Denver papers carefully. The news turned better. The courts had released not only Johnnie Neville, but all save two of the other men arrested at Cripple Creek, "on their own recognizance." A letter from Pettibone brought Orchard a draft for another one hundred dollars.

October came on. Orchard read in a local paper that Mr. Fred Bradley, the prominent mining man, had returned home from a business trip to Alaska. It was now time to start work. Orchard had already looked the ground over. Bradley lived with his family in a big three-story residence flat at the corner of Leavenworth and Washington streets, a building that today would be termed an apartment house. While ranging the neighborhood, Orchard noted a Room for Rent sign on a house on Washington Street, across the street and only a few doors from the apartment house but on a higher level. He asked the landlady, Mrs. F. E. Seward, to show him what vacant rooms she had. One of these seemed perfect for his purpose. Its windows were on a level with windows in the Bradley apartment, which was no more than a hundred feet distant. He found he "could look right into it." Orchard was elated. He engaged the room and moved in. He was now Mr. Berry.

Without showing undue haste, Orchard-Berry began to study

the neighborhood. Cater-corner from the apartment building where the Bradleys lived was a combination saloon and grocery. The Italian proprietor, a Mr. Guibinni, was genial and talkative. From him, over a drink or two, Orchard learned that Guibinni's place was favored by practically everyone in the neighborhood, including the family of Mr. Bradley, the great mining man from across the street. The Bradley servants bought most of the Bradley groceries there. It wasn't long before Mr. Guibinni introduced Mr. Berry to the Bradley's cook, Mrs. Crowe, and the maid. Mr. Berry invited the girls to have a drink. Everything went fine. One night a little later, Mr. Berry took them downtown to a show.

From the two servants, Orchard learned something of the daily routine of Mr. Bradley. Almost invariably he had breakfast in time to leave the apartment for his office at eight o'clock. The time of his return varied considerably. It might be well before six o'clock. It might be as late as ten. Orchard learned that five other families lived in the same building. All entered and left it through a big archway at the front.

Having received from Pettibone still another draft for a hundred dollars, which was "needed for preparations," Orchard bought a sawed-off shotgun. For a few nights he stood, the weapon under his coat, on the corner opposite the apartment house, waiting opportunity to shoot Bradley as he was about to enter the archway. But no chance offered. He put the gun away and looked again at those ten sticks of dynamite in his little black valise. Though he favored explosive above all other means, he was still in a quandary as how best to do the job on Bradley. Some twenty-odd people used the main entrance to the apartment building every day. He didn't want to waste a bomb on just anybody.

At this stage of the project, he got a curt letter from Pettibone. It did not contain the five hundred dollars Orchard had written he needed to carry on his plans. With it came no money at all. The letter said simply to "call it off," obviously meaning the affair concerning Bradley. Had the boys at headquarters tired of his inaction?

Orchard had been spending too much money gambling. His ready cash was running low. He was irritated that Pettibone had not even mentioned his request for money. He was hurt. He felt put upon. Did Pettibone and Haywood refuse him cash because they thought he dared not return to Denver without having done away with Bradley? Whose fault was it, anyway, that Orchard had been sent to San Francisco without first discovering that his target was in Alaska?

It is not difficult to understand Orchard's reasoning. Like hatchet men before and since, Orchard felt an importance as tender as it was exaggerated. Here he was, the spearhead of terrorism of the Western Federation of Miners, being denied money needed to finish a job which, no matter how well it turned out, called for him to risk arrest, and perhaps even the capital penalty for murder. The nearly three months during which he had lived at ease were as nothing. Goonlike, he thought them little enough compared to the cold fact that he now had to make good, *to kill a man*. He sat in his room feeling sorry for himself, and resentful.

It seems to have been characteristic of Orchard the terrorist that his periods of really great energy were broken by long spells of what looks to have been no more than loafing. The man was not lazy. True, he enjoyed gambling, drink, and women. But not just loafing. He needed to be doing something. What did come over him at times, however, were brief periods during which he seemed wholly unable to make up his mind what to do next. It was just such a moment of indecision that later was to prove disastrous.

Now, in his room on Washington Street in San Francisco, he decided on a method which he was to call so desperate and horrible that he "would gladly have let it die in my breast." At a drugstore he purchased a quantity of strychnine crystals. Next morning, in the early dark, he arose and went to a vacant house that stood just behind the apartment building. There he waited. After what seemed a long time he heard the distant clop-clop of a horse on the pavement. The sound ceased intermittently, while a delivery was made, then resumed, and moved nearer. It was still dark when the wagon came in front of the building. By then Orchard had climbed to the roof of the vacant house from where he could look down on the outside stairs which led up to the several apartments. He watched as the man placed so many bottles at this door, so many at that. When the man had gone, Orchard came quickly down to the back yard, then crept silently up to the back porch of the Bradley apartment. He noted that one bottle of milk and one of cream had been left. Removing the cap of each he sifted a generous dose of poison into the bottles, stirred the liquid, and replaced the caps with the deft touch of a man who once drove a milk wagon in Burke Canyon. Then he hurried back to his room.

No matter how horrible the means selected, which he had every reason to believe might kill not only Bradley, but also his wife and two sons little more than babies, to say nothing of the two servant girls, Harry Orchard was no man to shirk his plain duty. He sat at his ease in his little room, with its fine view of the apartment; and observed with no little interest the Bradley family at their breakfast. He saw the cook preparing the breakfast food. He saw the maid take it to the table. He watched while Mrs. Bradley helped one of the youngsters, and Mr. Bradley had his oatmeal and coffee—with cream. Yet, though he watched every move closely, nothing unusual happened. All seemed as routine as could be.

Orchard was mystified. Had he put too little of the stuff into the bottles? Though he knew little about poisons, he felt certain that he had sifted sufficient strychnine into the liquids to cause some sort of action. Possibly strychnine required a little time before it began to take effect. He didn't know. But now he saw Mr. Bradley finish his second cup of coffee and light up a cigar; saw him rise from the table, go into the hall, put on coat and hat, and leave for the office, apparently as healthy as ever. In another few moments, the maid was clearing away the dishes. It had been just another breakfast at the Bradley's.

Puzzled and vaguely uneasy at the failure, Orchard walked out into the bracing, salt-laden air, where little mists were moving, and went into Mr. Guibinni's small barroom. He needed a drink, perhaps two. While tossing them off, something on the bar back caught his eye. It looked like a bottle of milk, and behind it was a smaller container, cream size. Making a joke of it, Orchard asked the Italian if he had added milk to his usual line of bar goods. This served to start the talkative fellow to telling of an odd happening.

The maid from Mr. Bradley's, Guibinni said, had come in that very morning bringing the bottles of milk and cream. Both she and the cook had tasted the milk. It was "terrible bitter." Now she wanted milk and cream from the store. She left the milkman's bottles with Guibinni, asking him to "have them analyzed." He himself had tasted the milk, the Italian said, and it sure was bitter as hell. "Taste it yourself," he said, proffering the bottle from the back bar. "I don't like milk," said Orchard.

The failure of the poison attempt brought an end to the period of indecision that had dogged Orchard. He threw it off as if it were a blanket. Reflecting that his knowledge of chemistry, gained from the informal course under Professor Pettibone in Denver, had included nothing but explosives, he now consigned strychnine and all other such trumpery to the Devil. Let the shoemaker stick to his last. Let the dyno man stick to No. 1 Gelatin, or any other form of the marvelous substance invented by Mr. Nobel, the Swedish genius.

From the neighborhood plumber Orchard bought a twelve-inch length of lead pipe of five-inch diameter. Working happily and swiftly in the medium he thoroughly understood, he fashioned a bomb containing six pounds of dynamite, to which he added sugar, potash, and caps. It was to be a set bomb, and its mechanism was thus: a cord attached to the cork of a small vial would, when pulled, release acid to flow through a hole in the pipe to the caps inside. Detonation would result.

"While making the bomb in my room," Orchard related, "I tested it to make sure the cork would come out of the bottle without moving the bomb itself. I flattened the pipe into an oblong shape and packed it with the dynamite but did not put in the caps. I fastened an empty vial in place. I drilled a hole. Then I put the whole thing on the floor of my room, attached one end of a cord to the bottle stopper, the other end to a screw eye in the door of my closet. Then I pushed the door shut to pull the cork from the vial. It worked fine. I knew that the doors to the apartments opened inward. This would cause the same action as closing the door of my closet."

For all this care, Orchard now made a stupid mistake which, had the Devil himself not been guarding his efforts, should have caused his arrest. He left the room to go downtown, and also left the screw eye in the closet door, the string with it, and at the other end of the string the bottle stopper. His landlady must have been a markedly incurious woman. While Orchard was out, she came in to make his bed and tidy the room. She could scarcely have missed seeing the rather odd arrangement of string, screw eye, and cork, yet she "never gave any sign she noticed it." (It turned out that she had thought her roomer was an inventor.)

Orchard was already familiar with the morning routine of Mr. Bradley. Now he sought to make certain that the mining engineer would not be away on some trip or other on the morning selected. From a downtown telephone he called Bradley at his home. Saying he had come in from Goldfield, Nevada, just then undergoing a wild rush of prospectors, he asked if Mr. Bradley would be interested in some good mining property there. Mr. Bradley was interested. He suggested that Orchard come to his office next morning at nine o'clock.

Late that night Orchard went to the apartment building, walked up one flight, and fastened a screw eye in the Bradley's door, then returned to his rooming house, where he carefully wrapped the bomb in store-type paper and tied it with store-type string, the whole making what he considered a very neat package.

The next thing was to lay plans for a smooth getaway. Telling his landlady that on the morrow he was going away for a brief trip, he paid her the rent. He hid the neat package on a shelf in the closet, then took his valise downtown to check it in a saloon. He returned to his room, to catnap while the night hours passed, slowly enough.

Orchard was up betimes to watch the Bradleys at breakfast. When Mr. Bradley started on his second cup of coffee, Orchard went down to the street, crossed over, and walked into the apartment building as if he owned it. Then came the ticklish moment when he had to place the bomb on the mat just outside the Bradley door, and attach the cord to the screw eye he had already fastened in the door.

All now was in place, waiting for Mr. Bradley to finish his second cup, light his cigar, and leave for the office. Orchard emerged from the building and got aboard a streetcar for downtown. Less than five minutes later, Bradley lighted his cigar, put on his coat and hat, and went out the door. The bomb let go.

Six pounds of No. 1 Gelatin, confined in a casing of lead pipe, wreaked havoc with the front of the building. The entire front stair was blown out onto the street. Bradley went with it, falling to the sidewalk amidst shattered timbers and broken glass. Windows were broken up and down Leavenworth and Washington streets.

Orchard did not even hear the explosion. Doubtless the noise was muffled by the surrounding buildings. There was also the pounding of the streetcar. He got off at Taylor Street. Finding himself tired from late hours, he got a room in a nearby lodging house, paid the woman a week's rent, and lay down to go instantly to sleep. In a short time, there was a rap at the door. Orchard roused to ask who was there. "It's the sheriff," came a voice. "Open up." Orchard was now quite awake. He called out to wait a minute until he got dressed, meanwhile wondering if somebody had spotted him while laying the bomb and had followed him. He dressed quickly. He took a revolver from his valise, then opened the door. Only the landlady was there, and she was weeping that it had indeed been the sheriff, that he was in the house even then, to remove her furniture which had been seized by a court order.

Orchard was understandingly relieved. "It was such a happy surprise to me," he once told a reporter, "that I left the house without asking the landlady for the rent I had paid her, nor mentioning the annoyance that had been caused me there." Orchard obviously liked to recall his generosity on this occasion, but the reporter was more taken with the courteous forbearance in regard to that "annoyance."

It was now around four in the afternoon of November 17, 1904, and Orchard was anxious to see what the newspapers had to say about the explosion. He bought a copy of the *Evening Bulletin*. Search it as he would, the paper contained not one line he wanted to see. "I began to feel uneasy," he recalled. "If the bomb had not gone off, then somebody must have found it in time. They would have seen how it was rigged to the door, and, if detectives started to investigate the neighborhood, they might learn from the woman where I roomed about the screw eye and string in the door of my closet."

By now, he had made up his mind that for some reason or another the bomb had not exploded. Everything seemed to be working against him. He was almost broke again. He suddenly recalled that he had had nothing to eat since the night before. Going into a restaurant to order a meal, he picked up a copy of the *Evening Post*. There, splashed all over the front page, were pictures and a story to tell him of the destruction caused by his six pounds of dynamite.

Reading the account, he learned that Mr. Bradley "would probably die, or at least lose his hearing and eyesight." In either case it would show what happened to enemies of the Western Federation of Miners. Or, would it? Reading on Orchard learned that the explosion was "believed to be due to leaking gas" which had ignited when the mining engineer lighted a cigar as he left his apartment. Yet, no matter what the paper said, Haywood and Pettibone would know what and who had blown up the Bunker Hill & Sullivan official. It would show them that he, Harry Orchard, was the man who got things done, who blew things apart. No sooner had he finished his hurried meal than he wrote a note to Pettibone asking for money. This note he wrapped in a copy of the *Evening Post* and mailed this evidence of a mission completed to Denver.

Next day he was elated to read the San Francisco *Call*'s account, which began with the statement that "an explosion of gas" wrecked the building, and went on to say, "F. W. Bradley was the innocent cause of it" when in the hall "he scratched a match to light his cigar." The city fire marshal, who had "made a careful inspection," was of the opinion that "gas escaping from a grate in the apartment of M. E. Cummings, San Francisco Park commissioner, had furnished the explosive material." No trace of the bomb apparatus was mentioned. Orchard sent a copy of the *Call* to Denver, too. Federation headquarters must have been impressed. Almost at once he received three hundred dollars—by Postal Telegraph.

Whether from curiosity or mere bravado—and the latter was present in Orchard's make-up—Orchard could not resist a visit to Mr. Guibinni, the grocer and saloon man. Dropping in casually for a drink, Orchard learned that the voluble Italian himself was of the opinion the explosion had been caused by a bomb, but that Mrs. Bradley was positive it had been the work of gas. For several weeks she had smelled gas constantly in the hallway, she insisted. Guibinni had heard talk that the owners of the building were going to file suit against the gas company.[7] Mr. Bradley was still under medical care, reputedly blinded for life.

Orchard was at a loss to understand how the mining engineer and official had managed to survive so powerful a charge of explosive that had gone off virtually at his feet. He had reason to believe, however, even if mistakenly, that he could brag truthfully that Fred Bradley would never more trouble the Western Federation of Miners.

It was time now to return to headquarters where, so Orchard thought, he would be welcomed as befitted a hatchet man who could blow up a building, maim a union enemy, and see the whole thing charged to a gas utilities company. Pretty fine work.

First, however, he committed an act as naive as it was potentially dangerous to his liberty. At a pawnshop in downtown San Francisco

---

7 They not only sued the gas company but collected damages. Still later, when Orchard saw fit to explain matters, the gas company sued the apartment owners for recovery.

he bought a secondhand uniform of a private soldier in the United States Army. Orchard had never been a soldier. Possibly he didn't know that more than a few criminals had been caught when they sought to disguise themselves as soldiers. In prisons all over the country were men doing time who had been picked up by police while posing as soldiers and had been unable to answer simple questions about the Army or to tell what regiment they belonged to. Orchard compounded his error by adding a pair of spectacles to his "disguise," not knowing that the recruiting service automatically refused men with impaired eyesight.

The Devil, however, was still with Harry Orchard. In an Army uniform, he arrived without incident in Denver, got a room in a lodging house not far from George Pettibone's home and store, then phoned the Western Federation's unofficial chemist that he was back from the front. Pettibone replied that he would be over in a little while.

14.

Poor Merritt Walley

With Pettibone when he came to call on Orchard was Steve Adams, not long since returned from his expedition to northern Idaho. Orchard hardly waited to receive their congratulations for the bombing in San Francisco but started immediately to take Pettibone to task. Why, he wanted to know, hadn't Pettibone sent him that five hundred dollars when he needed money so bad; and why had Pettibone written him "to call it off" just when Orchard had everything lined up to dynamite Fred Bradley?

Pettibone replied they had been alarmed by threats of Johnnie Neville. When Neville was released from the Cripple Creek jail, he came direct to Denver to tell Haywood and Pettibone that they'd better pony up a piece of cash or he would go to authorities and tell all about the explosion at the Independence depot, including who paid to have it done. He suggested twelve hundred dollars as his idea of cash just then. They stalled him for a few days, but he returned again, more determined than ever. It was at this point, Pettibone said, that he and Haywood thought it best to "lay off" for a while, and he had written Orchard to that effect. When Neville persisted in his blackmail demands, the federation men had about come to the decision to kill him when somebody remembered that Neville had collected insurance on his bankrupt saloon which Orchard had so accommodatingly, and cleverly, set afire. "We told Johnnie we'd go to the police with that story," Pettibone related. "That shut his mouth. The last we saw of him, Johnnie came in to say he was going to Goldfield, Nevada, to open a saloon."

Orchard was curious to hear how Steve Adams had made out on

his trip to the Coeur d'Alene country. This really had nothing to do with Western Federation affairs, but was prompted by Jack Simpkins, an Idaho miner who was also a member of the federation's executive board; and the trip, Steve explained to Orchard, had come off fine and dandy. Fine and dandy turned out to mean that Steve and Simpkins had shot and killed two claim jumpers, then buried them far back in the wilderness.

The dead claim jumpers were obscure nobodies named Tyler and Boulle. Their deaths were not only unmourned but suspected and welcomed by the few people who were in a position to know that they had suddenly disappeared. In fact, no person living then or later could say that Tyler and Boulle had been murdered. That is, nobody except Steve Adams and Jack Simpkins. Yet, because the two dead men were presently to play important parts in the affairs of the Western Federation of Miners, it is perhaps well here to indicate the manner of their deaths.

Beginning in a small way in 1901, a movement of homesteaders into the St. Joe country of northern Idaho had grown into something of a rush. Immense stands of virgin white pine were the magnet. Lumbermen of the lake states, where the timber was petering out, already had their agents and cruisers in northern Idaho, buying stumpage by the thousands of acres. An individual could have a hundred and sixty acres of government land merely for the asking, so long as he would agree to erect a cabin and make certain improvements, which were far from onerous. On came the homesteaders, among them Jack Simpkins, the miner and Western Federation official, to file a claim on Marble Creek, a tributary of the St. Joe River, which flowed into Coeur d'Alene Lake.

Scores of other men were doing the same thing. They came from everywhere—loggers from Wisconsin, farmers from the Dakotas, city fellows from New York and Boston. Frank Therriault, a woodsman from New Brunswick, had been among the first. On his claim beside Marble Creek, he established a sort of rough-and-ready trailside inn, a regular stopover place for those coming in and going out. In 1904, when his cabin was designated a polling place for the precinct, he was astonished that more than three hundred votes were cast by men who emerged from the woods in all directions.[8]

Claim jumpers were present almost from the first. There is no need here to go into their methods, other than to say that they squatted illegally on homesteads already claimed by others, sold out for what they could get, then went away or stayed to defend their ground against all comers. Among the most active of the claim jumpers were the Tyler and Boulle already mentioned. They appear to have been hard men.

But they were no harder men than Jack Simpkins and Steve Adams. Steve met Jack at Coeur d'Alene city, took a boat with him up the St. Joe to Marble Creek, then went overland some twenty-five miles to Simpkins's homestead. Armed with rifles, they first captured Tyler, held him prisoner overnight, and shot him dead next morning. They then ambushed Boulle, reputed a desperate character and shot him. They buried both men where they had fallen. Then Simpkins returned to his home in Wardner, where he lived when not "proving up" on the homestead. Adams remarked to Orchard and Pettibone that both elk and deer were thick in the Marble Creek country. "Best hunting, I ever seen," he said.

The discussion in Orchard's room continued, and Pettibone let his two hatchet men know that things in Colorado were going far from well for the unions. Secretary Hamlin of the mine owners' group had just reported that thirty-five hundred men were working in the Cripple Creek mines as of December 1, adding that of these more than two thousand had been members of the Western Federation before the strike. The mines now employed no men who admitted membership in the union. The federation attempted to strike back. It prepared and printed a poster headed "Scab List," on which appeared the photographs of thirty miners, listed by name and number, with the admonition: "Remember the names and the faces. You will meet them again." At the bottom of the poster was a line: "Second Edition. More Coming."

Though it must have been fairly obvious that the strikes at Cripple Creek and Telluride were broken, the federation continued to warn "good union men" to keep away from those districts. Pettibone told Orchard and Adams that headquarters had more work for them to do.

For some reason, it was thought best for Orchard to move into the house where Mr. and Mrs. Steve Adams were living. The two men were

---

8   So, he recalled when I interviewed him in 1943.—S.H.H.

told to "lay low" for a little while, which they did. Then Haywood asked them to come to his house. Big Bill mentioned four likely prospects. There were Chief Justice William H. Gabbert of the Colorado Supreme Court, who "had decided against federation president Moyer in a habeas corpus case"; Justice Luther M. Goddard of the same court, "who had written the opinion against Moyer"; Frank Hearne, manager of the Colorado Fuel & Iron Company, a recent importation from Pennsylvania, where he had won recognition among employers as a man to ride roughshod over "anarchistic unionists"; and Governor James H. Peabody, the same official who had declared the Cripple Creek region to be in a state of insurrection and sent militia to police the district.

It seems to have been suggested either by Haywood or Pettibone that Orchard and Adams team up for the purpose of killing the four men selected. It was to prove an unwise combination. Either man was bold enough. And hard enough. Working together they had staged the Independence depot dynamiting. They had run down Lyte Gregory, the mine dick, and killed him on the street. Adams had killed a mine superintendent, to say nothing of a couple of claim jumpers. Orchard had dynamited Bradley and blown two mine bosses to bits. Neither thug had revealed anything that could be called a twinge of conscience. Yet, both Orchard and Adams were drinkers, and, though Orchard's judgment might be impaired by whisky, he had always kept sober when there was working to do. On the other hand, Adams got dead drunk on occasion, work or no work.

So, they started out to get Judge Gabbert. With revolvers on their hips, and sawed-off shotguns beneath their overcoats, they spent a few evenings strolling around the Judge's Denver home, stopping occasionally to have a drink. Orchard complained that the Gabberts were great people to keep their blinds pulled closed after dark. But he did not complain overmuch. The weather was cold when it wasn't stormy, the saloons were warm and friendly, and the two men spent far more time in the bar than on the street. "We did not make any great effort to get Judge Gabbert," Orchard later admitted. "We had plenty of money and lived good. Had plenty to drink. We took things easy."

After a few nights of this, Haywood told them to drop Gabbert for the time and to go get Hearne, the aggressive manager of Colorado Fuel & Iron. The weather hadn't improved. Adams and Orchard "strolled around his residence some but did not make much of an effort to do anything to him." Pettibone pulled them off the Hearne beat and told them to go after Governor Peabody. Toting shotguns, the two men did more of their night strolling, and thought they saw guards lurking around the outside of the Peabody home. But they learned that the Governor usually walked to the Capitol every morning. Perhaps a good bomb would fetch him.

Snow began falling steadily as Orchard went off to get a supply of dynamite and Adams had a plumber make a lead case. This was to be similar to the Bradley bomb, only a good deal bigger. Into it went twenty-five sticks of explosive, along with the caps and a vial of sulphuric acid to set it off. By the time it was ready a good six inches of new snow lay on the ground.

Late that night, the two dyno men arrived near the Governor's residence on Grant Avenue. It was still snowing. All street and pedestrian traffic had ceased. The entire neighborhood was in the hush of the new blanket of white, sparkling in the light of street lamps to take a picture postcard of Denver on a winter's night. The two men quickly and quietly laid a wire from Grant Avenue to Logan Street on Thirteenth Avenue, then went away. It was up Grant that the Governor walked to the Capitol, leaving his house at nine.

Next morning, a little after eight o'clock, Adams and Orchard in a horse-and-buggy rig driven by Billy Aikman, late of Bull Hill, left for the scene. As they neared the place, Orchard got out and walked ahead, while the buggy waited. Finding everything clear, and nobody approaching, he signaled. The buggy came up and Adams passed the bulky package, wrapped in a piece of white cloth, to Orchard. The buggy drove on to stop two blocks away.

Orchard brushed away snow and lay the bomb on the bare ground. He checked the bottle of acid. He hooked the end of the long wire to a screw eye in the stopper, covered the bomb with the fluffy snow, then walked away to where the buggy stood waiting. Just before nine, the Governor came out of his house, a bodyguard with him. Far down the street Adams and Orchard got out of the buggy to stand in the snow, each holding the wire, as they had done at the Independence depot affair, waiting until Peabody and his man came along to where the bomb waited.

Just then, as if waiting for a stage cue, a large coal wagon drove out of the alley in the middle of the block and turned toward the buggy. Right behind its tailboard came another coal wagon. Adams and Orchard, standing there in the street, holding a wire, were astounded. The muted world of Colorado winter had prevented the big vehicles from giving any warning of their approach.

The Governor and his man had been moving ahead steadily, and now, as Orchard looked, he saw them hard on the spot where the bomb lay. It was no moment to yank the wire. Even the drunken Adams knew that. In another moment the Governor had passed the bomb, and the coal wagons were trundling past the buggy. As if still prompted by cues, five or six pedestrians walked onto the scene. One wonders if any of them, or the coal-wagon drivers, noticed the tableau of two men, frozen by astonishment, standing close together near a buggy, or if the scene was brought to mind, as it was more than a year later to Governor Peabody, when its significance became general knowledge.

What had seemed to Orchard like a premeditated massing of citizens and coal wagons lasted but a moment. Everything on wheels and feet, including the Governor and his man, disappeared immediately. The three men drove down the deserted block. Orchard got out to lift the bomb into the buggy, while Adams reeled in the wire. All hands returned to stow the stuff away in Adams's home, and to discuss their failure over a bottle. A night or so later, the two men made another attempt to set the bomb. The snow had gone, the ground was hard, so they took along a spade. This time they would plant the infernal machine right next to the walk that led from the Governor's front door to Grant Avenue. They had scarcely started digging when a watchman popped out from behind the house. They went away so hurriedly that the new spade was left beside the hole.

When Orchard and Adams went to federation headquarters to report "progress" on the Peabody case, Haywood listened to their story, then suggested sardonically that they put their "goddam bomb in Peabody's desk and hook it up to the roll top." He then told them to lay off Peabody and to go after Judge Goddard. Before any plans were made for Goddard, however, the two dyno men had an attractive offer to blow up a boarding house full of nonunion smeltermen in Globeville, in suburban Denver.

The boardinghouse suggestion came from Max Malich, a member of the federation's Smeltermen's union, who operated a store and saloon and was generally known as King of Globeville. He was a leader of the Austrians who composed a majority of the union smelter workers there. But the federation strike, though still nominally in force, had failed here as elsewhere, and the Globeville smelter was being operated with a nonunion crew of three hundred men, most of whom were housed in one great rambling hotel.

Max Malich told Orchard and Adams it would be simple to get into the hotel and plant a bomb. He knew a fellow who lived there who could be trusted, and he himself would lend a hand. Max also knew where they could get all the dynamite they wanted. Adams and Orchard went out to case the scene. It looked easy compared, for instance, to putting a bomb in the desk of the Governor of Colorado. Max took them out beyond the edge of town and pointed to a number of powder magazines. That night, in a rig driven by a close friend of Max, Orchard and Adams went out to the magazines. They took six hundred pounds of dynamite from one place, fifteen boxes of giant caps from another, loaded everything into the rig, and returned to Globeville, to bury the explosive in the cellar of a house Max had designated.

Globeville was to produce nothing to add to the reputations of Adams and Orchard, but it turned out to be an engaging sort of interlude. Between free drinks at Max Malich's hospitable bar, the two dyno experts experimented with powder and plaster of Paris and devised at least one number they thought would be effective when conditions called for a contact bomb to be thrown. "We first made a little ball of damp plaster," Orchard said. "We stuck this full of giant caps. When it had hardened, we stuck a wire nail into each cap, point inward. We shived the nail up with slivers of wood, so the nail would not press on the powder at the bottom of the cap but would do so if jarred ever so little. We got some rubber balls, cut them open, slipped them around the outside of the nails, filled the casing with four pounds of dynamite, then sewed up the rubber."

Taking a couple of the loaded rubber balls, Adams and Orchard visited Max's saloon, then went out into the country. Steve could hardly wait. He tossed one of the balls at a large cottonwood tree. It was stronger than he had thought. The explosion tore a huge piece out of the tree and had like to have knocked Adams flat. Badly shaken but pleased, Steve allowed that one of these balls would do to toss at Peabody, or Goddard, or whoever the high command suggested as next in line.

The two men were quite willing to prepare a special bomb for the boarding house, but federation president Moyer was against it, and asked pointedly why they did not accomplish the things they had been set to do. Judge Goddard, for instance. Well, then, Goddard it would be. Taking their sawed-off shotguns, the two men went forth to consider the chance of shooting Goddard through a window of his home. They sighted the place from several angles but did not get a look at their target. They decided that the next night might offer opportunity.

Steve Adams suddenly disappeared without trace and without a word to his wife or to Orchard. Day followed day with no word of him. Orchard set out to visit saloons and talk to bartenders. At one place the barkeep said he had heard that Steve had had a fight with somebody. Beyond that, he knew nothing, nor did anyone else Orchard talked to. One week later Steve returned home, obviously a chastened man, still shaky from six days in the city jail without a drink.

Orchard wormed the story out of him. Steve had gone downtown the day of his "disappearance." He had got drunk. And though he could remember nothing whatever about it, he awoke to find himself in jail charged with stealing a bicycle. The event had not even made a line in the police news. Orchard gave Steve a good lecture, not about whisky, which Orchard favored, but about getting drunk. "Haywood and Pettibone won't like it," he said with some truth.

Rum was getting the better of Steve Adams. Within a few days he got so drunk again that he had to be helped home. Pettibone told Orchard they would have to get rid of Adams. "He knows too much about things," Haywood added. "We can't afford to have him going around drunk."

Orchard left the Adams home, where he had been living all winter, and took a furnished room. He never saw Steve again in Denver. Haywood told Orchard he had urged Steve to get out of town, which he did at once. "He plans to take a homestead somewhere in Oregon," Haywood said.

It was now spring. Though the team of Adams and Orchard had not produced an explosion all winter, the latter appeared to be still in the good graces of the federation bosses, who had not yet given up the idea of destroying Governor Peabody. Peabody was no longer in office. He had resigned (the lieutenant governor succeeded him), and then returned to Canon City, where he had lived before entering politics. Haywood and Pettibone told Orchard to go to Canon City and see what he could do; and Pettibone, never short of ideas, came up with one he thought would ease Orchard's way.

Remarking that Canon City was a small place where strangers without obvious means of support were looked at askance, Pettibone suggested that Orchard become an insurance agent. Not a phony, but a genuine, documented agent. Orchard didn't mind, and some of Pettibone's influential friends were happy to assure the old-line Mutual Life that Thomas Hogan—for such was Orchard's name on the application—was a man to be relied upon. With a pocketful of nice new cards, agent Hogan was soon canvassing Canon City and taking in the lay of the land as regarding the residence of that town's most eminent citizen, Ex-Governor Peabody, who, incidentally, was the first but not the last ex-governor to attract Orchard's interest.

"I found I could no more keep my mind on insurance," Orchard remembered, "than I could fly." But, in keeping fairly close watch on the Peabody home, he concluded the best method to use here would be a time bomb, set off by an alarm clock. Telling the landlady where he stayed that he had to go to Denver, but would be back very soon, and to hold his room, he took the train to Denver, went to Globeville, the place where dynamite could be had for the asking, and from Max Malich got fifty pounds of powder and a box of caps. Putting these into a couple of valises, he stowed them briefly in Pettibone's store. At a nearby plumber's shop he asked the man to make him a lead bucket. Wanted it to hold a cactus plant, he explained. While the plumber was whacking up the bucket, Orchard went out to buy sulphuric acid and an alarm clock. Then, weighted down with considerably more luggage than was usual for an insurance agent, he returned to Canon City.

Orchard appears to have been invariably foresighted, or at least fortunate, in the matter of selection of rooming houses. His lodgings in Canon City overlooked the Peabody home; his landlady displayed no interest in what went on in her roomers' quarters. Orchard went ahead to hammer his lead cactus pot flat on one side, packed it with twenty-five pounds of No. 1 Gelatin, affixed the alarm clock and acid bottle with plaster of Paris, hooked wire from bottle to the alarm key of the clock, then made a dry run to make certain the apparatus would pull the stopper from the bottle. Sounds of all this activity must have been clear to anybody in the house, but no inquiry was made. Possibly the landlady thought they were exactly the sounds made by an insurance agent.

When he had the monstrous machine ready and in good working order, Orchard reflected it was big enough to blow the Peabody house apart. He was content. "I figured," he said, "we ought not to take any chances of missing Peabody."

Nothing came of this bomb. Once it was ready, Orchard seems not to have been overanxious to place it in or near the Peabody residence. Perhaps he was suffering from another of those spells which seemed to dog him—periods when he could not make up his mind what to do next. He excused himself, however, on the fact that just then he was joined by a William J. Vaughan, described as a close friend of Pettibone, who arrived at his rooming house. Vaughan explained that Pettibone suggested he and Orchard team up to write insurance.

There is nothing to show that Pettibone actually sent Vaughan to report secretly on Orchard's movements. Vaughan was full of talk about insurance, but never once mentioned the Western Federation of Miners. While he and Orchard were talking, the stranger seemed to be uneasy, glancing first here, then there around the room, as if looking for something. At last he let on what was troubling him. "I can hear a clock ticking," he said, "but I can't see no clock."

He heard a ticking, all right. Good craftsman that he was, Orchard wanted the running parts of his apparatus to continue in operation, hence had kept the clock wound. All that was needed to make ready was to hitch the wire from the vial cork to the alarm key. When Mr. Vaughan remarked about the ticking, he was virtually sitting on top of twenty-five pounds of dynamite, packed in lead and capped, in a big suitcase under Orchard's bed. The sudden remark did not shake Orchard. If Pettibone *had* sent this fellow to learn if Orchard was busy on Governor Peabody, he might as well know the truth. "That ticking," said Orchard slowly, "is a clock with the bomb in my grip." He pointed casually beneath the bed. He offered no explanation.

Vaughan displayed no further interest in what was occupying Orchard's time. It was at least possible he was upset to find himself so near the suitcase that ticked. He told Orchard that Canon City was no place to sell insurance, but that he, Vaughan, knew where the pickings were good. Let us go, said he, to the Arkansas River valley, down around Rocky Ford. The farmers there had been pretty much overlooked by insurance agents.

Orchard was losing interest in bombing Peabody. He welcomed the distraction suggested by Vaughan. Not caring to tote along the big suitcase, which weighed nearly fifty pounds, he asked his landlady if he might leave it while he was away for a few days. She didn't mind. Put it right under that table, she told him, where it would be in no one's way. (Orchard had let the alarm clock run down.) The two men went away, leaving the landlady—a kindly woman, Orchard remembered her—to keep house for the Peabody bomb.

At Rocky Ford, Colorado, Orchard and Vaughan hired a rig and started to canvass the farmers round about. At this point, they were the legitimate agents of a reputable company. Business was not too good. They presently met a Mr. Peterson who represented himself as general agent for a concern selling hail insurance on a policy so filled with fine-print "exceptions" as to constitute an outright fraud. "You can make a fortune with this policy," Mr. Peterson said. Orchard's interest quickened at once. "I liked it," he remembered, "because it was crooked." So, he and Vaughan switched to hail insurance, clearing as high as one hundred dollars some days, always making at least twenty dollars a day. It did not last very long, for at Las Animas Orchard found a letter from Pettibone, who wanted to see him in Denver.

LEAVING VAUGHAN AT LAS ANIMAS, Orchard took a train for Denver, but did not stop at Canon City to relieve the kindly old lady of the heavy suitcase in her living room. Pettibone reported that Moyer and Haywood had gone to Salt Lake City to prepare for the coming convention of the federation. He, Pettibone, was to follow them, but, before he left, he wanted to make sure Orchard was going to "pull something off" before the convention opened.

Sensing that Pettibone was irritated because he had failed to blow up Governor Peabody, Orchard was full of excuses for the delay. Pettibone said to never mind that, but to do something right off about Judge Gabbert, the same Chief Justice of the Colorado Supreme Court whom Orchard and Steve Adams had halfheartedly stalked vainly with shotguns. Pettibone said he would lend a hand. The two men repaired to the basement of Pettibone's store and made a bomb from a molasses can. Pettibone had previously cased Gabbert's routine.

It was a day when great men still walked to and from their offices, and it was Chief Justice Gabbert's pleasure to walk from his home to the Supreme Court in the Capitol buildings. The route brought him down Emerson Street to Colfax Avenue. At the junction of those thoroughfares was a vacant lot. Across this lot was a footpath which it was Gabbert's custom to follow. Working at night, Orchard and Pettibone dug a hole beside the path, buried the bomb, and covered it neatly with grass sod.

Next morning the two men observed that the vacant lot looked just as they had left it. Pettibone took his post where he could see the judge when he left his residence. Orchard stationed himself near the lot where the bomb lay waiting. Pettibone was to signal when the judge started. Orchard was then to take a lady's purse he had bought, go to the lot, lay the purse fair in the path, then hitch it to the fine wire in the grass that led to the bomb.

Pettibone gave the signal. Orchard started for the lot, but stopped when he saw another man pass the approaching judge and head for the lot. By the time the stranger passed the spot, the judge was too near to let Orchard attach the purse without being detected. Three more attempts on as many mornings were frustrated because other strangers appeared on the scene almost simultaneously with the judge. Orchard came to think the vacant lot at the corner of Emerson Street and Colfax Avenue was jinxed. And so, it was.

Pettibone now had to leave for the federation convention in Salt Lake City, but not before he had told Orchard to let nothing interfere with the dynamiting of Judge Gabbert. Pettibone obviously meant it as a warning, for he casually mentioned that here it was already summer and there was nothing at all to show for the winter's work.

Left alone to carry out the Gabbert job, Orchard went again to the vacant lot to consider the still waiting bomb. "I was afraid to touch it after it had stood so long," he said later. "I knew that the little windlass swung very easily. The least touch of the wire was sure to tip the bottle of acid." In such case, he thought that in hooking the purse to the wire, and doubtless in some haste, that—well, he decided the thing to do was to make and plant a second bomb.

Returning to the cellar beneath Pettibone's store, surely a den to please the most exacting nihilist, Orchard went to work on another bomb for Justice Gabbert. It was to be something of a new departure from convention. In the basement, standing silent and dusty on a shelf, he had noticed several old eight-day kitchen clocks. Orchard removed the main spring from one of these to see if it was strong enough to break one of the vials he used for acid. It was. He went ahead to make the bomb, the clock spring bent back and held by a piece of stiff wire that would be released by a casual pull of the wire—if and when Justice Gabbert reached for the purse. That night Orchard strapped the bomb under his coat, got aboard a bicycle he found in the cellar, and rode out to the vacant lot, where he planted the second bomb "as close to the first as I dared."

Riding the bike again next morning, Orchard was on the scene in good season. When he saw Judge Gabbert come out and start down the steps of his home, he rode ahead to the lot, attached the purse, then rode swiftly away. He was not there to see what happened.

Just as Judge Gabbert was approaching the corner of Colfax and Emerson, a friend hailed him. The judge paused. The friend came up. The two men talked a moment, then walked, still talking, not across the vacant lot, but around it. That was why Orchard, by then several blocks away, heard no welcome sound.

The vacant lot waited, the enticing purse fallow on the ground. Approximately fifty minutes after Judge Gabbert had taken the tack that led him around the lot, a good citizen of Denver, Merritt W. Walley, came along Colfax Avenue. He turned into the foot path across the lot to Emerson Street. He saw the purse. He stooped to pick it up.

A total of twenty pounds of dynamite, in the two bombs side by side, blasted a mighty hole in the ground, and fairly tore poor Merritt Walley apart. "The explosion," reported the *Rocky Mountain News*, "also shattered windows all over the neighborhood."

Harry Orchard heard the noise but had to wait for the papers to learn what had happened. He was much "disappointed" that the victim was a man he had never heard of. He was relieved, however, to read that police were at a loss to explain the matter. One news story suggested that "yeggmen had buried nitroglycerin there" and the unfortunate Walley "stubbed his toe on it." No report connected the outrage with mine-war terrorism. The murder of Walley was of no value to the Western Federation, by then in convention at Salt Lake City. It is doubtful that the delegates even read of the mystery. It suddenly occurred to Orchard that, if he was going to redeem his waning reputation, he must do something right away. He tried. One night soon he planted one of his old-style string-and-stopper bombs in a hole he dug against a gatepost in the yard of Judge Luther M. Goddard's home. Next morning, he went back there and took a desperate chance: in broad daylight he stopped in front of the judge's house, attached a fishline from the bomb to the swinging gate, and left. Nothing happened, either that day or the next.

Now thoroughly convinced that the Devil had deserted him, Orchard went to investigate. Though he knew well enough the properties of sulphuric acid, it was chemistry that had defeated him. He had attached the fishline to a pin he had pushed through the rubber stopper of the vial. The vial had been brimming full of acid. It had stood thus, Orchard recalled, for two or three days before he set the bomb by the gate. The acid had eaten away the head of the pin. When Judge Goddard, or some other lucky person, had opened the gate, the headless pin had slipped easily through the stopper. The rubber had closed instantly. Not a drop of acid had escaped.

All of which reminded Orchard of the dangers inherent in the sort of chemistry he practiced. He did not mean to add to them by removing this bomb at the Goddard gate. The lawn had been watered two or three times. The caps in the bomb were thus ruined. They would not explode even if acid did drip upon them. Let it lie. And there it was to remain unsuspected for seven months.

At about this time Orchard suddenly remembered the great time-clock bomb he had left many weeks before with the kindly old lady in whose house he had lived in Canon City. Just why he troubled himself about it is not clear. Possibly the continuous failure of his recent bombs "to do the harm contemplated for them," as he quaintly put it, caused some anxiety about his job and prompted him to any sort of activity that would make him appear busy for the good of the Western Federation. He took a train to Canon City and went boldly to the rooming house. The old lady was glad to see him, after all this time. No, the suitcase had not caused any inconvenience. It was right there where he had left it. He thanked her, struggled to the depot with the leather bound burden, and so back to Denver. Here he went first to Pettibone's cellar and left the bomb. It was a rather large thing to have lying around loose. A few days later he took it out and buried it somewhere.

By now the Western Federation's convention was over. Haywood, Moyer, and Pettibone returned to headquarters. Haywood and Moyer left again for Chicago, after Haywood told Orchard he had better "lay off a while." Pettibone, however, had other plans, one of which was to shoot Sherman Bell. A fearless if noisy fellow, Bell had been one of Teddy Roosevelt's Rough Riders in the Spanish-American War. As adjutant general of Colorado, he had commanded the militia which rode roughly over the miners during the Cripple Creek strike.

In a buggy, with Pettibone driving and Orchard holding a repeating shotgun loaded with buckshot cartridges, the two men spent a few nights in August (it was still 1905) trying to get a shot at the redoubtable Bell, either in his yard or in nearby Congress Park. They never so much as sighted their target. They were still trying when Moyer returned to Denver. Moyer was angry. He wanted no more rough work in Denver. Pettibone attempted to argue. Moyer fairly hit the ceiling. If anything were pulled off in Denver, he said, then he, Moyer, would be automatically arrested. If Pettibone and Orchard were so anxious to be busy, he went on, then let them go to Goldfield, Nevada, and do away with Johnny Neville. "He knows too much about us," Moyer said. "He's liable to get us into trouble any time. Go get him."

If Moyer was irritable and short of temper at this time, it was probably due to a rift between him and Haywood, of which Orchard, certainly, and possibly even Pettibone, suspected nothing.

15.

The Wobblies Are Born

Many years after they were dead, an aged hard-rock miner remarked that Moyer had been the brains and Haywood the spirit of the Western Federation of Miners. Whether or not this estimate is accurate, the personality of Big Bill was such as to have survived the passage of time and to come through as a vital thing, while Charlie Moyer and many other labor figures of the era are shadows.

Even in his heyday, Moyer was more a name to the rank and file of miners than he was a living man. He may well have been as courageous as Haywood, but he tempered courage with caution. He had better judgment than Haywood. Haywood was careless to a fault; he was wholly undisciplined. Haywood acted from emotion rather than reason. It was just these things that helped to make him the incomparable leader of the foot-loose working stiffs of the West—the miners, the loggers, the harvest hands, the boomers of all kinds. He was their friend. They called him Big Bill.

Moyer comes through the dust of years as the silent, secretive man-in-the back-room, the planner, the think boss, possibly wise and farseeing, but in any case, no man to lead a charge. Haywood shot from the hip. Moyer took careful aim, even when he missed. Both men were ambitious. Moyer was politic and could work with others. Heywood could work comfortably with nobody. By 1905, it is certain that Moyer, the federation president, was irked because Secretary-Treasurer Haywood was running things with little or no regard for the executive board of the organization. Worse, Haywood was devoting far too much of his time talking about a One Big Union of all wage-workers. The Western Federation, true enough, had officially indicated its favor of "amalgamation of the entire working class into one general organization." It had discussed the subject with other groups, including the railway unions. President Moyer had gone along with the idea, though subsequent events indicate he was more interested in getting rid of Haywood than in anything else.

On January 2, 1905, twenty-six men and one woman met in Chicago to plan for the One Big Union. Among them were Eugene V. Debs, who as Socialist candidate had received an astonishing four hundred thousand votes for President of the United States, and three delegates from the Miners—Moyer, Haywood, and John M. O'Neill. They gathered in the same hall on Lake Street where the celebrated "Chicago Anarchists" used to meet before the bomb went off in the Haymarket.

It was still a day for manifestoes, and the conference drew up a characteristic manifesto to formulate the Industrial Workers of the World: Class divisions had grown more fixed ... class antagonisms had grown sharper ... used-up laborers were thrown on the scrap heap to starve ... wages grew less ... working hours grew longer ... capitalist success rested on the blindness and internal dissensions of the working class ... the class struggle must go on until the workers took over the tools of production ... through working-class unity ...

The group voted to print and distribute two hundred thousand copies of the Manifesto, and to hold a convention in Chicago six months later. This convention opened on June 27 with delegate Haywood in the chair. Picking up a piece of board that lay on the platform, Big Bill struck the speaker's table a rousing blow. "Fellow workers," he roared, "the aims and objects of this organization shall be to put the working class in possession of the economic power, the means of life, and control of the machinery of production and distribution, without regard to capitalist masters." Pausing a moment for effect, Bill let his audience know who they were. "We are," said he, with happy analogy, "the Continental Congress of the working class."

There were a few more than two hundred delegates in the hall. One of them, George Speed, soon to become and remain as devoted and astute a Wobbly as ever graced soapbox, described this gathering as "the greatest conglomeration of freaks that ever met in convention." There was Mother Jones, the vitriolic old agitator from the coal mines who had begun to talk for the Knights of Labor back in the 1870's;

Lucy Parsons, widow of the hanged Haymarket anarchist; Robert Rives La Monte, a young intellectual who was later to debate socialism, in print, with H. L. Mencken; "Father" Thomas J. Hagerty, the big black-bearded former Catholic priest and editor of a labor paper; William E. Trautmann, leader of the radical United Brewery Workers and editor of that union's German-language paper; Charles O. Sherman, general secretary of the United Metal Workers; Daniel De Leon, "pope" of the Socialist Labor Party; Gene Debs, of the Socialist Party; and several score more members of left-wing unions.

Though one and all avowed their belief in the One Big Union idea, as outlined in the Manifesto of the Industrial Workers of the World, it was the binding influence of their common antipathies that brought them here in the first place. They hated the old-line unionism exemplified by the American Federation of Labor, with its divisions of crafts. Yet, this hate was not enough, nor nearly enough, to weld these heterogeneous elements into anything like unity. Too many of those present felt, each in his own heart, that he alone had a patent on the utopia that all longed for.

Debs was by far the most prominent man there. He was also the most engaging left-wing personality of the period, a tall, gaunt man, bald as could be, with a genial manner and a soft-voiced eloquence as convincing as it was pleasant to the ear. He had risen from callboy to locomotive engineer while still in his teens, then left the throttle to organize the American Railway Union and stage the strike at Pullman, Illinois, that put him in jail. He had gone on to organize the Socialist Party. Now, at this meeting in the Chicago hall, Debs said it was possible for the delegates to form one great sound organization of the working class based on the class struggle that would be "broad enough to embrace every honest worker yet narrow enough to exclude every faker."

Following Debs on the platform was De Leon, a professorial type with badger-gray whiskers, editor of *The People*, who ten years before had split the Knights of Labor into factions. No theologian made finer distinctions in affairs of dogma than De Leon could muster in socialism. He had long since drawn up a plan for a utopia which owed something to Edward Bellamy but also had a good deal of De Leon in it. And now he told the founding convention of the I.W.W. that "*before you take men into a union you must indoctrinate them*" with the ideas of socialism.

Haywood compared the two men as they addressed the group and reflected that Debs's ideas "were built upon his contact with the workers," while De Leon's only contact with workers "was through the ideas with which he wished to indoctrinate them." Bill disliked highfalutin words like "indoctrinate." He thought that the address revealed De Leon's incomprehension of anything like reality in the class struggle. The man was "economically hollow."

The delegates proceeded to draw up a constitution for the new union, together with its preamble, that was clear enough for the simplest mind: "The working class and the employing class have nothing in common ..." This was the nigh-magic dream that was to catch the imaginations of hundreds of thousands of tramps, hobos, bums, itinerant working stiffs of all sorts, who had never belonged to a union, and to transform them into Wobblies, as I.W.W. members were soon known, ready to die, and sometimes to kill, for the One Big Union.

Haywood was nominated for election as first president of the Industrial Workers of the World. He declined, offering the excuse that he had just been re-elected secretary-treasurer of the Western Federation of Miners. Charles O. Sherman, of the United Metal Workers, became the first head of the Wobblies; and their first secretary-treasurer was Trautmann of the Brewery Workers' union.

Moyer, Haywood, O'Neill, and the other miner delegates returned to Denver. With characteristic enthusiasm, Haywood got in touch with his brother-in-law, Tom Minor, a cowhand so proficient in the saddle that he took part in bronco-busting contests and told him about the new One Big Union. Haywood proposed the forming of a Bronco Busters & Range Riders Union. Letterheads, cards, and other literature were printed. The union's wage demands were listed: fifty dollars a month for range work; fifty dollars a day for riding in contests. The union seal showed a cowboy on a horse branded BBRR. Haywood agreed to act as secretary until organization was completed with a big membership. The cowboy union never got anywhere, possibly because Haywood could devote little time to it.

The strength of the new I.W.W. lay in the Miners' affiliation with it. Even so, De Leon was already privately referring to the Western Federation as "proletarian rabble"; he had immediately set out to capture control of the I.W.W. It is proper at this point to mention that De Leon succeeded, a little later, in splitting the One Big Union into two schisms that would probably have wrecked it beyond mending, had it not been for a chain of events set off by Harry Orchard, a man who had not the least interest in the Industrial Workers of the World. Yet, because of Orchard, Capital and Labor were brought face to face in a manner that caused all radicals to forget their factional differences— for the time—and to see their enemy clearly as the monstrous thing it was. This enemy was of course the "employing class" of the I.W.W. Preamble.

THE CHAIN OF EVENTS SET off by Orchard had its inception in a more or less casual discussion of a suitable target for his next bomb. This was in early August (1905), shortly after Moyer, Haywood, and other Miners' delegates returned to Denver from the I.W.W. meeting in Chicago, to find Orchard and Pettibone still making futile attempts to get a shot at General Sherman Bell. Moyer called them off, and in some heat said he wanted "no more rough stuff" in Denver. The man to be taken care of next, he said, was Johnny Neville, Orchard's old saloon-keeper friend, whom Haywood and Pettibone had frightened out of Colorado by threats to reveal the actual cause of his saloon fire at Cripple Creek. Moyer declared he had been unable to get Neville out of his mind. He had said as much before, and now he complained that nothing had been done. "If we don't get Neville," he said, "Neville will get us."

Neither Haywood nor Pettibone seemed anxious about Neville. They argued with Moyer. Pettibone still wanted to "do something about these fellows in Denver," meaning Bell and Judge Gabbert. Moyer wouldn't hear of it. Haywood declared that Frank Steunenberg, the ex-governor of Idaho, should have preference. He pointed out that four different men had been sent to Steunenberg's home town, Caldwell, Idaho, and had failed to do anything. The men, he said, were Steve Adams, Ed Minster, Art Baston, and a miner from the Coeur d'Alene country named McCarty.

Moyer warmed to this suggestion, saying in effect that, if Steunenberg were bumped off, they could write letters promising similar treatment to Bell, Gabbert, Goddard, Peabody, and others who had been "prominent in trying to crush the federation." Haywood agreed. Because Paterson, New Jersey, was generally believed to be "anarchist headquarters" in the United States, said Haywood, the letters could be mailed there, and the recipients would think it "was some of those foreign anarchists" who were planning to kill them. The men who got the letters, he continued, "would be afraid of their shadows, for, if we got Steunenberg, after waiting so long, then they would sure think we never forgot anyone who had persecuted us."

Pettibone would not mind if Steunenberg were killed, but he did not think it would be an easy task to get the ex-governor in a little country town like Caldwell. Haywood countered by saying he had been told Steunenberg was in the sheep business, that he often drove out alone to his sheep camps in the mountains; and further that he, Haywood, doubted Steunenberg considered his life was in danger because of the troubles in the Coeur d'Alenes. They were far in the past.

Finally, Moyer said to go ahead with the Steunenberg job, but that Orchard should route himself to Idaho by way of Goldfield, Nevada, and rub out Neville. This ended the discussions in regard to what one is almost forced to think of as the opening of the fall hunting season. As soon as he was ready to leave, Orchard was to get travel money from Haywood.

Though it had no bearing on Orchard's enterprise, an incident at this period, related later by Haywood, indicated the distrust that was growing between Haywood and Moyer. "I was sitting at my desk," Haywood tells it, "when Moyer came in and put down a telegram he had just received. I read it. It was from his wife, who was then in California, saying she was very sick and asking him to come at once." Moyer had put the telegram on Haywood's desk but said nothing. Haywood picked it up and took it into the other's office. "Charlie," he said, "I'm sorry your wife is sick. I suppose you'll have to leave right away." Moyer replied that he would leave Denver that evening. Moyer then put on his hat and went out. No sooner had he gone than Haywood went back to Moyer's office. Then:

"There on his desk (Haywood remembered) was a book of telegraph blanks, with the carbon paper on top. The thought struck me—why did he tear the blank off? I picked up the carbon paper, took it into my office, and read it in a mirror. It was a telegram from Moyer to his wife, asking her to wire him, to say she was ill and wanted him to come at once."

Haywood seems to have been genuinely shocked at the subterfuge. He would have made no objection if Moyer had said simply that he was going to California.

Now that the high command had agreed on the next subject for his attention, Harry Orchard busied himself with preparations for the lethal expedition to Idaho. That big package, the alarm-clock job containing twenty-five pounds of dynamite, a real old lifter referred to as the Peabody bomb, was going along too. It might come in handy. One could never tell about such things. Orchard retrieved it from where it had been buried, either in Pettibone's yard or somewhere near, and put it into his trunk. Haywood peeled three hundred dollars in bills off a roll and gave it to him for travel money. Orchard purchased a round-trip ticket to Portland, Oregon, good for ninety days with stopovers anywhere along the route and good also, if wanted, for a return to Denver by way of Seattle and Spokane.

The reason for inclusion of the two Washington cities in Orchard's itinerary related to an idea Haywood and Pettibone had been discussing for some time. This was to have a hideout, a sort of secret refuge to which the Western Federation could send men who for some reason or another needed to disappear, perhaps somebody on the lam, or merely members wishing to hide from the embarrassment of subpoena. The hideout Haywood and Pettibone had in mind might be a small farm, nothing more than a stump ranch with house or cabin, where men could hole up in comparative comfort. For obvious reasons, the hideout should be fairly close to the Canadian border. The plan, as Orchard understood it, was that eventually he and Pettibone would live at the hideout, ready to welcome and care for fugitives from "the injustices of Capitalist courts." It almost automatically occurred to Orchard that such a place near the international boundary would permit "us doing some smuggling there." To locate a place proper for such a hideout was to be one of Orchard's jobs while on his way to Caldwell, Idaho, by what surely was as circuitous a route as a man could well arrange.

Being by taste a man who liked to dress well in quiet clothes, Orchard now bought a black derby hat, a three-piece suit of conservative dark material, and a black valise into which he packed a revolver, a pump gun (repeating shotgun), and a couple of quarts of whisky. Then, one hot August afternoon, he watched to make certain that his heavy trunk was safely in the baggage coach and took a seat in the smoker of a Denver & Rio Grande train out of Denver, heading in a roundabout way for Caldwell, Canyon County, Idaho, and a sort of eminence.

16.

Murder is a Lonely Job

Almost four months were to pass between the sweltering August afternoon when Orchard's train pulled out of Denver and the snowy Idaho night in late December when one of the great hatchet men of all time reached the apex of his professional career. If four months seems on the face of it a long time to perform what basically was a simple piece of work, the delay is not inexplicable. To begin with, Orchard had not one but three assignments for this expedition. He was to "take care" of Johnnie Neville in Nevada. He was to locate a suitable place for a hideout near the Canadian border in Washington. He was to shoot, blow up, or otherwise get rid of Ex-Governor Frank Steunenberg in Idaho.

Then, there was Orchard's own recurrent indisposition. Not liquor, or women, or even gambling. He took these things pretty much in stride. They seem never to have prevented him from carrying out a project, nor to have delayed him overlong. His trouble, as must be clear by now, was the occasional inability to decide, to choose a course. All of his killings and maimings were done in cold blood. All (save for the shooting of mine detective Lyte Gregory) were accomplished by stealth. Stealth called for planning. The plans usually involved two or more methods of approach to the victim. Here was the rub—the "craven scruple of thinking too precisely" on the method. Orchard did not always admit to himself this difficulty but sought to excuse delay by what he called "dread." "I always dreaded to do these murders," he once complained to a reporter, "and usually put them off as long as I could, or rather as long as I had money."

He had money now in the pockets of his brand-new suit, whisky in his new valise, and a fine big time-clock bomb in his trunk in the baggage coach ahead. He stopped several days in Salt Lake City to see an old friend of mining days, Charlie Shoddy, a shadowy figure and somehow sinister, about whom little is known save that he and Orchard had left the Coeur d'Alenes right after the destruction of the Bunker Hill & Sullivan concentrator, back in 1899.

Shoddy in 1905 was working in a mine near Salt Lake City. He and Orchard had a grand reunion, talking over old times, and Shoddy remarked on his friend's fine clothes and obvious prosperity. He naturally wanted to know what line of work Orchard was following. Orchard replied he had found a new way of making a living without working too hard. He may have given a knowing wink, as from one sophisticate to another, when he spoke thus of his occupation, for, when Shoddy wanted to know more about it, Orchard intimated he might "have something" Shoddy could help with. It is more than possible Orchard mentioned Johnnie Neville in this connection. At least Orchard wrote Pettibone to that affect and even stated he had asked Shoddy to go to Goldfield, Nevada, for the purpose of "doing that job."

Orchard said good-bye to Charlie Shoddy and headed next for Idaho. Bearing Pettibone's warning in mind, that Caldwell was so small as to present unusual dangers for work of the nature he was to perform, Orchard got off the train at Nampa, nine miles east of Caldwell, to stop a few days in the Commercial Hotel. Knowing from Haywood that Steunenberg was in the sheep business, it occurred to Orchard that he might as well pose as a sheep buyer. In Nampa he became T. S. Hogan, from Denver, Colorado, a man looking for a chance to buy a few thousand sheep. He made inquiries in the hotel and got the names of several people who had sheep to sell, among them Frank Steunenberg.

Three days in Nampa gave Orchard a feeling he was acclimated. He had picked up a lot of talk on the methods of sheep men, learned the going prices, the places of shipment, and where the sheep were pastured at that time of year. He wanted to know these things before going to Caldwell.

In Caldwell he registered at the Pacific Hotel, and proceeded to engage Mr. Dempsey, the proprietor, in conversation, telling that gentleman that he, T. S. Hogan had been asked by a friend to stop off there and see if he could buy some lambs. Mr. Dempsey, eager to aid a guest, and doubtless happy to display his own knowledge of Idaho's important assets, gave Mr. Hogan an excellent lecture on the buying and selling of sheep, and mentioned, interestingly enough, that right there in Caldwell was one of the leading sheep men of the state, Frank Steunenberg. Mr. Hogan was most attentive. He learned, among many other things, that Mr. Steunenebrg was just then out of town, either at Mountain Home, where his sheep range was located, or in Boise, the state capital.

Orchard went out to look over Caldwell, a much smaller place than Nampa, and to observe the modest and well-kept home of the town's first citizen, its yard enclosed by a fence with a picket gate which, as Orchard may have recalled, was not unlike the gate of Judge Goddard's home in Denver. Then, having got the lay of the land, he checked out of the Pacific Hotel and took an afternoon train to Boise, where he registered at the Capitol Hotel. He was still T. S. Hogan. He remained but one night, then moved to the Idan-ha Hotel, after learning that Steunenberg was registered at the latter place.

The Idan-ha survives half a century later, retaining a fine flavor of the period, with its large rooms, high ceilings, and other reminders of turn-of-the-century charm. Orchard was given a room on the same floor where the ex-governor was staying. He started to investigate matters at once. Being a man who seems always to have devoted some little attention to the work and habits of chambermaids and other hotel help, he waited until noon, "when the chambermaids were off the floor," then tried a skeleton key. It readily opened the door. He went in to look around. This might be the place to use that alarm-clock bomb which lay in his trunk at Nampa.

Orchard next went down to the lobby and there got in with the Johnsons, father and son, who were local commission men handling sales of sheep, cattle, hogs, and other ranch and farm products. While they were talking, the elder Johnson pointed to a man standing in front of the hotel. "That's Governor Steunenberg," he said, "one of the big sheep men of Idaho." It was the first time Orchard had seen his next subject.

Orchard took an afternoon train to Nampa, returned to Boise in the evening, and had the trunk moved into his room at the Idan-ha. He unpacked the bomb, the Peabody job. He wound the alarm clock, pushed the bomb under his bed, and sat down to listen to its ticking. In

1905 most alarm clocks had an escapement that all save the stone-deaf could hear. In the comparative silence of the hotel room, Orchard's clock seemed to make a terrific lot of noise. It wouldn't do for the present work. Sitting in his chair, he contemplated the next move. He could put the bomb, minus the clock attachment, in Steunenberg's room, and hitch it to the door with screw eye and line. The clock ticked on while he turned over in his mind the probable sequence of events.

The bomb contained twenty-five pounds of dynamite. It would blow the hotel all to pieces, he reflected. It would kill a lot of people. "I really didn't care about that," he remembered, "so long as Mr. Steunenberg was one of them. What worried me was my own chance of being caught by the explosion." He was sure he could get the bomb into Steunenberg's room without being detected. He knew the ex-governor would be killed the moment he opened the door. But he could not be sure when he would return to his room. "A chambermaid might go into the room before Steunenberg did," he ruminated, "and that would spoil everything." This was no time to let a chambermaid's whim spoil everything ...

No, he would have to go back and start all over again and come up with a better plan. That was the worst of these things. You had to think it out straight. If you didn't, there'd be the devil to pay one way or another. Wasn't it always best to look before you leaped? He sure was glad he had listened to that alarm clock before he went out and left it under Mr. Steunenberg's bed in that quiet room. Glad he knew the habits of chambermaids, who always forgot something and had to return to a room to leave or to get whatever it was they forgot. You knew such things only because you got around. He, Harry Orchard, got around a good deal, but, come to think of it, he had never been in Portland. They were having a "world's fair" or something similar in Portland, so he read in the papers. He had missed the one they had last year in St. Louis on account of being tied up on the Fred Bradley job so long. He was routed to Portland on that yard-long ticket in his pocket. Why not go see the fair now? The change might help him to make up his mind about the Steunenberg business. Portland was on the direct line to Seattle. That was the region where Haywood and Pettibone wanted him to find a good place for a hideout. Why not go along now, see the fair, then travel on to Seattle? Like as not, half a dozen ideas about Mr. Steunenberg would occur to him. Riding the cars was a better place to think than sitting alone in a hotel room with a clock ticking. He still had plenty of money. He still "dreaded to do these murders." He put the big Peabody bomb back into his trunk. An hour or so later he was on the Union Pacific night train for Portland.

The Oregon metropolis was in festive dress and mood, decked out with electric lights and bunting for what officially was the Lewis & Clark Centennial Exposition; and proud that its first bid for international attention had already brought more than two million visitors to witness the state's big party honoring the noted explorers. It was quite a show. Orchard had seen nothing like it before. And, for all the two million customers, who included Charles Warren Fairbanks, Vice-President of the United States, and James J. Hill, the Empire Builder, to say nothing of Little Egypt, a famous if by then somewhat worn exponent of the dance, for all these, it is to be doubted that the exposition had a visitor more enchanted than the stocky, florid man with the derby hat and shiny black valise. Orchard remained nearly a week, taking in the Midway, seeing the exhibits "of seventeen states and sixteen foreign countries" and "the Biggest Log Cabin on Earth." He found everything quite marvelous, possibly because it helped him to forget the decision he faced of what to do about Frank Steunenberg.

He moved on to Seattle, where Pettibone had suggested he see an old friend named William Barrett. Barrett took him around the city and introduced him to real-estate men who were happy to show a prospective customer exactly the place he was looking for. By this time the autumn rains had set in. Orchard did not like so much moisture. He also thought the region cold, which seems a little odd in a native of Ontario who had lived in north Idaho and high Colorado. After a week of this, Orchard began to think the Puget Sound country was unfit for any hideout. But he had come with orders to investigate the region's possibilities for a specific purpose. To quiet Haywood and Pettibone he wrote the latter an unenthusiastic letter and enclosed a map of Puget Sound. That would hold them.

The wandering assassin now turned east, and a day later was made welcome at Wardner, scene of the Bunker Hill & Sullivan battle, by his old friend Jack Simpkins, the miner and homesteader to whom Steve Adams had recently lent a hand in removing the two claim jumpers on Marble Creek. Jack was still a member of the executive board of the Western Federation. Orchard liked him. Perhaps he would have liked almost anybody right now. "I told Jack," he said later to a reporter, "about my mission of death. I wanted company." The face of murder wore a lonely aspect. The heavy trunk he was toting around the country was becoming a burden. The aging bomb inside it was an accusation of a duty yet unperformed.

"I wanted company," said Harry Orchard. Jack Simpkins said sure, he'd go along to Caldwell with an old friend like Harry. Glad to help him out. He had a fine idea, too. "I'll make the trip official business," he said. "Silver City is only a little way from Caldwell. I'll go visit the local union there. I can charge the federation headquarters for my time and expenses." There is nothing more attractive to many people than legitimate dishonesty. And, besides, Jack would be doing Harry a good turn. Harry brightened perceptibly. He had been a little dismayed that his trunk with the much-traveled bomb had not arrived in Wardner. He had checked it from Seattle. Because of the nature of the contents, the missing trunk troubled Orchard a little. But not too much, now that Jack had agreed to accompany him to Caldwell. It would show up. Trunks always did. They could wait a few days.

Jack Simpkins came up with a dandy idea. It was late September. Good time to get a deer, possibly an elk. Let the trunk take its time; he and Harry would go hunting. Within hours the two men were on their way up the St. Joe River to Marble Creek. While shacking up on Jack's homestead, Jack showed Orchard where he and Steve Adams had buried Tyler and Boulle, the claim jumpers. After little more than a week the hunters returned to Wardner.

The big trunk was there in the depot. They took it to Simpkins's home, where Orchard removed the bomb. Just looking at it made Orchard tired. He related its long history to his friend—how he made it many months before in Canon City, Colorado, specifically to use on Governor James H. Peabody; took it to Denver and buried it; dug it up to take on his rambles to Salt Lake City, to Nampa, Caldwell, and Boise; tested its mechanism for sound in the Idan-ha hotel and found it too noisy; packed the accursed thing to Portland, then Seattle, and now to Wardner. It was just too big, too heavy for the light work in Caldwell, yet it was a well and carefully made job. Jack Simpkins was fairly running over with bright ideas. Why not, he asked Orchard, give the bomb to one of Simpkins's good friends who worked in a mine at Gem? The boys at Gem had been having a little difficulty with the management. A thing like this alarm-clock job might come in handy. Orchard was delighted to have it taken off his hands, and to know that, if it were used, it would be for the good of the Western Federation.[9]

With the Peabody bomb out of the way, Harry Orchard appears to have turned suddenly energetic again. He proposed to Simpkins a wild scheme to kidnap the young children of a Wallace miner who had struck it rich and was fairly rolling in wealth, and to hold them for ransom. Simpkins did not think this was a very good idea. Orchard next proposed a burglary job in Wallace. He had somehow learned that in the railroad depot there was a trunkful of valuable jewelry, the property of a salesman who was due to leave next morning for Spokane. Simpkins was willing. That night the two men broke into the baggage room of the depot opened the trunk, and found it contained nothing but shoes, which, being samples, were all for the left foot.

No little of Orchard's new if fruitless energy was due to the fact that his travel money was getting low. It was now the twentieth of October, high time to leave for Caldwell. On the way to Spokane, Simpkins told Orchard how he could raise a modest amount of cash: sue the railroad company for delay of his trunk. Jack had a lawyer friend in Spokane, just the man to sue the railroad, Fred Miller of the legal firm of Robinson, Miller & Rosenthal. They went to see him.

Sure, said Miller, he would be glad to handle the case of the delayed trunk, and about how much did Mr. Orchard figure his time was worth a day? Orchard replied that he was a mining promoter, that his time was worth at least ten dollars a day, plus expenses. Attorney Miller drew up a claim for sixty dollars. Orchard signed a document to the effect that his affairs had been injured to that extent. As the two men prepared to leave the law office, attorney Miller asked Simpkins a question. "Jack," said he, "what are you lugging in that little box?" It just happened to be ten pounds of No. 1 Gelatin which he was bringing along in case he and Orchard should have difficulty buying explosive in Caldwell.

"It's nothing but dynamite," Jack replied roguishly.

Miller laughed heartily at the joke too.

---

9 I can find nothing to indicate this bomb was ever used. There is a legend that it was tossed into the Coeur d'Alene River at or near Wallace.—S.H.H.

On or about the first day of November, Orchard and Simpkins checked in at the Pacific Hotel, Caldwell, Idaho, and registered respectively as T. S. Hogan and Jack Simmons. That evening they went out to case the Steunenberg residence. Next day, working together in their hotel room, they made a ten-stick bomb. It was one of Orchard's conventional jobs, set to go off when a string turned a windless holding a vial of acid, to drop the liquid on detonating caps. It was now Saturday night.

Late Sunday afternoon Ex-Governor Frank Steunenberg was seen in the lobby of Caldwell's other hotel, the Saratoga, talking with friends. When the two watching men considered the early November night to be dark enough, they got their bomb. Then, as Orchard remembered it: "We went to the street that led to Mr. Steunenberg's home. We placed the bomb close to the path where he would be most apt to pass, covered it with weeds, and stretched a wire across the pathway, staking the loose end of the wire. Then we hurried back to the Pacific Hotel, so we could prove where we had been, if necessary."

Sitting in the hotel lobby, waiting for the noise, called—as Orchard philosophically remarked—for patience. Two hours of patience was enough. The two men went over to the Saratoga Hotel. Steunenberg was not there. They walked down the street to where they had left the bomb. The wire across the path was broken. Still in place, hidden in the weeds, was the bomb. It was probably Steunenberg who all unknowingly had broken the wire. On checking the apparatus Orchard found that, although the windlass had turned clear over, it had turned so fast that no acid had run out of the vial. The vial was now almost but not quite upright again.

Orchard being the expert in such matters, it was up to him to take care of the live bomb. Even he considered this to be a very ticklish business. At first, he thought he'd leave it where it was, come what might. "But finally," he remembered, "I covered the mouth of the vial and took it out. I picked up the bomb and carried it over by the railroad track and covered it with weeds. Then we went back to the hotel."

Jack Simpkins must have found this sort of work depressing, for while the two men were having breakfast next morning it occurred to Jack—quite suddenly it seemed to Orchard—that it was time he went on to Silver City to visit the union local there. After all, he was a member of the federation's executive board. Duty was duty.

Moreover, he explained to Harry, that "if we did kill Steunenberg, it would be worse" for Orchard if he, Simpkins, were with him and they were both arrested. This rather astonishing presumption was apparently predicated on the fact that whereas Orchard was known as a union terrorist only "to the inner circle of the Western Federation" he, Simpkins, was widely known as one of the top men in the miners' union.

This seemed farfetched to Harry Orchard. If they did kill Steunenberg, and were arrested and charged with it, he could not see why either man would have a better chance than the other of getting out of it. He said so. But the reasoning had no effect on Simpkins. He obviously had had enough of Caldwell, of standing by while his friend fumbled in the weeds and the night with a bottle of sulphuric acid and ten pounds of capped dynamite. He jovially slapped Orchard on the back, told him to hang tough, to finish the job, and away he went for Silver City. From there, as Orchard knew, Simpkins planned to go on to Denver for a meeting of the federation's executive board.

Harry Orchard was now alone in Caldwell. The dreaded time had come. To face alone the job of murder suddenly seemed the most solitary occupation in the world.

17.

The Big One

As soon as Jack Simpkins left for Denver, Orchard checked out of the Pacific Hotel and got a front room in the home of W. H. Schenck, a longtime resident of Caldwell. From his windows he could observe the street used by Steunenberg when coming from and returning to his house. From the Schencks's he might also gain helpful information about Caldwell's first citizen and the routine of his family.

Frank Steunenberg was a large, rather silent man with the face of a Roman senator. About him was no trace of the pompous or ingratiating manners characteristic of politicians. "Rugged in body," said his friend, William Borah, of him, "he was also resolute in mind." And of Steunenberg's convictions, Borah thought, the man was "of the granite hewn." His only idiosyncrasy was that he never wore a necktie, nor would he explain, even to close friends, why he didn't.

Born in Knoxville, Iowa, Frank was the fourth child of Bernardus and Cornelia Steunenberg, immigrants from Holland. As a youth he was apprenticed to the publisher of the local *Register* and managed to spend a few terms at the agriculture college at Ames. He bought an interest in the newspaper, and married Evelyn Belle Keppel, a daughter of Dutch immigrants. The couple moved to Caldwell, Idaho, where Frank and his brother Albert purchased the weekly *Tribune*. Caldwell liked Frank Steunenberg. Her citizens sent him to the constitutional convention and helped to elect him representative to the first legislative assembly after Idaho became a state in 1890. Seven years later he was elected governor by a large majority.

Steunenberg's course during two terms as governor has been considered earlier. Orchard had naturally enough been thoroughly indoctrinated with the ideas of the Western Federation's leaders about Steunenberg. He was a man to be done away with. Orchard's sole interest in the man was in regard to his daily habits. It was becoming known in Caldwell that the ex-governor's habits had of late been undergoing a change. He would no longer do any sort of business on Saturday. Here was something that Orchard, still wondering where and when to set the bomb, found of more than casual interest.

The Steunenbergs had been Presbyterians when they arrived in Idaho. Though Frank never joined this or any other religious group, he attended church with his wife, who also taught a Sunday-school class. Mrs. Steunenberg later joined the Seventh-Day Adventist denomination. The two Steunenberg sons and one daughter attended the Adventist Sabbath school. Though the husband and father did not, as say, join the church, he not only welcomed Adventist ministers to his home but he himself accepted Saturday as the Sabbath. Strictly, too. Orchard learned that the ex-governor no longer bought or sold sheep on Saturday, that on Saturday he would not even enter the local bank, of which he was a director. He was never seen on Saturdays in the *Tribune* office. It was no use to call at his house. The big grave man told such visitors, quietly enough, that "no business matters can be transacted in this home on Saturday."

Orchard kept his lodgings in the Schenck home for nearly two weeks, during much of which Steunenberg was out of town. Orchard passed the time doing some modest drinking and gambling at the Saratoga Hotel, and talking about sheep. As was always the case when he wanted to, he easily made the acquaintance of many townspeople. With these he adopted the pose of a genial man of the world and business affairs. He seems also to have taken pains to make an impression on a young waitress employed in the Saratoga's dining room. It is not known how far their friendship had progressed before Orchard went away from Caldwell for good, but it was at least far enough to cause the young woman no little embarrassment later.

Orchard made it a rule always to read the papers, and one day he saw an item saying that Frank Steunenberg had been appointed by Governor Frank Gooding to serve on some state committee that was to meet in Boise. Orchard shook off his inertia. He got the bomb he had hidden in the weeds near the railroad track, put it in his valise, and told the Schencks he had business in Boise. He went there, too, but never unlimbered the bomb in the three days he stayed in Boise. Not once did he catch sight of Steunenberg.

It seems possible that the delay, and the two futile attempts to get his man, had begun to tell on Orchard's all but nerveless system. "I was lonesome," he said, "and disgusted. I wanted to have someone to help me." There it was again—not fear, or dread, or conscience, but merely a most gregarious man who wanted some close friend to talk to. While the overbearing spell was upon him, he went to the local telephone office and put in a long-distance call to Bill Easterly, his old friend of Cripple Creek days who was "running the miners' union" at Silver City, some forty miles south. Such calls in the Idaho of 1905 were rare, and Easterly must have been given a start. When Orchard got him on the line, he tried to talk the union official into joining him in "a certain proposition." Easterly knew what he meant. Jack Simpkins had just been in Silver City and told him what Orchard was up to in Caldwell. Like Simpkins, Easterly wanted no part of it. He made as much clear to Orchard. Orchard was terribly disappointed. Jack Simpkins had run out on him. Bill Easterly would not join him. In his desperate need for company, Orchard bought a ticket for Salt Lake City and left on the next train. He would go and have a visit with Charlie Shoddy.

Shoddy was his friend who had wanted to know what kind of business kept Orchard supplied with fine clothes, railroad tickets, and cash for liquor and other needs. Well, he'd go see Charlie and give him a chance to earn some easy money. Johnnie Neville was still alive ...

Orchard spent some three weeks in Salt Lake City. Just what he did there is a mystery. He may have talked to Shoddy. Again, he may not even have seen Shoddy. The record isn't clear. Orchard seems never to have cleared it. This isn't to say that he knowingly held something back. When he got around to it, there was so much to confess that a few minor items may have been overlooked in the haste to "unburden my guilty memory." It is known, however, that, while on this murky trip to Salt Lake City, Orchard got a letter from Pettibone saying that Johnnie Neville had "died suddenly in Goldfield, Nevada." This sounded about right for an unreasonable man who had threatened to give the police a few missing details about the explosion at Independence depot.

Orchard immediately wrote to both Moyer and Simpkins to remind them that it had been he, Harry Orchard, who had sent Charlie Shoddy to Goldfield with instructions to do away with Neville. This was a lie. Orchard had not sent Shoddy to Goldfield. "But when I knew of Johnnie's death, I thought I would take advantage of it." In his letters to the men at headquarters, Orchard suggested that they send five hundred dollars to Charlie "for his good work in Nevada." He advised that the money be addressed to "Mr. Charles Shoddy, General Delivery, Nampa, Idaho." And added that "Charlie will stop in Nampa while I am looking after things in Caldwell."

That is the last one hears of Charlie Shoddy. It is also the last one hears of Johnnie Neville, the man who knew far too much.[10]

It was mid-December when Orchard returned to the scene of his current project. This time he registered at the Saratoga Hotel, where the pretty waitress worked. During the coming two weeks they were to see a good deal of each other. But Orchard knew very well that his time was running out. A letter from Simpkins reported that no more blood money, which Haywood liked to call "remittances for assessment work," would be forthcoming from federation sources except through Haywood himself. That was clear enough; Orchard could look for more cash only when he had "got the Big One," meaning Steunenberg.

Christmas Day was a Monday, bright and only moderately cold in Caldwell. The watching Orchard saw Frank Steunenberg leave his home and go to the house of his brother. Orchard returned to the Saratoga. He got the shotgun from his trunk. With a stout cord around his neck he hung the barrel down one side of his body, the stock down the other. Putting on his overcoat, he went forth to watch and wait until his victim should return home. He might as well shoot him there in the dark and be done with it.

After a long wait he heard someone coming in the gathering night. It was the ex-governor. Orchard went after his shotgun. The cord somehow got tangled with the stock. Before he could put the weapon together, the unsuspecting man opened the gate to the yard, entered and closed it, then went into the house. For the next two or three hours, gun in hand, Orchard stalked around the yard and house, peering in windows, hoping. At last he could stand the cold no longer. Anyway,

---

10 Though it was not in his confession, Orchard testified in court that Johnnie Neville was poisoned in Goldfield. And that "Sherman Parker and W. F. Davis followed Neville to Goldfield and either in person or through an agent administered poison to him."

the last light in the house had gone out. All the family must be abed. The shotgun man broke down his weapon, hung its parts under his coat, and returned to the Saratoga.

The hotel was bright and filled to capacity with scores of dancers who had come for the gala event of the season, a Christmas masked ball. Orchard had known about it, figuring it would be just the night to shoot Steunenberg. The crowd of maskers in all sorts of getups and costumes would make for an easy getaway, even an alibi. He would shoot his man, return to the hotel, black his face, perhaps, and mingle with the gay crowd. Having now no need to black up or mingle, Orchard went wearily to his room, put away the shotgun, and so to bed.

Yet, not to sleep. He had bungled the job, the Big One. His working medium wasn't gunpowder, anyway. It was dynamite. This was no real excuse. It was hardly small comfort. He would get no money for an effort that did not produce results. *There will be no more remittances for assessment work* ...On went the dance. The music wafted up the stairs, along the corridor, and filled Room Nineteen where Orchard lay on his bed, staring into the dark. What a hell of a time to choose for a masked ball ...

Two days passed with no sight of Steunenberg. But on Thursday Orchard saw him board the morning eastbound passenger train. He had no idea where the man was going. Later in the day, however, while walking aimlessly around Caldwell, Orchard met Julian Steunenberg, the ex-governor's older son, on the street. He queried the young man and was told that Mr. Steunenberg had gone to his sheep ranch. He could be reached there by telephoning the exchange at Bliss. "He will be home tomorrow, anyhow," the young man said.

Orchard had the Union Pacific timetables in his pocket, if not in his head. Bliss was a hundred and twenty-five miles east of Caldwell. His quarry would likely return from Bliss on the train due in Caldwell in late afternoon. This train would stop at Nampa fifteen minutes on the way to Caldwell. Nampa was ten miles east of Caldwell. A new plan was taking shape in Orchard's mind. It was going to be a bomb after all. He felt better at once. This was the stuff. He went out again into those weeds, now brushed with snow along the railroad track, and took the ten sticks of No. 1 Gelatin from the wooden box. Distributing them in his pockets, he returned to his room in the Saratoga, to spend the rest of the day working happily on a new bomb.

Somewhere along the line Orchard had bought a small, light sheet-metal lockbox, the sort of container which only too many trusting people used as a home safe. Into this he put the dynamite. At one end of the box's top he fastened an alarm clock, at the other end a vial to hold the acid. He stuck both in place with plaster of Paris. This was to be a dual-purpose bomb, either time or contact.

Pausing in the midst of his labors in Room Nineteen, he dropped down for a couple of fast ones in the Saratoga bar, and returned much refreshed to prime the bomb and get it in working order. He put in a generous supply of giant caps. He filled the vial with acid. He hitched a fine wire to the stopper and then—because if chance offered he meant to use it as a time bomb—he connected the stopper wire with the alarm key of the unwound clock.

It had been a most satisfying afternoon's work. He washed up and went downstairs for another drink, and supper, served by the young woman whose love, as she was to admit only a little later, this fascinating Mr. Hogan had won.

Next morning was Friday. Putting the small yet powerful bomb into his valise, Orchard took the morning train east ten miles to Nampa, and there he spent much of the day waiting for the next westbound, known in Caldwell for no particular reason as the Cannonball. She would stop in Nampa for fifteen minutes. Orchard planned to get aboard the smoker, then go back through the train looking for Steunenberg. Having spotted him, he would set the valise under or near Steunenberg's seat, then leave the car. If by this time the train had not already started, Orchard would leave the train. In either case, he would not be in the same car with Steunenberg when the valise let go.

Because of the factor of time involved, Orchard could not connect the wire from the bottle stopper to a running clock until the Cannonball had arrived at Nampa. She might be late. He must also set the alarm mechanism to go off before the train got to Caldwell, or some twenty minutes after she pulled out of Nampa. She might be late in leaving Nampa.

Did the boys at Western Federation headquarters appreciate the kind of nerve required to hook No. 1 Gelatin to sulphuric acid in a railroad depot, with bells ringing, people rushing about, and trainmen urging everybody to step lively? Orchard didn't know, but that was what he was doing when the Cannon-ball pulled into Nampa on Friday afternoon. Not only did he connect the wire. He also set the clock. How many minutes he meant should pass before the unwinding key pulled the cork is not of record. But valise in hand Orchard boarded the train and set about to find the ex-governor.

The train was crowded, every coach. Orchard went through it once. No Steunenberg. Orchard heard the call for all aboard. The train jerked, then moved slowly through the yards and picked up speed. Orchard worked his way up through the coaches, the clock ticking busily away in the valise in his hand. Still no Steunenberg. The Cannonball whistled for Caldwell. Whether Orchard managed to get into a train lavatory to stop the clock's alarm mechanism or how otherwise he handled it, he was ready to get off the train, valise in hand, when it stopped at the Caldwell depot. Frank Steunenberg got off the train too. Orchard saw him with astonishment.

Harry Orchard spent an evening of "dark despair," much of it with the Saratoga's waitress. She noticed how cast down he was, and how bitter. When she gently chided him as being "too fine and wonderful a man for such moods," he told her he was really "no better than a monster," and gave the impressionable girl to understand his life and works had been filled with "horrible deeds and loathsome sins." She could not quite believe him, yet that night, alone in her room, she prayed for the soul of her beloved Tom Hogan.

SATURDAY, DECEMBER 30, 1905. THE last day but one of the year dawned windy and cold in Caldwell. Shortly after daylight snow began to fall. The wind increased. By noon a small blizzard had taken over the town. Citizens put away their shovels until the snowing should let up. Only those with errands were to be seen moving about through the twilight of the storm.

The Saratoga Hotel was snug enough. Orchard, still bitter from what he thought of as the meanness of fate, sat in the lobby with other guests and town loafers, making small talk about weather, sheep, and politics. By midday a poker game had gotten under way in the bar. Orchard sat in, with what small cash he could muster. By now he was considered almost a regular in the hotel.

At the Steunenberg home the ex-governor had arisen at his usual early hour. When he had the kitchen stove fire going, he laid logs in the fireplace. They were snapping cheerily by the time Mrs. Steunenberg and the children gathered for breakfast. Everything seemed right for another peaceful Adventist Sabbath. The Governor, however, appeared worried. His wife asked if anything was wrong. "My dear," said he, "the good and the evil spirits were calling me all night long." She was startled at "this solemn reply." But happy, too. Was her husband all but ready for the Decision—"the Decision to follow his Savior?" One should bear in mind that Mrs. Steunenberg had not long since been converted to and baptized in the Adventist faith. "Do not resist the call of the good spirits, papa," she said.

During breakfast the telephone rang. It was one of the Governor's business associates. "No, George," his family heard Mr. Steunenberg say, "I will not be available today. This is our Sabbath, our Sunday. Any other time. Not now." He hung up. The afternoon wore on. The storm abated somewhat. A man called at the door. He was an agent for the life-insurance company with which the Governor had a policy. Mr. Steunenberg invited him to come in. The agent mentioned the fact it was time to pay a premium on the policy which was due to expire on this, the thirtieth of December. "I know it," the governor said, "but I cannot talk business now on the Sabbath. After sunset I will take care of the matter." He suggested he would meet the agent in the Saratoga Hotel, come evening.

Time in the Saratoga dragged on. The poker game continued. Orchard paused for midday dinner and got a smile and a few tender words from the waitress. Outside the storm seemed to have blown itself out. There was increasing activity in the streets. Caldwell's few street lamps went on with the early dusk. Orchard played a few more hands. Then he came out into the lobby to find Mr. Steunenberg there, talking with a man. It was now past sunset. The life-insurance policy was being renewed.

Noting that the governor had removed neither hat nor overcoat in the warm lobby, Orchard made up his mind. This was to be it. The Big One. He went up to his room. He wrapped the sheet-metal box in a newspaper, and with the package under his arm returned to the lobby. The clock on the wall showed the hour to be six-fifteen. Steunenberg was a prompt man. He was certain to start for home almost immediately. Orchard went out of the hotel and started down the long snowy street that led to the Steunenberg residence.

The great hush brought by the new snow blanketed everything

as Harry Orchard went to work laying his last bomb. It took but a moment. "I put the box down close to the gatepost," he remembered. "I tied a piece of fishline into the screw eye in the cork. I tied the other end around a picket of the gate. Opening the gate would jerk the cork from the vial and let the acid run out. To make sure the bomb would go even if he did not open the gate wide enough to pull the cork, I arranged the cord, so the Governor would strike the line with his feet as he passed in. I covered the box with snow and went away."

Making haste, though not yet running, Orchard headed back downtown. Steunenberg had already left the hotel and was walking briskly toward home. The two men passed in the night without a word. Then Orchard started to run. He hoped to be inside the Saratoga when the noise came. He didn't quite make it, but he was pretty close to the hotel when the quiet dark of the village was shattered by the tremendous explosion, and Orchard spoke aloud to himself. "There she goes," he said, and a moment later walked into the Saratoga bar.

At the ex-governor's home Mrs. Steunenberg was preparing dinner, the daughter, one son, and an adopted baby girl with her. The older son, Julian, a student at Walla Walla College, was in Caldwell for Christmas vacation. But he was downtown. His mother expected him at any moment. Perhaps he would come with his father.

The blast seemed to shake the night. The house trembled. Every window was shattered. The entire west side of the house was in splinters. A big clock toppled from its shelf and landed fair on young Frank Steunenberg, aged five, who was lying on a couch beneath the mantel. Mother and children were stunned a moment from the shock. Then the biting cold wind came rushing through the empty sashes.

Thirteen-year-old Frances was the first to recover. She ran outdoors into the yard to find her father a heap in the snow. He was still breathing. The girl ran to neighbors for help. Frank Steunenberg was carried into the house, where he died twenty minutes later, still unconscious. By then Julian had come home.

As soon as he walked into the Saratoga bar Harry Orchard took a quick drink, then lent a hand (it was steady, the bartender noted) to do up a New Year's gift which the bartender had been fumblingly trying to wrap. Always a handy man with his fingers, Orchard made a neat job of the package, then went in to supper. His waitress friend, like everybody else in the village, had heard the explosion. She did not yet know what it was. Orchard did not tell her. She noticed that he ate little that night. She even remarked on his poor appetite. Minutes later, when Orchard had left, she heard that Governor Steunenberg had been blown up in his own dooryard. It set a train of thought going through her mind, the horrible possibility there might be a connection between the explosion and Mr. Hogan's marked loss of appetite. If this supposition in a naive mind seems a little too much to accept, all one can do is to reject it. We have the woman's word for it, sworn to in court: she had been unable to shake off the feeling that had come over her on that tragic night, namely, that the man she considered her lover was somehow connected with the death of Governor Steunenberg. She lay long in bed, weeping with her suspicions, and at last, she admitted, had prayed God to take care of Hogan's soul. She seems not to have given any thought to the victim.

By the time Orchard finished his bleak supper, the news about the ex-governor of Idaho had been sent far afield. When it reached Frank Gooding, the Governor, at Boise, he asked the Union Pacific for a special train to take him and a few selected officials and friends to Caldwell. Among those invited to go was Joe Hutchinson, a one-time mining man who had been Steunenberg's lieutenant governor during his first administration and, more importantly, was considered a leading expert on explosives. The Union Pacific men worked fast. Within an hour after Governor Gooding's request, a two-car special was at the Boise depot, steam up, ready to start the thirty-mile run to Caldwell, with a green light all the way.

By the time the special pulled out of Boise, Harry Orchard had gone upstairs to his room in the Saratoga.

18.

A Man Almost Unnerved

In the annals of crime, it seems an almost universally accepted proposition that the criminal must soon or late commit some small error that will result in his apprehension. It is probable that Harry Orchard had come to believe he was an exception. Better men have made the same mistake. Orchard's own criminal career had begun with arson almost a decade before the explosion in Caldwell. For three years he had been a professional and busy killer; yet, he not only had never been arrested, he had hardly been suspected in the many murders and acts of violence in which he had been involved. He was still the shadowy figure just beyond the pale of identity, the John Doe and Richard Roe of uncounted warrants that had never been served.

Now, in Room Nineteen of the Saratoga Hotel, Orchard committed the necessary error. Let him tell it in his own words.

"I was going," he said, "to take some things out of my room and throw them away. There were some bits of dynamite, some pieces of fuse, several giant caps, and a bottle or two of acid. I emptied the acid into the washbowl and put the bottle into my side pocket, planning to take it downstairs and throw it away. It wasn't two seconds after I put that bottle in my pocket when a flash like a pistol shot rang out in the room and the coat was nearly all torn off my back."

Little wonder. Familiarity with explosives over a long period had made Orchard careless. When he came into his room that night he was carrying in a pocket a spare detonator or two. The bottle he had just put into the same pocket was not quite empty. A few drops of sulphuric acid remained. It dribbled out, reached the caps, and the coat of the Western Federation's dynamite man hung in smoldering shreds.

"I immediately understood what had taken place," Orchard recalled, "and it almost unnerved me for a moment."

One grants that it would have almost unnerved anybody. But no one apparently heard this second and minor explosion on a tragic night in the little village. The town was undergoing an excitement such as it had never known. Orchard had another coat in his room. He slipped it on and went downstairs to the hotel lobby. Talk was all on the murder of Steunenberg, and that a special train was bringing Governor Gooding and other state officials to Caldwell. Orchard went back to his room.

In Number Nineteen was still a smell of burning cloth. Orchard opened a window. He sat down on the bed. "Something, I cannot tell you what, came across me," he remembered. "I got to thinking of the many incriminating things in my room. Besides the fuse and caps, I recalled that I had some sugar and some chloride of potash in my things. I also had a small amount of plaster of Paris, a batch of screw eyes, and an electric flashlight. I had a gun in my valise." He knew well enough that these items would be hard to explain if his room were searched. "But still I sat there," said he, "and didn't do anything about them. After that cap went off in my pocket, I seemed to lose my reasoning power."

It wasn't every day that a man had his coat blown from his back and shoulders. Possibly the explosion in his pocket had unnerved him. There was a westbound train passing through Caldwell early that evening. Had he acted promptly, Orchard could have taken it. There was a later eastbound train. By then it is doubtful that he would have been allowed to leave town. But he made no effort to do so. He just sat there in the hotel doing nothing, making no further effort to clear his room, in which were all the requisites of a practicing assassin.

The arrival of Governor Gooding's special train brought new excitement to the Saratoga, which already was crowded. Orchard threw off his lethargy to the extent of going downstairs. In the lobby men were being dispatched to surround Caldwell. Telephone calls were being made to nearby communities. A Citizens' Committee was being formed to offer a twenty-five-thousand-dollar reward for evidence leading to the capture of the murderer. To this sum Governor Gooding added another five thousand dollars.

Nobody looked at Orchard with suspicion. He was, after all, a son of star boarder at the Saratoga. He had been in Caldwell a good deal of the time for more than three months. The hotel regulars liked him. He bought a drink as often as the next man. In the almost continuous poker game he neither won too much nor too often. He was always affable, kindly, courteous. More important, he was a "common-looking fellow you wouldn't pick out for any peculiarity of looks or personality."

Orchard and one of the hotel clerks had become friendly, and along toward midnight they walked together out to the Steunenberg residence. "It was not," as Orchard remarked, "a pleasant sight." But this in no way prevented him from having a good night's rest. On return from the murder scene, he went to bed and there he remained until almost noon the next day, which was Sunday.

At a late breakfast he read in the Boise *Statesman* an account of the mysterious explosion. No suspects were mentioned, but the paper cited "a fishline on the gate at the Steunenberg house" which Joe Hutchinson, the state's explosive expert, thought offered a clue. As soon as he finished his meal, Orchard went up to his room and there removed the remaining line from a reel in his valise and flushed it down the water closet. He also destroyed several letters and papers he knew would be incriminating if found.

The possibility that he might come under suspicion was taking hold of his imagination. The story in the paper had said no one would be permitted to leave Caldwell until cleared by authorities. "I thought what a fool I had been," Orchard mused, "not to have cleared every suspicious thing out of my room the night before." He dared no longer attempt to move the remnants of dynamite, the plaster of Paris, and other indications of his calling. One thought led to another, and he suddenly remembered that his trunk had been lying for two days in the baggage room of the Caldwell railroad depot. It was too late to do anything about that, either. He must now, as he had done at times before, trust to the kind of luck that had saved him in pinches in the past.

No matter what his luck, it seems unlikely that Orchard could have cleared himself at this stage of affairs. And his next move was fairly stupid, almost as if calculated to center suspicion on him. Out in the street in front of the hotel a group of men were standing and discussing the one topic of interest in the town—the bombing of Caldwell's best-known citizen. Orchard walked up to them. In a matter-of-fact way he asked if anyone could tell him where he might buy a band of good wethers, which are sheep. It was much too casual. Somebody in the group answered him curtly, and he went away.

A little later that afternoon, Joe Hutchinson showed a length of fishline to Charles Steunenberg, brother of the murdered man. "This string," he said, "was what your brother kicked to touch off the bomb." Within an hour, as Charles and a friend, George Froman, were passing the Saratoga, Froman pointed out a man who was sitting in the lobby behind the large window. "That's the man who did it," he said. When Charles Steunenberg asked why he thought so, Froman replied to the effect that Hogan (Orchard) had "been hanging around here for months doing nothing," that he seemed to have no means of support, and that a number of times he had inquired of people if they knew "when Governor Steunenberg would be home again."

If anything more were needed to direct suspicion, Harvey K. Brown, the high sheriff of Baker County, Oregon, who just happened to be in Caldwell on other matters, supplied it. Brown was an old-time miner. Catching sight of Orchard in front of the Saratoga, and being told that he was a sheep man, name of Hogan, Brown spoke to his colleague, Idaho Sheriff Moseley of Canyon County. "I know that feller," said Brown. "He isn't a Mr. Hogan. He is Harry Orchard, who used to be active in the miners' union in the Coeur d'Alenes."

Joe Hutchinson and Sheriff Moseley got busy. Orchard was out wandering the streets, asking about sheep, and going again to view the splintered gate at the Steunenberg residence. With a passkey, the two men entered Room Nineteen of the Saratoga. On the inside doorknob they found two towels tied together and hung to cover the keyhole. On the commode was a short piece of fishline that matched the quality of that found on the gate. Scattered about were bits of plaster of Paris. In Orchard's grip was a badly torn coat, and also a trunk check.

Hutchinson and Moseley hastened to the Caldwell depot to open Orchard's trunk. In it was enough stuff to have gone far toward convicting a saint—a few sticks of dynamite, a sawed-off repeating shotgun, several changes of clothing "fit to disguise one for almost any walk of life," and a collection of what a reporter described as "burglars' tools" but which were probably the tools Orchard used in his craft of custom-made infernal machines.

Exactly why Orchard was not promptly arrested is not now clear.

He knew he was under suspicion. The Oregon sheriff, ex-miner Brown who had recognized him, came later in the afternoon to tell him so. Orchard insisted he was T. S. Hogan, a simple sheep man. Brown suggested that he accompany him to see Moseley, the local sheriff. Orchard agreed. What happened then, the way Orchard recalled it, was that Sheriff Moseley said, "he would have to take charge of the things in my room, and that I was not to leave the hotel."

In view of the nature of the crime, this sounds altogether too free and easy, yet there is no evidence to contradict Orchard's assertion that he was not put under arrest but went to bed that night—it was New Year's Eve—in Room Nineteen of the Saratoga Hotel.

On Monday, 1906 dawned bright, clear, and bitterly cold. Orchard had breakfast, shaved, got into his best clothes and his black derby, and walked to the Commercial Bank Building, in the upstairs of which Sheriff Moseley had just called to order a meeting of the Citizens' Committee. Uninvited, and certainly not expected, Orchard walked into the meeting, and, when a pause in the proceedings seemed to offer the chance, he asked courteously enough of the chairman if he might speak a word. The permission was granted. "I understand I am under suspicion," he said, "and I should like to clear myself."

There is no record of what Orchard said at this meeting. Whatever it was, it must have been pretty good. He finished what he had to say, then strolled, a free man, back to the Saratoga and remained there until late afternoon when, at last, Sheriff Moseley decided to arrest him. Orchard was neither surprised nor perturbed. With his usual great good nature, he accompanied the officer and was lodged in Caldwell jail. Jail was a new experience. In his forty years he had never been arrested.

Next day, when Orchard's last victim was to be buried, flags flew at half-mast throughout Idaho. Schools and state offices were closed. The funeral was perhaps the most impressive the state had known. Attorney William E. Borah of Boise, soon to be a United States Senator, delivered the funeral oration, in which he called Frank Steunenberg "Idaho's first martyr." It is to his lasting credit that Borah warned against accepting implications of guilt until evidence was in. "Let us not," he said, "believe this is the crime of any class or any portion of our citizens or that it finds sympathy with anyone other than the actual perpetrator." Borah knew what the implications were. They were clear and were already known to all who read the papers: Frank Steunenberg had been assassinated at the instigation of radical mine union interests because, back in 1899, as governor, he had asked for troops and declared martial law in a district where conventional law no longer existed.

A wave of apprehension and fear spread over Idaho. Even children felt it. James Stevens, the author, was then a schoolboy in Weiser, on Snake River. One of his most profound memories was of his teacher informing the school, that snowy morning, in a hushed voice, that there would be no classes that day because Ex-Governor Steunenberg had been assassinated and was to be buried. Mr. Stevens recalls that for many months every stranger was eyed closely, by adults and children alike, lest he be another anarchist—by far the most sinister word of the period—like him who set the bomb at the picket gate in Caldwell.

The press of much of Western United States was prompt to supply the implications mentioned by Mr. Borah, and to identify by name the group responsible for the murder; it was the Western Federation of Miners. Even before his confession, Harry Orchard was referred to in editorials as merely the tool, the professional hatchet man, for the miners' union. And in a Denver paper Sherman Bell, Adjutant General of Colorado, predicted that Orchard would confess his guilt and name his accomplices.

Orchard was held eighteen days in the Caldwell jail. Newspapers must have been kept from him, or he would have read in the Boise paper that the State of Idaho had engaged a celebrated private detective to investigate the Steunenberg affair. This was James McParlan, of whom more later. Three days after McParlan arrived in Caldwell, where he did not talk with Orchard, the prisoner was taken to the state penitentiary in Boise, and there placed in solitary confinement.

For ten days Orchard was permitted to see no one. His meals were handed to him in silence. He was given no reading material. Then, a guard came to take him to the warden's office. In the office were Warden Whitney and a man Orchard had never seen. The warden remarked that the stranger, whom he did not identify, would like to talk with the prisoner, then left the two men together.

The stranger introduced himself merely as a detective, and Orchard faced a man of stocky build who looked older than his sixty-one years. His alert eyes peered through gold-rimmed spectacles. His magnificent red if graying mustache swept out and down, then curved, in the manner popular with so many chiefs of police of the era. His hair was thin and gray at the temples. His ears were set close to his head. He was dressed conservatively, while his stand-up-and-turndown collar and cravat with a huge knot, in which was a stickpin, were already archaic, being more in the mode of 1890 than of 1906. In his coat lapel was an emblem of the Elks lodge.

McParlan's voice was low, musical, soothing. In it was the soft quality of the Old Sod where he was born, in County Armagh, in 1844. Orchard didn't know it yet, but he was being worked on by the master of all undercover men—a protean fellow of high intelligence, almost no formal education, and a native charm of virtually fatal fascination. This is no hyperbole. Back in the mid-seventies, at least ten members of the Molly Maguires, a secret society of Irish Catholic coal miners, were hanged because they could not resist McParlan's charming ways. He was now to charm Harry Orchard as he had charmed the murderous Mollies, though with different results. He merits consideration.

At the age of twenty-three, James McParlan emigrated to the United States, where he neither joined the New York City police department nor went to digging ditches. After clerking in stores, he moved to Buffalo and was by turns a teamster, a deck hand on a Great Lakes vessel, a logger in Michigan, and a bartender. Such a variety of occupations helped to fit him for his later career; and to the jobs mentioned he added experience in Chicago as a private coachman, a policeman, and finally proprietor of a combination liquor store and saloon. The Great Fire of 1871 wiped out his business. Within a year he became an operative for Pinkerton's National Detective Agency. It is of interest to know that Allan Pinkerton himself put McParlan on the payroll.

As a novice, the young operative displayed such abilities that in 1873, when the Pinkerton agency was engaged by mine owners in the Pennsylvania anthracite region to destroy the Mollies, McParlan was chosen to get the evidence needed. As "Jimmy McKenna," he turned coal miner. Having been born and reared a Catholic, he was soon a member of the Ancient Order of Hibernians, from which the terrorist Molly Maguires were recruited. Playing to perfection the part of a typically devil-may-care son of Erin, he drank, brawled, danced, and sang his way into the higher councils of the order. Two years later the trap was sprung. Some three score alleged Mollies were arrested. Ten were convicted on murder charges and hanged. Another sixteen were sent to the penitentiary. McKenna-McParlan was the great hero of the affair, or the deep villain, depending on the point of view one held in regard to the coal mine operators and the Mollie Maguires.

Detective McParlan remained with Pinkerton, and, when conditions in the Colorado and other Western mining regions seemed to warrant it, the agency sent him to open a branch in Denver and take charge of its operations. It was to him, incidentally, that undercover man Charlie Siringo sent his reports of union activities in the Coeur d'Alenes. Here now was McParlan in the warden's office of the Idaho penitentiary, taking stock of Harry Orchard, a sociable man who, as McParlan had reason to believe, had been softened somewhat by ten days of loneliness and silence in solitary.

"Did you, my boy," he asked in a soft appealing voice, "ever hear of the Molly Maguires?" Yes, Orchard knew of the Mollies, and, as McParlan talked on, it suddenly occurred to Orchard that this "gentle old man," as he thought of him, was the notorious detective about whom Bill Haywood had spoken so bitterly. "Are you James McParlan?" Orchard asked. "I am," said the detective, "and I am here to give you some sound advice, if you will take it." Orchard replied that he did not need any advice. The detective paid no heed to the blunt refusal.

On went the soothing voice. "If you are innocent, as you say, of this horrible crime with which you are charged, my lad," it intoned, "then you have been the victim of most unfortunate circumstances." There was a little more talk about the crime of murder, then McParlan changed the subject. "Do you, young man," he asked, "believe in God?" Orchard was a little vague, but indicated he thought there was a Supreme Being. McParlan then drew from Orchard the admission that his parents had been God-fearing people who took their children with them to church, sent them to Sunday school, and were strict in keeping the Sabbath. "I am most glad to know that," said the detective. He stood up to indicate that the interview was over. Orchard was returned to his cell.

This was merely the first of several discussions between McParlan and Orchard. The latter went back to his silent cell filled, he said, "with a wild surge of hatred" toward the detective as "the sworn enemy of organized labor." He thought of McParlan as "the rich man's tool." But Orchard was not ignorant of the methods of detectives. "I always prided myself I could mix with any of them," he said, "and not tip my hand."

Yet, he welcomed anything that removed him even if temporarily from the terrible silence of his cell.

Legend has it that, during early evening after the first interview, the terrible silence in Orchard's cell block was astonishingly broken by the sweetly melancholy chords of a melodeon, moved there at the request of Detective McParlan. There was no Ira D. Sankey to sing the words, and none was necessary. The plaintive melody was familiar:

Where is my wandering boy tonight,
The boy of my tenderest care?

The prison walls may not have softened, but the boy who had wandered far from his home in Ontario, what of him? The little organ swelled as the refrain reached the climactic line, then diminished, and faded. The organist struck a new chord and wafting through the corridor of steel and stone came "The Ninety-and-Nine," an appealing hymn that had brought vast numbers of sinners face to face with their God, at least for the moment. Dwight Moody had recognized its power. "It will," said he, "move a man of granite." Harry Orchard was less than granite.

Two days later, McParlan and Orchard met again in the warden's office. "My boy," said the detective, "it is bad enough to live a sinful life. It is much worse to die without repenting one's sins." Then he took up the subject of murder and followed it from the times of King David to those of the Molly Maguires, and even by allusion to the murder of Frank Steunenberg. "There is no sin that God will not forgive you—if you repent." Then, as if it had just occurred to him, McParlan mentioned there had been cases where men had turned state's evidence and given witness for the prosecution. In such cases, he said, the state did not and could not prosecute them. What was more, McParlan went on in his soft, kindly voice, what was more, men could be a thousand miles from where a murder took place and yet be guilty of the crime. "Not only morally guilty," he said, "but they can be charged with conspiracy and convicted."

The trend was becoming clear to the prisoner. McParlan, however, was far too astute to weary a man. He dismissed Orchard, remarking that they should meet again soon, and added something for the prisoner to mull over. "I am satisfied," said he, "that you have been used only as a tool by the Western Federation of Miners which have a gang of murderers at their head. Your salvation, my lad, is to make a clean breast of it. Repent. Do not face the awful consequences of dying in your sins."

That night the unseen melodeon resumed its pleading, and in the dark of his cell Orchard "prayed to God," he said, "in a halfhearted way." There was another meeting with McParlan, and another night when the organ throbbed, to conjure up the sweet sadness of things long forgotten, of broken promises, of hopes long buried. At some point or other during this period, the warden gave the prisoner a religious pamphlet. "It was left here for you," he said, "by the widow of the man you murdered." In the mail, too, came a Bible sent by "a devout physician, Dr. David Paulson of Hinsdale, Illinois."

Meanwhile, of course, Detective McParlan continued to see Orchard almost daily. One morning, after an eternity of night during which Orchard sat on the edge of his little cot, there suddenly came "something which seemed to say to me there was still hope." He told McParlan he was ready to confess, not only about the murder of Frank Steunenberg, but "of my awful life of crime from the beginning."

Part Four:

Eminence

Part Four

Eminence

19.

Confession

Much of three days was needed for the clerk in the warden's office to take down the extraordinary confession of Albert E. Horsley, a name that appeared in the first paragraph and was not again mentioned in the entire document. Orchard might be hanged even if his soul might, as he hoped, be born anew, yet he could never shed the alias so casually assumed nine years before. The confession was to stamp him indelibly as Harry Orchard, the Dynamite Man.

The confession was a sizable document which in its original form must have run to something like one hundred thousand words. The reader already knows much of what it contained. A recapitulation is not necessary, save only to emphasize at this point that it criminally involved Moyer, Haywood, and Simpkins, all officials of the Western Federation of Miners, and Pettibone, a close friend and unofficial adviser. Steve Adams was also implicated in the business.

The confession appears to have been made to McParlan during the early part of February. All word of it was kept secret until the twentieth. The delay was intentional. It permitted Idaho authorities to make three arrests by perpetrating what a celebrated attorney and many other people were to term an infamous kidnaping.

If Orchard told the truth, then he was merely a tool, the hatchet man for the Western Federation. The Western Federation meant Moyer, Haywood, Pettibone, and to a lesser extent Jack Simpkins. They were his accomplices. If he was guilty of Steunenberg's murder, then so were they. At the time of Orchard's confession, the whereabouts of Simpkins was unknown. The other men were in Colorado, hence beyond the jurisdiction of Idaho. To be tried they must be extradited.

To be extradited a man must be a fugitive. None of the three men was a fugitive. They were accessories to the crime. Under general interpretation of the laws it was impossible to extradite an accessory; but the United States Supreme Court had often held that the right of a state in which a crime had been committed to try an *abducted* person could not be questioned, whatever the means used to secure his presence.

With Orchard's confession still held in secret, Idaho's Governor Gooding sent deputies to Denver to apply for extradition of Moyer, Haywood, and Pettibone. Governor McDonald of Colorado granted it. The Idaho deputies had been well coached in law matters. They knew they must use great care if they were to get their men. The law had usually if not always been interpreted to mean that a fugitive from justice facing extradition "may challenge the fact by habeas corpus immediately upon arrest."

February 17, 1906 was a Saturday. Courts would be closed until Monday. Until then it would be difficult if not impossible to get a writ of habeas corpus. Late Saturday the sheriff of Denver, accompanied by the Idaho deputies, made the arrests. They took Moyer at Denver's union station as he was about to board a train for Iola, Kansas, where he was to visit the Smeltermen's Union. They found Pettibone at his home in Denver. Haywood was in a rooming house in downtown Denver near the Western Federation office. Haywood described his arrest.

There was a knock at the door. "Who's there?" he asked.

"I want to see you, Bill." It was a deputy sheriff whom Haywood knew. "I want you to come with me." Haywood asked him what was up. "I can't tell you now, but you must come." Haywood got into his clothes. "Where are we going?" The deputy said to the county jail. Haywood protested. "Where's your warrant?" "I haven't any warrant," said the deputy, and added, "We've sent a messenger out to find Richardson. We couldn't get him on the phone." This was Edmund Richardson, long an attorney for the Western Federation.

At the jail Haywood was told that Moyer and Pettibone had already been arrested. When the Denver sheriff came in, Haywood demanded to know what it was all about. "They're going to take you to Idaho," he was told. "They've got you mixed up in the Steunenberg murder."

Haywood remained in a cell until about five o'clock in the morning, which was Sunday the eighteenth. He was taken into the jail office.

Moyer and Pettibone were there. All three men were handcuffed. Each was put into a separate carriage with—says Haywood—three guards, and the caravan drove through the dark deserted streets to the Oxford Hotel. From here they were marched to the Denver railroad station. A Union Pacific special train was waiting. The prisoners and guards were put aboard one car, and what seems to have been a sizable group of Colorado and Idaho deputies, lawyers, and such boarded another. Within a few minutes the train pulled out of Denver, running north and west.

Bill Haywood looked his guards over. One was a Bob Meldrum from Telluride. "I have never seen a human face," Haywood recalled, "that looked so much like a hyena. His eyes were deep-set and close together. His upper lip was drawn back, showing teeth like fangs." Big Bill had a flair for describing "tools of the Capitalists." Later, Bulkeley Wells, Colorado mine manager and militia officer, came in with a bottle of whisky to treat the prisoners. Haywood never exhibited any antipathy toward capitalist-made liquor. "I had a drink," he said, "though I handled the glass awkwardly on account of the handcuffs." Wells told the prisoners they were on a special train that would arrive in Boise the following morning. The tracks were cleared, and the special did not stop in the larger towns. It took on coal and water at little way stations. The curtains were pulled shut. It arrived in Boise on schedule Monday morning. The three prisoners were taken to the penitentiary and put in separate cells. Next day Orchard's confession was given to the press.

It is improbable that many confessions have been read with greater interest in so many different places. The owners of the Vindicator mine high in the Rockies learned who set the infernal machine that killed two of their superintendents. The people of Independence, Colorado, learned who blew their railroad station and thirteen men to Kingdom Come; and the survivors, several amputees among them, would never forget the names of Harry Orchard and Steve Adams. In Denver, the list of unsolved crimes was reduced by two, for Orchard cleared the mystery of Merritt W. Walley's death and that of Lyte Gregory, mine detective.

In San Francisco, officials of a public utility company were elated to know that leaky gas pipes had not been responsible for destruction of an apartment house at the corner of Leavenworth and Washington streets, as a court had found, and prepared to bring suit for recovery of damages paid to the owner.

Homesteaders along the St. Joe River in northern Idaho read what Orchard had to say about the activities of Jack Simpkins and Steve Adams and understood why two men named Tyler and Boulle had not been seen in more than a year.

When Judge Luther M. Goddard came to one paragraph in the confession, he put down his newspaper and went out into the yard of his home. There in a gatepost was a rusted screw eye. In the earth nearby was a slight depression. Police were sent for and came to dig up a box bomb that contained "thirty-seven sticks of giant powder."

The insurance company which had paid a claim to John Neville, on account of a fire in his saloon in the Cripple Creek mining district, could reflect on the subtleties of arson through the medium of George Pettibone's standard Greek fire mixture.

There were of course many others who read the confession with varying emotions and always with interest. It naturally hit hardest in the ranks of the Western Federation of Miners. It damned the union as worse than the Molly Maguire savages of an earlier era. Even if Orchard's assertions turned out to be, as Haywood said they were, a pack of black hearted lies, they were so shocking that a great majority of Americans immediately tended to believe "there must be some fire where there is so much smoke."

No matter what the outlook, however, several of the Western Federation's larger local unions rallied to the defense at once. The Silverton, Colorado, miners sent five thousand dollars to the executive board. The Telluride union matched that sum. The miners around Goldfield, Nevada, sent six thousand. A local of the United Mine Workers contributed five thousand. Many thousands of dollars more were to be added to these spontaneous efforts which gave hope to the arrested men.

The ranks of counsel took form almost at once. That for Moyer, Haywood, and Pettibone was headed by E. F. Richardson of Denver, whose associates were to be Edgar Wilson and John Nugent, of Boise, Fred Miller of Spokane, and Clarence Darrow of Chicago. The prosecution was in charge of Owen M. Van Duyn, district attorney, and James Hawley and William E. Borah.

The defense at once demanded the prisoners be taken from the

Idaho penitentiary and confined in jail at Caldwell, in Canyon County. This was done, but later, when a change of venue was granted, they were returned to Boise and this time confined in the Ada County jail there. Orchard remained in the penitentiary.

Eighteen months were to pass before Haywood, the first of the three defendants, was put on trial. The long delay was occasioned, first, by progress through the courts of defense counsel's demand for a writ of habeas corpus; and second, by another trial, a sort of curtain raiser to the main event. In the habeas corpus matter, the Idaho Supreme Court denied a writ, Justice James F. Ailshie holding that "The fact that a wrong has been committed against a prisoner ... can constitute no legal or just reason why he should not answer the charge against him when brought before the proper tribunal. The commission of an offense in his arrest does not expiate the offense with which he is charged."

In his reasoning, Justice Ailshie cited a case in which "an assassin on the Oregon bank of the great waterway [Snake River] that marks our western boundary" had, by firing across the stream, killed a man in Idaho. Another citation involved a Mrs. Botkin of California who, to remove a rival, sent a box of poisoned candy to a woman in New Jersey. The implications were clear—Haywood and Moyer and Pettibone had while in Colorado sent an assassin with a box of No. 1 Gelatin to Idaho. Defense counsel appealed. But the United States Supreme Court decided, eight to one, to uphold the lower court. The three men could be put on trial for the murder of Steunenberg.

Long before the habeas corpus matter was settled, and the main show could begin, a curtain raiser was provided by Steve Adams. This was the fellow who had been Orchard's partner in several crimes in both Colorado and Idaho. At the time of Orchard's arrest, Adams was living on a homestead in Baker County, Oregon.

The prosecution realized the need for corroboration of the testimony Orchard was prepared to give in court. It would not be enough to show the Western Federation of Miners responsible for a large number of atrocities. Even though a jury was convinced that Orchard told the truth and found the defendants guilty, the higher courts would not accept moral certainty as legal proof. But if a second party should confess to a hand in the same crimes, then Orchard's story would stand a better chance of acceptance in the higher courts, should the case be appealed.

Jack Simpkins, a member of the executive board of the Western Federation, had been named by Orchard as his accomplice in the Steunenberg murder. But Simpkins had vanished so completely and covered his trail so well that detectives could not locate him. Steve Adams, however, was known to be living in Oregon. True, he had not been in Caldwell at all; but Orchard had implicated him in other crimes. He might do.

Soon after the arrest of Haywood, Moyer, and Pettibone, and just before Orchard's confession was given to the press, McParlan asked that Steve Adams be arrested. Sheriff Brown of Baker County, Oregon, made the arrest, telling Adams that "they don't think you are implicated in the Steunenberg murder. They want you as a witness. If you will go to Boise and corroborate their stories, you will come out all right and won't be prosecuted." A day later Adams was put into the same cell with Orchard in the penitentiary.

Steve Adams was understandingly both nervous and confused. He did not yet know that Orchard had confessed and implicated him in most of Orchard's crimes and also in those having to do with Mine Superintendent Collins in Colorado and the two claim jumpers in northern Idaho. Orchard went to work with a will on Adams to get him to "make a clean breast of everything." He talked about "reforming and asking God's forgiveness." This seemed not to move Steve very much. Then Orchard told him of his own confession and remarked: "I have told the truth and am going to stand by it, let the consequences be what they will to myself or anyone else."

If Adams was not somewhat startled by this statement, it was because "he was a man of iron." He was not of iron. The sequence of following events is not clear, but it appears that both Detective McParlan and Governor Gooding took Adams in hand, with the result that Adams signed a confession corroborating Orchard in a number of crimes. His wife and children were then brought from Oregon and given a small house just outside the penitentiary walls.

The habeas corpus matter was meanwhile making its way through the courts. As soon as the United States Supreme Court had upheld what he referred to as "the kidnaping," Clarence Darrow arrived in Boise.

20.

Orchard, the Witness

In 1906 Clarence Darrow was forty-nine years old, a big hulking man with the shoulders of a gorilla, long unruly hair that fell down across his forehead, and a deeply furrowed face so mobile that in one and the same hour it was seen as "demoniac" and "jovial" and "ascetic."

The affair that brought him to Idaho was to make him internationally famous. He had already achieved something of a reputation as a "radical," because of his defense of Eugene Debs in the American Railway Union strike, his work for the United Mine Workers, and his long championship of John P. Altgeld, the humane Illinois governor who had pardoned three of the "Haymarket Anarchists." Darrow had also acted for several corporations, including the Chicago & Northwestern Railway. In 1906, however, his close friendship with Debs, the Socialist leader was sufficient to brand Darrow as dangerous in the eyes of many Americans. He was not in the least surprised to find that Boise's greeting was chilly.

After conferring with his clients, Haywood, Moyer, and Pettibone, and with other counsel for defense, Darrow centered his attention on the case of Steve Adams. Without the corroboration of Adams, he felt, Orchard's unsupported testimony could never convict. He was refused permission to talk to Adams in the penitentiary. Whereupon Darrow dodged the detectives set to watch his movements and went to Baker County, Oregon, where he talked with Mr. Lillard, an uncle of Steve Adams. Darrow convinced Lillard that if Adams would repudiate the confession he had made to McParlan, then he, Darrow, would defend Adams if the latter were brought to trial. Lillard, who seems to have thought of his nephew more as "a poor, misguided boy" than a professional killer, was persuaded by Darrow to go to Boise, talk with Adams in prison, and get him to repudiate the confession.

This was done. Lillard told Darrow he was sure Adams would stick to the repudiation. Darrow immediately demanded a writ of habeas corpus, thus forcing the state to show cause for holding Adams in jail. The prosecution was ready to meet this move. When the court ordered Adams to be released, he was met at the penitentiary gate by the sheriff of Shoshone County, handcuffed, and taken to Wallace in the Coeur d'Alene region of Idaho. Here he was charged with the murder of Tyler, the claim jumper. Jack Simpkins, of course, knew as much or more about Tyler's death than Adams, but Simpkins was not to be found.

James H. Hawley, one of the attorneys who was to prosecute Haywood, Moyer, and Pettibone, had his name entered for the prosecution of Steve Adams in Shoshone County. Darrow went there to defend the man. Many years later, when he came to write his autobiography, Darrow recalled the Coeur d'Alene country with lyric prose seldom encountered elsewhere in the book. He thought the region had a natural charm and beauty one rarely found. It was marked with steep slopes "of firs and flowers, and funiculars and flumes." Its rich mines of copper, zinc, and lead had brought wealth to the section and its people. "Or," he added, "at any rate to *some* of its people." Darrow saw the Coeur d'Alenes romantically. They had been settled by homesteaders, "the sort that, following Daniel Boone, had slowly made their way from Virginia ... to the farthest limit of the unexplored world in Texas. The majority of them were men skilled in woodcraft."

Because the state had found "a lonely grave in the forest and unearthed the bones and decayed clothing" which were alleged to be the remains of Tyler, the claim jumper, and which they were to use as a corpus delicti in the Adams case, Darrow felt it necessary to view the scene of the crime and to talk with homesteaders in the area. The "great trackless wilderness along the St. Joe River" appealed to him. He talked to homesteaders along Marble Creek and discovered that "their natural instincts were against claim jumpers." Through it all he saw "shadow pictures of Robin Hood and the greenwood tree, and Daniel Boone with his long rifle and buckskin shirt blazing the trail for a new civilization." Both the region and Steve Adams's trial were "as interesting and remarkable" as any Darrow was to know in his long life.

Getting a jury was none too easy. Every day the courtroom was filled with picturesque miners and woodsmen. Dressed in widow's weeds was the mother of Fred Tyler, the deceased. Darrow's stand was that the prosecution of Adams was humbug and fraud. "The powerful interests which are behind this case are not interested in Steve Adams." They—and by "they" he meant the mine owners of Idaho, Colorado, and elsewhere in the West—merely wanted him convicted "to get him back into their hands where he was before." He must be forced to renege on his repudiation of his confession. He must be ready to corroborate Harry Orchard and thus "hang Haywood, Moyer, and Pettibone" for the crime "of defending the working class. This is a fight between capital and labor …"

The jury's first ballot was seven to five for acquittal. Two days later the vote was the same. The jury was dismissed. The judge refused to admit Adams to bail. He was held in the jail at Wallace. Both Darrow and Hawley returned to Boise. The main show could now begin. The State of Idaho must try Haywood, Moyer, and Pettibone on Harry Orchard's confession alone, or with such support as could be had from witnesses other than Steve Adams.

William Dudley Haywood was selected to be tried first. The trials were to be held in Boise, the state capital, after a change of venue from Canyon to Ada County. Judge Fremont Wood was to preside, a just and brave man who had studied law at Bates College in his native Maine, then came West to become a pioneer district attorney in what was then the Territory of Idaho. Even Darrow was to find Judge Wood to be "fair and judicial." The court calendar set the Haywood case to begin May 9, 1907, or some fifteen months after the tree men were arrested.

Few trials have had more advance advertising. Haywood had no more than landed in the Ada County jail than he prepared a startling poster which was printed and distributed by the thousands from Western Federation headquarters. It displayed a picture of a train of passenger coaches streaking through the Rockies and labeled "The Kidnappers' Train." With it were photographs of Moyer, Pettibone, and Haywood, fairly loaded with handcuffs. In large type across the top of the poster was a slogan from Debs:

AROUSE, YE SLAVES! THEIR ONLY CRIME IS LOYALTY TO THE WORKING CLASS!

Debs had of course got into the battle at once. He contributed a regular column to the *Appeal to Reason* of Girard, Kansas, an uninhibited weekly given to black studhorse headlines interspersed with brilliant red titles and borders. Since its founding in 1897, the *Appeal* had never been long without a good Menace. It was first to publish Upton Sinclair's *The Jungle*. It regularly attacked the Tariff, the United States Supreme Court, and the White Slave business. Its favorite "news" was a Martyr Story, in which the martyr, usually a Socialist, was pictured as a Christian at the stake, with the unholy Romans—the Capitalists—lighting the fires around him. Then the paper could start a Martyr Defense Fund. Even illiterates found these stories inflaming.

And now, with three Western Federation martyrs in the Boise jail, the *Appeal* laid in a fresh stock of vermilion ink and columnist Debs went into action. In a violent manifesto he said that Capitalist tyrants were trying to put innocent men to death. This called for a revolution, and "I will do all in my power to precipitate it." Then he demanded that "the workers form an army and march to Idaho to free these martyrs to the cause of Labor."

Haywood prepared another poster for the Western Federation to distribute. It quoted Adjutant Sherman Bell of Colorado: "Habeas Corpus be Damned; We'll give 'em Post Mortems."

Labor unions staged parades of protest in many cities. There was to be no sitting on the fence. Either you were for Haywood, Moyer, and Pettibone, or you were against them. Even the President of the United States was not immune to the hysteria. In a private letter that was made public, Theodore Roosevelt wrote that, whether or not these three men were guilty of the Steunenberg murder, they were "undesirable citizens." Columnist Debs was quick to make a proposal in the *Appeal*, and within a week union men the country over were wearing buttons on which was inscribed "I Am an Undesirable Citizen." Meetings were held in all of the larger cities and in many mine towns. A defense fund reported variously to total from one hundred to two hundred and fifty thousand dollars was raised. As Haywood's trial got under way, Chicago unions staged a parade in which marched nearly four thousand men, women, and children, many carrying red banners.

When the trial began there were present in small Boise reporters "of fifty-four newspapers and press associations" and staff men from possibly twenty periodicals. The town was further crowded by observers of all shades of opinion, including labor organizers, free-wheeling reformers, and assorted politicians. In New York city, where he had just arrived from Russia, the dramatist Maxim Gorki was induced to send a sympathetic telegram to Haywood. Whereupon Gorki and his common-law wife were evicted from the Manhattan hotel where they were staying.

Just after Haywood's trial got under way, Ethel Barrymore came to town with her touring company to present a revival of *Captain Jinks of the Horse Marines*. She found the Idan-ha Hotel "full of extraordinary people." Most everybody seemed to be armed, and she was shown a bedroom where the mattress was raised to reveal Winchester rifles. When she asked what was happening in Boise, she was told simply, "This is the Haywood trial. The whole town is a fort."

Miss Barrymore obviously had never heard of Haywood or the other prisoners, nor of "a man named Clarence Darrow and a man named William Borah," but she was game to learn and eagerly accepted an invitation to attend the trial. She happened to have a seat next to "a dreamy-looking man whose name was Gifford Pinchot." She saw Harry Orchard on the stand, and this "great Killer," she thought, looked like a respectable grocer, "a little like Mr. Hobbs in *Little Lord Fauntleroy*." The jury appealed to her. They were "the most wonderful-looking men I've ever seen." They had "the bluest eyes, used to looking at great distances." They made her think of "Uncle Sam without the goatee."

She thought Mr. Darrow was a thorough actor. "He had all the props, an old mother in a wheelchair and a little girl with curls draped around Haywood. I don't know whether she was his daughter or just one of Mr. Darrow's props." Miss Barrymore asked if she might meet Orchard, and was taken to the penitentiary, where they exchanged greetings in the warden's office. Orchard was "very polite and quiet." He said, "I've heard a lot about you, Miss Barrymore," and the famous actress responded, "I've heard a certain amount about you." She went away thinking that "this killer of twenty-six people" was "just like somebody in a store."

ORCHARD WAS STANDING UP WELL on the witness stand. In spite of the savage cross-examination by Richardson and Darrow, he remained perhaps the coolest person in the court. "His performance on the stand," wrote the *Oregonian*'s reporter, "has been marvelous. At no point has he tripped ... On cross-examination he did not vary a hair's breadth from the tenor of what had been said. Old hands around the court express astonishment."

The defense hoped to prove that Orchard had killed Steunenberg not at behest of Haywood and the Western Federation but because of a personal matter. Darrow brought out the fact that Orchard had owned a one-sixteenth interest in the Hercules mine in the Coeur d'Alenes; he had been forced to flee the region, said Darrow, when Governor Steunenberg had brought in troops after the dynamiting of the Bunker Hill & Sullivan and had sold his interest for a pittance. For this, Darrow said, Steunenberg had been murdered. A personal grudge.

Not at all, said Orchard. He had sold his interest in the Hercules in 1897, long before the trouble and troops. Steunenberg had nothing to do with it. To corroborate Orchard, prosecution put one James McAlpin, a miner from Burke, Idaho, on the stand. He readily admitted that Orchard "was dishonest and a liar" and that his "greatest fault was gambling." McAlpin said that he, McAlpin, had sat in a poker game, one day in 1897, when Orchard lost two hundred dollars to a William Chapman. Knowing Orchard to be unreliable, Chapman had insisted on payment then and there. Whereupon Orchard gave Chapman a bill of sale for his interest in the Hercules, a mine that later panned out better than well. "No, sir," said Orchard, "I had no feeling about Governor Steunenberg one way or the other. But the 'Inner Circle' of the Federation had it in for him."

Before Haywood's trial began, the defense agreed among themselves that Richardson should handle most of the cross-examination and that Darrow should guide matters and make the final appeal. Richardson was a fierce fellow, given to hard, fast attacks. Now he sought to show what an inhuman monster Harry Orchard was. Orchard did not mind.

Q. Why did you shoot Lyte Gregory *three* times with a sawed-off shotgun?
A. He didn't go down until the third shot.
Q. You kept pumping until he did go down?
A. Yes, sir, I kept pumping until he went down dead.

Richardson sought to ridicule Orchard because once when he donned a soldier's uniform, as a disguise, he added a pair of glasses.

Q. Didn't you know that soldiers don't wear glasses?
A. I didn't know it, no.

Mr. Hawley of the prosecution entered the discussion: "You forgot Mr. Roosevelt at San Juan, Mr. Richardson."

"*He* wasn't a soldier," Richardson shouted.

"And he wasn't at San Juan," declared Mr. Nugent of defense counsel.

When the laughter subsided, Richardson made a long statement in regard to Orchard's all-around depravity and dishonesty, then asked:

Q. It was your habit to lie about everything, wasn't it?

A. Yes, sir, whenever it suited my purpose.

FOR MANY DAYS RUNNING RICHARDSON led Orchard back over the mazes of his confession, trying to wring from him deviations that would indicate he was what Richardson had called him, namely, "the most monumental and loathsome liar of record." But the tricky questioning did not bring the deviations. Orchard described the mining regions of Idaho and Colorado so accurately that those who knew the country recognized it. He had the dates and times of explosions correct. He assessed the havoc wrought accurately. Nor did he once lose his good nature or raise his voice during the abuse of sarcasm and condemnation heaped upon him by the defense attorneys. And, unlike so many leading figures in criminal trials, he did not wander from the subject. Whatever the question, he answered it with directness.

Richardson brought the witness to the time when Orchard had toted a bomb into the Idan-ha Hotel, Boise, with the idea of planting it in Governor Steunenberg's bedroom there.

Q. This bomb would have blown the hotel to pieces, wouldn't it?
A. Yes, sir.
Q. And you were willing to do this?
A. Yes, sir.
Q. Did you expect to stay in the hotel that night?
A. No, sir.
Q. You were willing to kill everyone but yourself?
A. Yes, sir.

Not once did Orchard seek by euphemism or explanation to mitigate the long series of horrors he had perpetrated. He was merely a professional killer. Reporters noted that his countenance and voice showed emotion only once while he was on the stand. This was when Richardson was attacking him, not as a heartless murderer but as something worse—a "furtive, sneaking, depraved deserter of wife and little children, a monster whom the Devil himself would consider unfit to breathe the sulphurous fumes from the lowest levels of the Pit that has no bottom." Orchard was seen to brush his eyes. His usually cheerfully placid countenance contracted.

ORCHARD WAS INVARIABLY ATTENTIVE WHILE witnesses were testifying, as, for instance, when Mrs. F. E. Seward, who had been his landlady briefly in San Francisco, was on the stand:

Q. What do you recall of the accused, Mrs. Seward, when he was a roomer at your place?

A. He had a very heavy valise in his room.

Q. Is that all?

A. I often found wood shavings and what looked like lead scrapings on the floor. I noticed he had put a screw eye in the closet door. There was a string in the screw eye and it was attached to a bottle stopper.

Q. Didn't these things make you suspicious?

A. No. I made up my mind he was an inventor.

P. L. McCleary, a chemist of San Francisco, took the stand to testify about his analysis of milk left at the Bradley home. He said it had contained "between forty to sixty grains of strychnine."

Q. How much strychnine, Mr. McCleary, is sufficient to cause death?

A. Two or three grains are sufficient.

Poison or dynamite, Harry Orchard was consistently a heavy loader.

During a period of eight days the prosecution presented these and other witnesses to prove that Orchard had actually committed the crimes to which he had confessed. Browbeat as he would, Defense Counsel Richardson failed to shake the corroborative witnesses to any extent; while, as for Orchard, reporters variously saw him emerging from every attack "a magnificent witness," "wholly invulnerable," a "man determined, courageous, pert, resolute." It was a stunning performance. What the press seems to have overlooked was the fact there was little evidence then or later, save by inference, that Orchard had killed Steunenberg on orders of Haywood or the Western Federation of Miners.

DARROW DID NOT LIKE RICHARDSON's methods. He grew morose as the trial proceeded. One evening, when he went to the big cell to confer with Moyer, Haywood, and Pettibone, he was so down in the mouth that Pettibone sought to comfort him. "Cheer up, Clarence," he said, "Don't you know that we are the ones they are going to hang?"

Though both Moyer and Haywood grew moody at times, Pettibone remained cheerful, even jovial. Somebody had given him a pyrography set, a fad then in vogue but which fifty years later should perhaps be explained as the art or craft of making patterns or pictures on wood or leather by burning the material with a red-hot instrument; and it was only natural that the man who had taught Orchard and others how to make and use Greek fire should enjoy working designs with a glowing pen kept hot with a miniature bellows. Conventional material to work on being absent in the Boise jail, Pettibone used the tops of cigar boxes, which in that day were made of wood. Haywood thought that his friend "turned out some very fine specimens."

Haywood did a good deal of reading during the evenings and on Sundays. "I went through Buckle's *History of Civilization*," he recalled, "and extended my acquaintance with Voltaire. I read many English classics, including *Tristram Shandy*, the *Sentimental Journey*, and Carlyle on the French revolution. I also read Marx and Engels. Upton Sinclair's *The Jungle* kept me awake a whole night. I also started a correspondence course in law." Moyer read a lot, too, but left no record of its nature. The bad feeling already mentioned between Moyer and Haywood grew bitter, and many days passed when they did not speak to each other. The new I.W.W. group had split into two factions, and the Western Federation of Miners had withdrawn its financial support, quite possibly because of Moyer's influence with James Kirwin, who had been acting in Haywood's place as secretary-treasurer of the federation. Bill Haywood, even while on trial for his life, still had great ambitions for the group that was soon to become known as the Wobblies.

Haywood, somewhat surprisingly to those who knew him best,

turned out to be an excellent witness, answering questions put by both prosecution and defense with quiet moderation. He did no ranting. He gave no lectures on the innate depravity of mine owners. He did not snarl about "Capitalist civilization." Indeed, his gentleness on the stand seemed to belie his well-known bellicose attitude of a man who believed in force and used it when he could. He flatly denied, though without his natural bellow, any connection with Orchard or knowledge of his movements. Orchard, he said, was merely one of several thousands of miners he knew casually. What was more, he went on, Orchard had long been suspected of dealing with agents and detectives of the mine owners.

In his confession Orchard had admitted to "seeing" detectives for Cripple Creek railroads and giving them information in regard to attempts of strikers to derail trains. Richardson and Darrow, in cross-examination and summary, did all possible to impress the jury that Orchard was no more a tool of the miners than he was of the mine owners.

Prosecution Counsel Hawley worked to some purpose on witnesses to prove to the jury that Orchard had told the truth in everything he had done, no matter how low it placed him in their eyes, and therefore must be telling the truth about the murder of Steunenberg. His approach to a witness was not unlike that of Defense Counsel Richardson. James Hawley was sixty years old in 1907, a gigantic man with a walrus mustache, who had been an Idaho pioneer of 1862. He worked in the mines while studying law, became a lawyer, then a circuit court judge who covered the circuit on horseback. It was told of Hawley that, more than once when a man was convicted, he would handcuff the prisoner and ride him down to Boise and the penitentiary. Of him, Borah said that he had "defended more men and got them acquitted and prosecuted more men and got them convicted than any lawyer in America." Hawley had developed considerable eloquence. Darrow considered him "an old typical pioneer lawyer of the West, a man of ability."

George Kibbe Turner, who was covering the trial for *McClure's Magazine* saw Haywood as built with the physical strength of an ox, a man with a big body, a big head and a square jaw, who had "risen from the bowels of the earth" to become a sort of religious zealot, with Socialism his religion. He had a good brain. He had come up struggling and fighting, giving blows and taking them. He could see nothing "beyond the wrongs to his working class." Turner thought Haywood tough, and warped. Given also Haywood's idealism, "and you had a leader who will bend his people to his own beliefs. We do not expect to find such a leader patient of obstacles, nor far-sighted, nor politic."

Turner's first emotion on seeing Orchard was astonishment. "This is the confessed assassin of eighteen men," he wrote. "In appearance he is like nothing so much as your milkman—the round-headed, ruddy-faced, sandy-mustached milkman, with his good-natured diffidence, breaking easily into an ingenuous smile." But he said Orchard's face showed plainly that "it is no permanent amusement to be a hunted beast." Turner thought it a wanton waste of time to discuss the question of Orchard's sanity, for "he is sane to the point of bleakness. It is a mind direct, practical, concrete, absolutely devoid of imagination. It is this last quality which accounts for the man's utter lack of fear." Turner wrote that Orchard had followed his career of murder as practically as a farmer followed the plow. In an earlier time, Orchard might have been "the invaluable instrument of some petty European sovereign as the most fearless and workmanlike of bravos."

Sane or not, Orchard was worked over by Dr. Hugo Munsterberg, Ph.D., Leipzig, 1885, and M.D., Heidelberg, 1887, who since 1892 had been professor of psychology at Harvard University and who declared that, amazing though Orchard's confession was, the man was telling the truth.

Darrow thought it worthwhile to bring eighty-odd witnesses to the stand to show Orchard was lying in one or more details. Five of these claimed to have heard him make threats against the life of Steunenberg because of Orchard's loss in the rich Hercules mine. On cross-examination Hawley showed all five witnesses had been or were members of a miners' union. Hawley pretended to be aghast that the defense should have put such witnesses on the stand, implying that all of them "were a party to this conspiracy."

After seventy-eight days of grueling legal action, during which Darrow and Hawley displayed great energy and some of the finest invective the press had been privileged to hear, the reservoirs of witnesses for both the state and the defense were exhausted. It was time for Mr. Darrow to make his final plea for Haywood, after which Mr. Borah was to give the closing argument for the state.

21.

Mr. Darrow & Mr. Borah

Mr. Darrow's closing argument for the defense occupied almost eleven hours. Boise was jammed with people, only a small number of whom could get into the courtroom; but the weather was blistering, and all the courthouse windows and doors were open. The lawn and virtually all space around the building was filled with the hopeful, the worried, and the merely curious. Whichever they were, they heard a master of spoken prose, and some caught glimpses of him through the windows.

Dressed in a slouchy gray suit, a wisp of hair falling across his forehead, he liked to walk up and down before the jury, his left hand in a coat pocket, right hand holding his glasses and making gestures of attack, of appeal, astonishment, contempt. His mobile and deeply furrowed face synchronized perfectly with the gestures. So, did the organ that was his voice, emitting snarls where needed, a shout or bellow on occasion, then a purposeful phrase cloaked with an emotional hush, and a whisper of accusation, or pity.

Clarence Darrow was addressing the jury. He was also telling the United States through the assembled men of the press that the trial of Big Bill Haywood was an inquisition as damnable as that of long ago which had burned religious heretics at the stake. The modern inquisition was composed of "the mine-owners of Idaho and Colorado" who with their vast resources of influence and money had subverted the state. The tool of this hellborn combination, namely Harry Orchard, was a true monster who "sought to hand over his friends to the executioners."

First, however, Darrow wanted the jury to know just what the Western Federation of Miners was. It was the federation, not Haywood, he said, that was on trial. And the federation did not exist without good reason. It had come into being to protect at least in some measure the wage slaves from their masters, the greedy and grossly brutal mine operators' associations. Mr. Darrow proceeded to instruct the jury—and the United States—in regard to the plight of the workers in the mines, the mills, and smelters of the Rocky Mountain region.

Before the unions came, these men had worked twelve hours a day in the gloomy bowels of the earth, where the haste and carelessness of hard-pressed overseers had resulted in fires, explosions, and cave-ins beyond knowing. Injury or death always accompanied the meager wages. Conditions were no better above ground. The dreadful fumes of arsenic arose from the ores being treated to paralyze the arms and legs of the workers. Their teeth loosened and fell out. Five years, Darrow estimated, was the average life of men under such conditions.

The local unions had tried to improve matters and had, Darrow said, to some extent succeeded in doing so; yet they quickly discovered they were no match for the mine owners, who banded together in districts to crush the local unions. The need was clear. A few farsighted and courageous miners had formed the Western Federation, which a majority of the unions had joined, and the federation had spread out its protective wings to the helpless and almost hopeless workers.

With new strength, the federation had put a stop to the worst abuses, and had gone on to build and maintain hospitals, reading rooms, and union halls for the comfort and education of its members. It had supported the ill. It had buried the dead. It had cared for the widows and orphans. The Western Federation was becoming so effective, Darrow said, that the fearful mine operators' associations employed secret spies to join the various unions, to take part in Western Federation deliberations, then to betray their associates. "Labor unions," Darrow admitted, "are often brutal, they are often cruel, they are often unjust ... I don't care how many brutalities they are guilty of. I know that their cause is just."

Attorney William E. Borah was not asleep, and he arose to object. "This is merely a murder trial," he said. "We are not fighting organized labor."

Darrow shifted to the subject of Harry Orchard, to wonder aloud whether in Idaho or anywhere else "a man can be placed on trial and lawyers seriously ask to take the life of a human being upon the testimony of Harry Orchard." He paused to contemplate for a moment the object of his unspeakable loathing, who remained placidly cheerful. Then Darrow fairly exploded. "For God's sake," he cried, "what sort of a community exists up here in the state of Idaho that sane men should ask it? Need I come here from Chicago to defend the honor of your state? If twelve jurors could take away the life of a human being because a man like Orchard pointed his finger at him to save his own life, then I would say that human life would be safer in the hands of Harry Orchard than in the hands of a jury that would do it. A man who would believe Orchard would strike a blow against his own manhood and the manhood of all men."

Again, Darrow reiterated the charge he had repeatedly made throughout the trial: "This case, gentlemen, is a case of Harry Orchard from beginning to end. There is nothing at all left in evidence without him."

No matter that Borah called this a murder trial, Darrow now returned to the "class war." "Mr. Haywood," he said, "is not my greatest concern. Other men have died before him. Whenever men have looked upward and onward, worked for the poor and the weak, they have been sacrificed. They have met their deaths, and he can meet his." He turned to direct a baleful glance toward Attorneys Borah and Hawley. "But, you shortsighted men of the prosecution, you men of the mine-owners' associations, you people who would cure hatred with hatred, you who think you can crush out the feelings and the hopes and the aspirations of men by tying a noose around his neck—you who are seeking to kill him not because he is Haywood but because he represents a class—don't be so foolish as to believe you can strangle the Western Federation of Miners when you tie a rope around his neck. If at the behest of this mob you should kill Bill Haywood, he is mortal; he will die, but I want to say that a million men will grab up the banner of labor at the open grave where Haywood lays it down, and in spite of prisons or scaffold or fire, in spite of prosecution or jury or courts, these men of willing hands will carry it on to victory in the end."

Being no man to place too much trust in the retentiveness of the minds of jurors, Darrow now reminded them again who was responsible for this farce of a case against Haywood. It was the Mine owners Protective Association. "The mine owners of Colorado and Idaho," he cried, "are pulling the wires to make *you dance like puppets.*

They gathered these officers of the Western Federation of Miners and sent them here to be tried and hanged." He was also thoughtful of who would have to foot the expense. "Idaho is holding the bag," he told the twelve Idaho farmers and ranchers. "And you men of this jury will have the pleasure of working to pay the deficiency warrants which have been issued by the State to meet the expenses of the prosecution."

For more than ten hours Darrow held the courtroom, and much of the crowd outside, in thrall to his spoken prose. He was never much of a writer, but when on his feet, his great and subtle brain heated to intensity with whatever cause he made his own, he was nothing less than magnificent. Lyrical at times, brutally blunt at others, speech flowed from him like a river, and like a river it was filled with moods, with lights and shadows, with musical cadences as appealing to the ear as its content was moving to the mind, or at least to the emotions. Now he was almost done. It remained for him only to remind the jurors whom he, Clarence Darrow, represented, and to remind the jurors of their responsibility. Not alone to justice, but to humanity.

"I speak for the poor," he told them. (The voice came up from the deeps of misery.) "I speak for the weak, for the weary, for that long line of men who, in darkness and despair, have borne the labors of the human race. Their eyes are upon you twelve men of Idaho tonight. If you kill Haywood, your act will be applauded by many. In the railroad offices of our great cities men will applaud your names. If you decree his death, amongst the spiders of Wall Street will go up paeans of praise for these twelve good men and true. In every bank in the world, where men hate Haywood because he fights for the poor against the accursed system upon which the favored live and grow rich and fat—from all those you will receive blessings and unstinted praise."

Railroads. Banks. Wall Street. In 1907 these things were symbolic words. They conjured up automatically what in many minds were the most sinister forces in the United States. Darrow knew his jury. True, they were not miners. All were or had been farmers. Eleven of them were more than fifty years old. Among them, it seemed likely, must be more than a residue of Populism, the left-wingers of the nineties. That residue of antagonism toward railroads, banks, and Wall Street might of itself be enough to turn the trick. If not, then there remained pity, or at least a feeling of sympathy for the industrial lowly.

"But," said Mr. Darrow in closing, "if your verdict should be 'not guilty' in this case, there are still those who will reverently bow their heads and thank these twelve men for the life and reputation you have saved. Out on our broad prairies where men toil with their hands, out on the wide ocean where men are tossed and buffeted on the waves, through our mills and factories and deep under the earth, thousands of men and of women and children—men who labor, men who suffer, women and children weary with care and toil—these men and these women and these children will kneel tonight and ask their God to guide your hearts."

Darrow's was a masterly summation for the defense, shrewdly calculated to touch jurors in their tender spots, brilliant in its insistence on the class-war motif and devastating in its strictures on the mine operators. In view of the fact that he had developed a vast dislike for Haywood, as was later known, it is perhaps not surprising that Darrow said far less about him than he did of the Western Federation.

Before Borah took the floor for the closing argument, Prosecutor Hawley launched a speech filled with invective against the Western Federation which some present thought did little more than bear out Darrow's assertion that it was the federation and nothing else that was on trial. In any case, Hawley was grossly intemperate. In his closing address, Borah was both temperate, as the moderation of criminal lawyers was then considered, and pretty effective too. There was possibly less poetry in him than in Darrow, yet he marshaled the evidence with consummate skill and with considerable dramatic power. He moved to attack Darrow almost at once.

"Gentlemen," he said to the jury, "if Orchard had not turned state's evidence, he would now be on trial and the eminent counsel from Chicago would be defending him with all the eloquence he possessed instead of denouncing him as the most despicable monster on earth." Yet, after sixty days of trial, during which Orchard had been subjected to the fiercest sort of examination, counsel for the defense had been unable to shake his testimony in the least. Now Mr. Borah reminded the jury what this trial was about. It was about murder, and more.

"I saw that night," he cried, "that bleak winter night with the blood of my dear friend marking the white earth. I saw Idaho dishonored and disgraced. I saw murder—no, a thousand times worse—I saw Anarchy unfold its red menace ..."

(Anarchism was then the epitome of subversiveness.)

Mr. Borah continued: "What a scene we have passed through in these sixty days of trial! Twenty-odd murders proven and not a single man punished. Many blown to pieces. Think of it—laboring men trying to earn their daily bread, trying to plant the dimple of joy upon the faces of prattling babes, trying to drive the shadows from the simple hearth—blown to an unrecognizable mass because they were not union men!" Yet, the prosecution was not fighting union labor. "This trial has no other purpose or implication than conviction and punishment of the assassins of Governor Steunenberg."

Mr. Borah went on to outline the conspiracy which resulted in the murder at the picket-fence gate in Caldwell. One reporter thought Borah's presentation of the state's case could be "likened more than anything else to the setting of a series of mines to blow up the defense." This was the strength of the state's case and "it was greater than the force of the direct proof." Another reporter, O. K. Davis of the *New York Times*, declared that the evidence marshaled by Mr. Borah was "terrific, crushing, destroying."

In the final moments of his argument, Mr. Borah told the jury what they were facing and asked them a question. "Right here at home," he said, "we see Anarchy, that pale, restless hungry demon from the crypts of hell, fighting for a foothold in Idaho! Should we compromise with it? Or should we crush it?" Then he brought the jury back again to the tragic and bereaved home in Caldwell. "I only want," Mr. Borah told the jurors, "what you want—the gates to our homes—the yard gate whose inward swing tells of the returning husband and father, shielded and guarded by the courage and manhood of Idaho juries."

If there were lumps in throats when Mr. Darrow had finished, there were eyes misty when Mr. Borah was done.

Judge Fremont Wood now instructed the jury. It is improbable that any judge was ever put in a more awkward position than this veteran of nearly forty years' experience at the Idaho bar who had just been elected to the bench. His law partner for many years had been Edgar Wilson. As soon as it was established that Judge Wood would preside at Haywood's trial, lawyer Wilson was engaged by the defense as counsel. He had never tried a criminal case, and no reason could be assigned for his employment unless—as one court observer put it—"the defense believed Wilson's long association with Lawyer Wood might have some influence upon Judge Wood." Throughout the trial Wilson sat with defense counsel, mute save for a moment when Darrow instructed him to rise and ask Judge Wood to throw the case out of court. (In later years Judge Wood intimated that, had it not been for Mr. Wilson, he might have done so.)

One need have no knowledge of the judicial mind to appreciate the position of Judge Fremont Wood. On the one hand, he must have known that most of his friends of forty years, together with former clients and conservatives the country over, felt certain that Haywood was a public enemy and would be convicted. On the other hand, radicals everywhere had all along been denouncing Wood as a mere puppet, "a tool of the plutocracy." What both sides may not have taken into consideration was the possibility that Judge Wood was not only a just man but also a most courageous one.

Now that the lawyers were done, he instructed the jury. There was no pettifogging. What he said was clear as crystal. "Gentlemen," he told the twelve men, "under the statutes of this state, a person cannot be convicted of a crime upon testimony of an accomplice, unless such accomplice is corroborated by other evidence."

It was now late Saturday afternoon, July 27. The jury retired. Early Sunday morning guards took Haywood from his cell to the courtroom to hear the verdict. Not guilty. Big Bill arose and shook hands with the jurors. The foreman, Thomas B. Gess, told him that the first ballot had been eight not guilty, two guilty, two not voting. By half-past three in the morning, a fifth ballot showed no change. The jurors agreed to sleep briefly on it. About five o'clock the count stood eleven to one for acquittal. A bit later the one holdout gave in.

Much of Boise was stunned. The usual Sabbath morning quiet of a small city seemed intensified. As one citizen recalled it, "the community was so confident of conviction that the shock was all but paralyzing."

Now a free man, and back in his cell only to pack his things, Haywood noted that, although Pettibone greeted him joyfully and shook his hand, Moyer did not even rise from the chair where he sat reading. "That's good," was all he said. The same afternoon Moyer was released on bail of twenty-five thousand dollars furnished by Butte Miners Union No. 1. Pettibone was to be tried next. He seemed cheerful when Haywood said good-bye and left for Denver.

It still remained to try Pettibone and Moyer. The prosecution announced that before either of these men went on trial, Steve Adams was to be tried again on the charges of having murdered the claim jumpers.

At almost the same time, the federal government announced it was to put lawyer Borah on trial for "irregularities" while acting as an attorney for the late Frank Steunenberg in some land deals. Borah had already been elected United States Senator. He had asked to be excused from taking his seat until the Haywood trial was over. It was now over. The land-deal indictment was generally regarded as a political move. In any case, Borah withdrew from prosecution of Steve Adams and of Pettibone and Moyer and defended himself successfully in the land-case trial. He had little difficulty in quashing the indictment.

Then, before Prosecutor Hawley could prepare for the second trial of Steve Adams, something like a thunderbolt took the headlines from Idaho. On September 30, 1907, at about half-past ten at night, Harvey K. Brown was blown up and fatally mangled when he opened the gate to his home in Baker City on the upper reaches of Powder River in Oregon's Blue Mountains. Baker City was one hundred and fifty miles west of Boise, on the main line of the Union Pacific railroad to Portland.

22.

The Enigma of Harvey Brown

The assassination of Harvey K. Brown was a stunner. Coming in the midst of the sensational trials in Idaho and after more than a year of disclosures about bombings and dynamitings, it made a profound impression, not only in Oregon and Idaho, but wherever newspapers were read in the United States. Both in method and timing it seemed as if calculated to serve as warning—warning that the "Anarchists" were still paying off old scores, that their reign of terrorism was to continue. Consider that Brown like Steunenberg was murdered at the gate of his own home, at night, and by explosive. Bear in mind that Brown was slated to be a witness in the approaching second trial of Steve Adams.

Who was Brown? On the night of the Steunenberg murder, he just happened to be in Caldwell on business. He was then sheriff of Baker County, Oregon. It was he who identified "Thomas Hogan" as Harry Orchard. A few days later, at the request of the State of Idaho, he had arrested Steve Adams, who was then homesteading near Baker City. He had persuaded Adams to waive extradition and to accompany Captain Swain, of the Thiele Detective agency, to Boise and to give himself up. Adams had done this, so he later told Darrow, because Brown had given him to understand he would not be prosecuted for anything—that is, if he would act to "corroborate Harry Orchard's confession" in regard to the Steunenberg murder. Adams, it will be recalled, made a confession of partnership with Orchard in several other crimes, then repudiated it. He was then tried on a charge of murder in the claim jumpers case. The jury disagreed. He was about to be tried a second time when the bomb went off at the gate of Brown's home.

The explosion broke windows up and down the street. Brown was terribly hurt. He died the next day, but not before he requested that the district attorney be sent for. To him Brown made a statement, and died soon after, leaving a widow and a daughter, Ethel, aged thirteen.

Harvey K. Brown's life was filled with pioneer flavor. Thirty-six years old at the time of his death, he was a native of Baker County who at sixteen had been a stage driver on the run from Baker City to the Elkhorn mines. He had been a miner in the Sumpter Valley; and at Sumpter town operated a livery stable. In 1901 he was elected sheriff and re-elected to a second term. He operated a small mine of his own.

Baker County had come into existence as a result of a modest gold strike and a typical rush to the diggings. In 1907 perhaps two score mines were still operating, mostly in the Sumpter Valley. Life in that region was more characteristic of mining districts than of the cattle, wheat, and sheep country which ranged over so much of eastern Oregon. Baker County was specifically known for its free-and-easy attitude about saloons and gambling houses. They never closed. During his second term, however, Sheriff Brown proposed to close them. He did not succeed in doing so, but the accompanying publicity gave him the urge to run for the office of governor of Oregon. He was defeated. At the time of his death he occupied himself with his mine and real estate interests.

Why was Brown killed? Here we come to an enigma of such density as to make one believe the affair was the work of a master of riddles, a killer dedicated to a labyrinth of possible clues. There were many clues. Each was to glimmer brightly, one after the other, like foxfire in a swamp, then go out.

The method was remindful of Harry Orchard and Steve Adams, who, by then, had been in jail or prison for more than a year. The plagiarist placed the Brown bomb just inside the gate. It was operated by hand. The attached wire ran along the top of the picket fence about twenty-five feet to the street corner, where it dropped to the ground and continued in a gutter for another forty feet to a telegraph pole, around which it made a couple of turns. At the end of the wire were brass knuckles, a piece of offensive armor popular with plug-uglies and smalltime thugs. The significance of the brass knuckles was nothing more than that its owner was familiar with the ways of strong-arm criminals. Schoolboys of the time knew as much from the columns of *The National Police Gazette*, in which advertisements for brass knuckles appeared regularly.

So much for the method. As to motive, the immediate and automatic opinion of most Baker people was that their prominent townsman had been murdered by agents of the Western Federation of Miners. Had it not been Brown who identified Harry Orchard? And while her mortally wounded husband still lived, Mrs. Brown told District Attorney Lomax that "Harvey has been in low spirits lately." He had told her, "I am a doomed man. I have been slated for removal." The dying man's statement to the district attorney seems not to have been published, though Lomax gave a reporter the gist of it: Brown laid the bomb to the fact that he "had done work for the State of Idaho on the Orchard case." Unnamed friends of Brown were more explicit. They said he had recently confided to them that he "did not want to take the stand against Steve Adams" for the simple reason that, if he did so, he would *never escape from Idaho alive*."

Thus, the first news story sent out from Baker City indicated that Ex-Sheriff Brown was a victim of the same anarchists responsible for the death of Ex-Governor Steunenberg. Then, somebody in Baker City remembered that Brown, while sheriff, had received anonymous threats "because of his efforts to put a stop to booze and gambling." Mrs. Brown commented that no threats of such nature had been received by her late husband "in a long time." What was more, the lid on liquor and gambling in Baker County had never been really closed and it had been distinctly off well over a year. All places were operating as if Brown had never raised voice against them. Yet, reporters interviewed a local preacher, a fanatical "temperance" man, who insisted that Brown had been done in by "murderous rum-sellers."

Four days after the explosion, and three days after Brown had died, opinion returned to place the Western Federation as the guilty party. A close friend of the family let it be known that only recently Brown had increased the amount of his life insurance from ten thousand to twenty-seven thousand five hundred dollars. The widow added that her late husband had become so uneasy, during recent months, that he told her they would "move to California to live before winter came."

Interviewed in Boise, Clarence Darrow told the press that "the effort to make it appear" that the Western Federation was responsible for the outrage was "quite in keeping with the Policy of the prosecution to make it appear that the federation is to blame for every crime in the world." That, of course, was propaganda. But Darrow also gave the press a fact or two. "Harvey K. Brown," he said, "was friendly to the defense of Steve Adams. We paid him to go to Wallace to testify for Adams. To testify that he, Brown, had told Adams he would be properly cared for if he would corroborate Harry Orchard." When the reporter got that down, Darrow added that "Brown was to have been a most important witness for the defense when Adams was put on trial a second time." If this was true, it was most confusing. It was to become more so.

The Baker City police seemed confused. So, did men from the sheriff's office. Even the bloodhounds brought from Walla Walla hardly knew which way to turn. By the time the dogs arrived, the scene of the crime had been trampled over by a good part of Baker City's population. There being as yet no real suspect, and no sign of clothing left behind, there was nothing to offer the hounds as a scent to work on. The animals wandered aimlessly around the Brown yard, sniffing. After quite a while they moved, though with no enthusiasm, toward "the home of a woman known to be a friend of Western Federation people." The dogs seem not to have come very near the house, yet officers got a search warrant. The woman made them welcome, telling them to look where they would. They did. Nothing "of a suspicious nature was found." The dogs went back to Walla Walla.

By this time Baker City had attracted many of the reporters and press association men who had been covering affairs in Boise. They thought that the investigation of the Harvey K. Brown murder had been badly bungled from the start. Private Detective Swain of the Thiele agency complained that the local police were doing nothing and wanted no help from anybody in doing it. There were also a dozen or more officious citizens who were independently "developing clues" and listening to the imaginative stories of those neurotic individuals who have always bedeviled the investigation of crime.

For instance: Although nobody was ready to swear that he or she had been an actual witness to the explosion of the bomb, there was presently a growing army of patent liars who had caught fleeting glances of a mysterious trio moving through the pitch-dark night of ill-lighted Baker City. According to whom you talked with, this trio was variously three men, or two women and a man, or two men and a woman. And there were those who were certain that one was "a man dressed as a woman." In any case, these three wraiths went hither and yon during the night of murder, walking the streets, moving cross lots, ranging the railroad yards, and even fording the Powder River.

On October 7, in the nearby mining hamlet of Granite, a man known as Frank Tucker became drunk in the Fawn saloon and said that *he* knew who killed Harvey K. Brown; that the bomb had been made of nitroglycerine and white-pine sawdust; and that he, Frank Tucker, had been offered one hundred dollars to participate in the job. He was arrested by Town Marshal Thornburg and taken to Sumpter, metropolis of the mine district, for questioning. By the time reporters arrived in Sumpter, Frank Tucker turned out to be "a harmless logger who has boozed until he has lost control of his faculties."

Tucker had no more than been disposed of when, at Colfax, trading center of the Palouse wheat-growing country of Washington, a Frank Page was arrested because he had bragged that "he knew all about the killing of Brown." Whether or not his "knowledge" was derived from the bottle isn't known. He was soon turned loose.

On the same day, in Pocatello, Idaho, an unnamed man who was known to have been an intimate friend of Brown told police that, for many months before his murder, the ex-sheriff had been "trying to run down Jack Simpkins." Though the informant was not then or later identified in the press, he must have been taken seriously by both reporters and police. Here might be a motive for the destruction of Brown. Simpkins was the Coeur d'Alene miner, member of the Western Federation's board of directors, who—according to Orchard—had engaged Steve Adams to help with the murder of the two claim jumpers; and who, moreover, had spent some time with Orchard in Caldwell casing the town in preparation for the assassination of Frank Steunenberg. It will be recalled that, simultaneously with Orchard's arrest, Simpkins disappeared so completely that neither the Western Federation officials nor detectives for the state of Idaho had been able to find him. Both the prosecution, and possibly too the defense, wanted to talk to Jack Simpkins.

Corroboration of the information in Pocatello now came from T. S. Hammersley, chief of police at the Oaks, an amusement park at Portland, Oregon. Hammersley had formerly been a police officer in Baker City. He had worked on cases with Sheriff Harvey K. Brown. Brown had been in Portland shortly before his death to talk with Hammersley. What he told the Portland officer indicated that Brown had indeed been looking for Simpkins.

"Brown had an undercover man in the miners' union at Bourne, Oregon," Hammersley said. Bourne was a mining camp in the Sumpter Valley district of Baker County. Hammersley intimated that this undercover man was getting information about Simpkins for Brown. Brown learned from some source that Simpkins was "sweet on a girl in Walla Walla, Washington." Brown went to Walla Walla and discovered that Simpkins had been there at least three times during the past summer, and that on one of these visits "had purchased a violin in a Walla Walla music store."

And that was the last one hears of Jack Simpkins. It is a tantalizing thought—Simpkins, the direct-actionist, the mine union official, the man who knew what to do with claim jumpers, stealing quietly into old Walla Walla to make love and to buy, of all things, a violin. Was the instrument a gift to his sweetheart, or for his own use? The record doesn't say. Harry Orchard and Steve Adams both knew Simpkins as a jolly fellow, but do not mention any musical instrument. Nor do they leave any idea of his appearance. Yet he once posed for a picture.

It was an official photograph, taken in 1905, of "The Executive Board of the Western Federation of Miners," and shows ten soberly self-conscious men at a paper-strewn table. Nine are seated. The tenth is "L. J. Simpkins," and he stands with hands resting in comradely fashion on the shoulders of board members James Kirwan and Frank Schmelzer. He appears to be of medium height, and round-shouldered. His nose is more than merely large; it is prominent. His mustache is a sweeping affair, possibly the heaviest among the seven displayed by the executive board. When it came time for him to disappear, shaving such a rich ornament as that mustache would surely have changed his visage, but the enormous nose had to remain. Yet Brown never caught up with him, nor did any other detective.[11]

---

11 Sometime after the disappearance of Simpkins, a personable woman was engaged as nursemaid to the children of B. R. Lewis, well-to-do lumberman of Spokane. She was both efficient and likable, and remained more than a year. Only when she left did she tell her employer she was the wife—not the widow—of the still-notorious Jack Simpkins. The Lewises never again heard from or of her.

As October approached its end, the motive for killing Brown seemed to grow as clear as the mystery of who killed him deepened. The motive for murder concerned Brown's connection with the arrest and confession of Steve Adams. A contributing factor may have been Brown's search for Jack Simpkins, but this seemed less likely.

What was still far from clear was *which* side, the prosecution or the defense, would profit more, or even at all, by Brown's removal? Thiele Detective Captain Swain pointed to what he termed "two very good reasons why the Western Federation wanted Brown killed." One was their standard practice "to terrorize and intimidate all witnesses against Haywood, Adams, and the others." The second reason, which took into consideration the claims of both prosecution and defense—that each had paid Brown "for work done"—was that the Western Federation wanted Brown killed "because of what they thought was his duplicity." He had "talked Adams into a phony confession." He had later accepted Western Federation money to testify for Adams in the trial at Wallace. Meanwhile, he was "taking prosecution money for trying to run Jack Simpkins to earth." The confusion was compounded when J. W. Lillard, an uncle of Steve Adams by marriage, told the press that he, Lillard, had "in his possession his own canceled checks to prove" he had paid Brown to go to Wallace to testify for Adams.

Harry Orchard was interviewed by a reporter. His opinion was that "Harvey K. Brown was murdered as revenge for work Brown had done in helping the State get evidence in the assassination of Governor Steunenberg."

Attorney William E. Borah, about to take his seat in the United States Senate, was of the opinion that "no evidence yet uncovered points toward the Western Federation" as the party guilty of Brown's murder.

The affair of Harvey K. Brown is as deep a mystery today as it was in 1907. It is not mentioned in the several biographies of Clarence Darrow, or in Darrow's autobiography. Of all the many summaries of the Steunenberg-Orchard-Haywood case, only that of Mark Sullivan devotes so much as a line to the assassination of Brown. Sullivan puts it in a footnote, remarking that "it was generally supposed to be in retaliation for his (Brown's) identification of Orchard and to prevent his being a witness in the subsequent trial of one of the inner circle of the Western Federation of Miners." Half a century later the fading folklore of Baker County seems to agree with Sullivan. Yet not even folklore names the killer of Harvey Brown. It seems almost certain he was a lone operator, for in fifty years there has been no leak by an accomplice. Whoever he may have been, he left no fishline or plaster of Paris in a hotel room. He did not mix giant caps and sulphuric acid in a pocket. Possibly he committed what is called a perfect crime, a crime without a suspect. Less rare than a perfect crime, but rare enough, is a perfect disappearance. Jack Simpkins accomplished the latter feat. It would be tempting to relate Simpkins to Harvey Brown's murderer, were there anything to go on. But there isn't. One must leave him—or them—safe in the snug harbor of the port of missing men.

No matter what Harvey K. Brown was to testify, the second trial of Steve Adams was pretty much a replica of the first. It was held (after a change of venue) in Rathdrum, a farming community in Kootenai County, Idaho. Though ill with an ear infection, Darrow made the long and arduous trip from Boise to take charge of the defense. Richardson had returned to Denver. Hawley prosecuted without the help of United States Senator Borah.

Though Darrow was "much in agony" from his ear trouble, he boarded and roomed for nearly two months at the home of Mr. and Mrs. William Cleland, who gave him a "warm welcome and tender consideration." Mrs. Cleland was rehearsing a piece she was to play and sing at an entertainment to be given by the Eastern Star ladies. It was the popular "Redwing," and, "at times when I seemed to be in less distress," his landlady would slip into the parlor and soon the melancholy story of poor Redwing, "weeping her heart away," would permeate the house. Years later Darrow remarked that the melody and words had never left him, and he expected they would be haunting his ear "when I am falling into the final sleep."

Darrow ref erred to the second trial of Steve Adams as dealing mostly "with a skeleton in the forest." The skull of the claim jumper, with the bullet hole, together with the bones, lay for days on a table in the courtroom. "Once more," as Darrow remembered it, "the doctor lovingly handled the skull and, pointing to the fracture, gave it as his scientific opinion that the deceased had come to his death by a shot piercing the skull. Again, lawyers wearily put on witnesses and examined them and cross-examined them by the hour. Over again the story was related to the jury, impressing upon the twelve men their evident intelligence, the importance of the trial in the affairs of the universe, and urging them to be fair and honest though the heavens fall."

As at the first trial, the jury could not agree and were discharged. Adams, however, was not set free. He was returned to Boise and installed in a house in the penitentiary yard, where Mrs. Adams kept house for him. Darrow tried to have Adams admitted to bail. The court refused.

The infection in Darrow's ear grew steadily worse. By the time Pettibone's trial came up on the docket, Darrow had been to see specialists in Portland and San Francisco. He was confined to his bed in the St. Francis Hotel in the latter city when a wire from Boise advised him that Pettibone's trial was to begin. He sought to get more time but was refused. Darrow's doctor thought that returning to Idaho might be fatal to Darrow, and Pettibone telegraphed cheerily that it would be fatal to *him* if Darrow didn't come. Darrow went.

Pettibone's trial was something of an anticlimax. Though the courtroom was filled to capacity every day, nothing like the tense excitement that attended Haywood's trial developed. Harry Orchard took the stand to repeat his confession. Instead of abusing him as a monster, this time Darrow treated him with pseudo kindness and consideration, even pity, seeking to have the by-now-sophisticated witness elaborate on his more horrible deeds. For instance, he asked if Orchard knew how many guests were in the Idan-ha Hotel when he registered there with his black valise. He inquired if Orchard had known that "the man living in the top flat of the San Francisco apartment house had a tiny girl." He reminded Orchard of the abandoned wife and children in Ontario, and wondered aloud, and ever so kindly, "if you have considered how it would affect them to know of your life in the West."

DARROW'S ILLNESS GREW WORSE. EVEN Pettibone urged him to quit. He returned to the courtroom once more, to sit propped up in a chair and to tell the jury "what we expect to prove." Then he told the court he was compelled to leave the case. He went to Los Angeles, where he entered the California hospital and was attended by a whole battery of specialists. He was pleased, though not surprised, seven days later when a telegram informed him that Pettibone had been acquitted.

The latter was freed and returned to Denver. The case against Moyer was dropped. So was the prosecution of Steve Adams after a jury in Telluride, Colorado, where he had been moved from Boise, failed to convict him on a charge of shooting Arthur Collins, manager of the Smuggler-Union mine there.

It was now March. The year was 1908. More than two years had passed since Orchard's arrest and confession. Of those who had been indicted in the murder of Frank Steunenberg, only Jack Simpkins and Orchard remained to be tried. Simpkins was not available. Orchard was arraigned before Judge Fremont Wood, who had presided at the Haywood and Pettibone trials. Orchard changed his plea to guilty. Judge Wood sentenced him to death by hanging and set May15 for the time of execution. Having done as much, the judge made judicial recommendation to the Idaho Board of Pardons of commutation from death to life imprisonment. It was granted by the Board with the approval of the jury and the lawyers for the prosecution. It is of interest to know that Orchard himself refused to sign the application.

In passing judgment upon Orchard, Judge Wood made it clear he believed the man had spoken nothing but the truth, and that he considered Haywood and Pettibone guilty. No statement did more to clarify an affair which for more than two years had bewildered honest people and left them to wonder if Western United States had been taken over by dynamite-laden thugs wearing the false face of Labor, or by cynical and greedy mine operators posing as the Law. With a minimum of legal phraseology, Judge Wood explained why Haywood, though guilty, had been freed. He told why he believed Harry Orchard. He sounded a warning. And without oratorical reference to Capital or Labor, or to Patriotism or Anarchism, he stated the purpose and duty of American courts.

"I am more than satisfied," said Judge Fremont Wood of Boise, Idaho, "that the defendant now at the bar of this court awaiting final sentence has not only acted in good faith in making the disclosures that he did, but that he also testified fully and fairly to the whole truth, withholding nothing that was material, and declaring nothing which had not actually taken place. During the two trials to which I have referred [Haywood's and Pettibone's], the testimony of the defendant covered a long series of transactions, involving personal relations between himself and many others.

"In the first trial he was subjected to the most critical of cross-examinations by very able counsel for at least six days, and I do not now recall that at any point he contradicted himself in any material matter, but on the other hand disclosed his connection with the commission of many other crimes that were probably not known to the attorneys for the State. Upon the second trial referred to, the same testimony was given, a most thorough and critical cross-examination of the witness followed, and in no particular was there any discrepancy in a material matter between the testimony given upon the latter trial, as compared with the testimony given by the same witness on the former trial."

Remarking that it had been his particular province to observe and follow Orchard during the trials, Judge Wood went on to give his reasons for belief in the witness.

"I am of the opinion," said he, "that no man living could conceive the stories of crime told by him and maintain himself under the cross-examination of the attorneys for the State, unless upon the theory that he was testifying to facts and circumstances which had an actual existence within his own experience. A child can testify truly and maintain itself on cross-examination. A man may be able to frame his story and testify falsely to a brief statement of facts involving a short single transaction and maintain himself on cross-examination. But I cannot conceive of a case where even the greatest intellect can conceive a story of crime covering years of duration, with constantly shifting scenes and changing characters, and maintain that story with circumstantial detail as to times, places, persons, and particular circumstances, and under as merciless a cross-examination as was ever given to a witness in an American court—unless the witness thus testifying was speaking truth—fully and without any attempt either to misrepresent or conceal."

Coming now to the juries and their verdicts, the judge observed that the truth of Orchard's testimony was in no manner impugned by the fact that Haywood and Pettibone were found by the juries to be not guilty. "The statute of the State," he declared, "imposes a bar of conviction on the testimony of an accomplice alone, no matter though he be believed by the jury, unless there is other and independent evidence tending to connect the defendant on trial with the commission of the crime. In each of the cases tried, the court, at the written request of each of the defendants, instructed the jury that a verdict of not guilty did not mean that the defendant on trial was innocent, but rather that his guilt had not been proved beyond a reasonable doubt in the manner and form prescribed by law. For these reasons it is at once apparent that verdicts of the juries referred to are not necessarily at variance with the views here expressed."

Having thus clarified the law of evidence as it applied to the cases of Haywood and Pettibone, Judge Wood thought it worthwhile to touch on another matter. "I want," said he, "to take the opportunity to say to the associates in crime of this defendant that they cannot by such acts terrorize American executives and prevent them from performing their plain duties, and they cannot prevent American courts from declaring the law exactly as they find it." This, too, was clear enough. It could have left little doubt as to Judge Wood's opinion in regard to the high command of the Western Federation of Miners.

When the judge was done, Harry Orchard was returned to the penitentiary where he had already spent more than two years, "awaiting disposition" of his case, a sort of transient boarder, so to speak, who might be hanged, or even released. This time, however, he was in for life, and life for Orchard turned out to be quite a span. When he was officially dressed in at the Idaho prison, only a few more than fourteen hundred unfortunates had preceded him. The number on his uniform was 1406.

Part Five

Retirement

Part Five

Retirement

23.

A Ward of the State

Orchard was for forty-eight years an inmate of the Idaho penitentiary. This was a considerable stretch, in the argot of convicts, and in time one came to hear the brag, at least in Idaho, that No. 1406 was the oldest prisoner in the United States in point of service. This was far from the case. In Massachusetts was Jesse Pomeroy, a sadistic killer of little children, who remained in prison seventy-six years and died there, in 1952, aged ninety-two.

Yet, Harry Orchard's spectacular crimes and longevity combined to set him apart from the common run; in the scale of values among convicts, which is not wholly unlike the various ratings of fame outside prisons, he was something of a celebrity. He seems not to have been particularly pleased with the distinction until time began somewhat to fade it. By then time had also worked to make him into the Old Nestor of the penitentiary, a part he played extremely well, and which one feels he enjoyed immensely.

Unlike another and even more notorious prisoner who wrote poetry in *Reading Gaol*, Orchard was not to find prison a place where only what was good in men "wasted and withered away." True, the early period was hard going, and as with the *Reading* convict each day was like a year, "a year whose days are long." In those days, the walls were strong, and bars *did* make a cage. But then came the "miracle" which caused Orchard to think of himself as the Man God Made Again. It is clear from the diary he kept during much of forty-eight years, and from his letters and other writings, that, of all those seventeen thousand and five hundred days, the incomparable moment came for him on the ninth day of January 1909, when he was baptized in the prison's "big plunge bath" by W. W. Steward, a pastor of the Seventh-Day Adventist Church. From that moment until his last, Orchard was not only a "model prisoner" but a most industrious one and probably as happy a lifer as could be found anywhere.

His first occupation as a convict was taking care of the pigs and chickens whose quarters were just outside the Big Wall. He asked for the job, possibly the most unpopular at the pen, knowing that only trusties were permitted outside the prison. Warden Whitney remarked that he "would trust Orchard anywhere," and Harry started work with a will, and intelligence. He repaired the worst pens and sties, built new ones. He borrowed books and trade papers dealing with hogs and poultry from the Boise Public Library. He liked both the work and the comparative freedom. But his reputation soon brought an end to the arrangement. When it became known that "this villainous man" was a trusty, cries of protest and alarm were made by Boise people. The warden felt constrained to move him inside.

For a while he worked as a meat cutter in the commissary. Later he was set to work in the shoe shop and here he displayed such ability and ambition that he was put in charge and the department enlarged until twenty convicts worked at making shoes for wards of the state in the penitentiary and other institutions. In his spare time Orchard set his talented fingers, so used to delicate work in other fields, to the making of fancy bridles. For these he got as much as forty dollars each. When the shoe shop was done away with because of the objections of union labor, Orchard began making fine hair and clothes brushes. This craft lasted him for several years, and from his income of "many hundreds of dollars" he sent all but one tenth to the wife and daughter he had abandoned in Ontario. The tithe was for the Lord's work. "There are many passages in the Book," he said, "to support this sound Bible system of finance. I commend it to all."

Sometime around 1930 Orchard was permitted to build the little house within the Big Wall where he lived almost to his last day. Meanwhile, he suggested starting a flock of turkeys. The big birds, along with chickens, became a source of pride. He read everything on poultry he could find. He tested foods, corresponded with experts in animal husbandry at agricultural colleges. At the least sign of any of the many distempers to which turkeys are prone, he was quick to isolate and treat the ill. The chicken and turkey flocks each grew to thousands of birds.

It seems unfortunate that nearly all of those portions of Orchard's continuous diary which were published had to do almost wholly with spiritual matters and are repetitious. One would have liked to know what comment, if any, he made when in 1909 he learned of the death of George Pettibone; and the passing later of other figures such as Steve Adams and Charlie Moyer. The diary is said to contain "notations on commonplace events" such as visitors, pardons for convicts, prison breaks, suicides, runaways brought back; of "repeaters," hangings, changes of wardens, and prison rules. But the published extracts are mostly to tell of Orchard's "daily walk with God."

It is not the plan of this book, nor is it within the competence of the author, to pass judgment on Orchard's conversion. He told this story himself in the book he was working on when I visited him, and which was brought out many years later.[12] By the time I met him, Orchard had long since entered the Old Nestor phase, an authority on poultry, hogs, and several crafts, on Idaho weather, prison history, on the Bible and the reformation of criminals. He told me, a little wistfully, that many of his efforts to bring fellow convicts to penitence and reformation had doubtless failed. This was so, he thought, because "God's promises all have a condition. They do not come automatically for the asking." It was something you had to work at, hard and long. Yet, he never became discouraged. He continued to tell other unfortunates how it had been in the old bad days with Harry Orchard. "I found myself," he told them, "a hopeless, helpless wreck, high and dry upon a bleak barren shore." But he had appealed to God for mercy, for pardon, and they were given to him.

He did not mean he would lose God's grace by indifference. Most of the early portions of his diary that were made public contained a line of five capital letters thus: "G D S, B G," which stood for "Good day spiritually, Bless God." They varied on occasion to appear as

---

12   *Harry Orchard, The Man God Made Again,* by Harry Orchard in collaboration with LeRoy Edwin Froom. Another book which deals in part with Orchard is *Greater Love,* by Frank W. Steunenberg, Mountain View, California: Pacific Press Publishing Association. This work is dedicated to its author's parents, the late Governor Frank Steunenberg and his wife. Both books are published by departments of the Seventh-Day Adventist Church.

"Very G D S, Bless God," or even "Splendid etc. etc." Now and again, however, after what one judges must have been notable struggles with the Archfiend, he admitted the fact and wrote it plain: "Not Very Good Day Spiritually."

In the opinion of Elder Frank Steunenberg, son of Orchard's last victim, there were three influences of an "outward nature" which brought about Orchard's "ultimate decision." In a letter to me he listed them as follows: "First, the fact that there had appeared in the newspapers a statement of forgiveness on the part of my mother; Second, my mother sent him a little religious inspiration book, *Steps to Christ*, and other literature; and Third, the gift of a Bible by Dr. David Paulson of Illinois." Elder Steunenberg added that, contrary to a persistent legend, his mother "did not go to the prison and plead with Orchard to become a Christian, as the story has often been told."

Soon after Orchard's confession to Detective McParlan, the prisoner attended a Sunday afternoon service held in the penitentiary by the Reverend Edwin S. Hinks, dean of St. Michael's Cathedral (Episcopal) at Boise and asked if he might see the good man alone. "Almost immediately," wrote Dean Hinks, "he came to the point on which he desired my expression of opinion: Was he, as a murderer, shut out from hope of God's forgiveness?" The dean replied that neither in the Old Testament nor in the New Testament Scriptures "was there a single word to preclude a penitent from an honest approach to God, whose forgiveness and pardon are full and free." Quite soon Orchard was at work preparing his confession for publication as a book, remarking to Dean Hinks that his object was to present a warning against taking "the first steps in a path of reckless living that so rapidly ends in pain." The cleric was glad to write a personal note of introduction for the book, in which he had some interesting things to say of Orchard.

"As I comprehend the transformation of Harry Orchard," he wrote, "from reckless criminality to a penitent willing to tell the truth, I feel that the world should understand that his change of front was not in the order of religious conversion, then moral perception, leading to confession. No! It seems to me the order was first physical, second moral, and finally religious.

"He was wretched behind stone walls, lonely as cut off from freedom and old associations; hence he fairly craved the sympathy which he got in the unburdening of his mind to McParlan. ... This confession, to my mind, evinces the first real, moral change in the man." Which seems to say that a regime of solitary confinement has its points.

24.

He Reads the Papers

Number 1406 did not merely vegetate for forty-eight years. He used up a lot of energy in the shoe shop and on those hogs, chickens, and turkeys. He obtained the comfort of religion. He enjoyed the security of the pen. He also read the newspapers, a habit he had acquired in the days when he himself was making no little news that more often than not appeared on the front page.

Now in prison, Orchard was what editors like to call a Constant Reader. He read not only the Boise paper but also the *Spokesman-Review* of Spokane, whose news field included the Coeur d'Alenes. The boon of the Spokane daily was due to "a former north Idaho banker" who, because of some slip or other, was for many years an inmate of the penitentiary. The fallen Midas had managed to retain sufficient cash to subscribe to the Spokane paper and was happy to pass it along to his fellow convict every day.

From two excellent daily papers Orchard kept up with affairs, both foreign and domestic. He could have read, not long after the Idaho trials, of the death in Denver of his old friend George Pettibone and learned of the automobile accident which killed E. A. Richardson, the Western Federation attorney who had so ferociously cross-examined Orchard at the Haywood trial.

Bombs were still going off. Within a year after his baptism in prison, Orchard could have read of the explosion, at one o'clock in the morning of October 1, 1910, in the *Times* building, Los Angeles, when twenty employees were killed. The press agreed it had been a "unionist bomb," but Job Harriman, the Socialist attorney, investigated matters, then announced the explosion was due to leaking gas in the plant of this "notoriously antiunion newspaper." Reading this in the Boise pen, the man who had blown Fred Bradley into the street may well have guessed where Harriman got *that* idea.

Though James McParlan still lived, the hero detective of the *Times* affair was a younger man, William J. Burns, who arrested the brothers McNamara, James B. and John J., and one Ortie McManigal, whom at least one newspaper referred to as "a man of the Harry Orchard type." Eugene Debs was still active, and in the *Appeal to Reason* he wrote that this case was to be a "repetition of the Moyer-Haywood-Pettibone outrage. Be not deceived by the slimy Capitalist press," he warned; but "Arouse, ye hosts of Labor, and swear that the villainous plot shall not be consummated!"

It was a long affair. Some two years later Ortie McManigal had turned state's evidence, was free, and had "disappeared"; the two "McNamara Boys" had confessed and were in prison; and a whole slew of hatchet men of the International Association of Bridge & Structural Iron Workers had been tried on various charges, in a dynamite conspiracy, and most of them convicted. The prosecution, as Orchard may have been interested to read, offered six hundred and twenty exhibits in evidence—pieces of exploded bombs, fuses, cans of nitroglycerin, and other ordnance. To a newer generation, the name of McNamara came to mean terrorism much as Harry Orchard's had meant in the past.

Clarence Darrow turned up again as counsel for the defense. This time things went badly for him. Without notice to him, their chief attorney, the McNamaras changed their not-guilty pleas to guilty. The case ended in fiasco. Darrow was then tried twice for jury bribing, resulting in a hung jury and an acquittal.

Reading of the many bombings and the wholesale arrests and convictions, old hatchet man of the of the Western Federation of Miners must have been grateful all over again for the peace and security of the penitentiary, to say nothing of his having been born anew.

Poor Charlie Moyer, still head of the Western Federation, was getting into the news again. He was having more troubles than one man should be made to bear. While a strike for union recognition in Utah and Nevada was being lost, local unions in the copper country of Michigan's Keweenaw Peninsula got out of hand and, against Moyer's advice and even pleading, voted to strike. Their demands centered on "doing something about" the new one-man drilling machine which not only was "too heavy for one man to set up" but was resulting in fewer jobs. Moyer did not believe the unions were strong enough to win the strike. He tried to have it arbitrated. Matters were dragging along thus when, on Christmas Eve (1913), the women's auxiliary of the Western Federation held a party for miners' children in a hall at Calumet, Michigan. Hundreds of youngsters and their parents crowded the premises. At the height of the merriment somebody shouted "Fire!"

Next day, newspapers the country over, including those in Boise and Spokane told of seventy-two lives lost by fire or in the stampede of panic. On the night after the tragedy, Charles Moyer, in a hotel room at nearby Hancock, was taken by unidentified thugs, who beat him, shot him through the back, dragged him through the streets, and put him aboard a train for Chicago. No one was ever arrested for the outrage. Three months later the district union called the strike off. The Western Federation's historian, Vernon H. Jensen, was to write that "the defeat in Michigan irreparably weakened the organization."

Worse, much worse, was coming, as the "biggest copper camp on earth" broke into the headlines. Bill Haywood's Wobblies, the I.W.W., had been active in Butte with the idea of wrecking the Western Federation before it could carry out Moyer's plan to amalgamate with the United Mine Workers of America. In June 1914, close on the heels of a most riotous celebration of Miners' Union Day in Butte, Moyer arrived to find that the Western Federation's union had been voted out of existence and a new union formed, of which one Muckey McDonald had been elected president. Moyer also discovered that the federation union's cash and records had disappeared. He called a meeting in the federation's staunch old union hall. "That night," recalled John Sullivan, a Butte miner since 1884, "that night was the one Butte never forgot."

Safe in the penitentiary, reading the ex-banker's Spokane paper, Orchard saw that the tables had been turned and that the Western Federation had become the target of demolition squads. Moyer was just making a speech to the one hundred or so faithful federation men who showed up in the hall. Outside in the street some three thousand other miners gathered. They were merely waiting for something to set off the expected wide-open brawl. A miner named Bruneau supplied it. Waving a union card in his hand, he started up the stairs to the meeting place. Somebody there started to shoot. Bruneau went down.

The crowd outside blew up.

The street mob shouted to "kill the Federation fakers." Guns appeared at every window in the hall and opened fire. The street cleared, save for two men bleeding all over the sidewalk. Within a few minutes many of the mob returned, this time with rifles and revolvers. They began to shoot into the hall. There was no return fire. Moyer and the "federation fakers" had escaped out a back door.

While the street crowd milled around, a delegation of their fellows—Wobblies, said the press—went to the West Stewart mine. At gun point they forced the engineer to lower them down the shaft. They forced a shift boss to lead them to the powder magazine. They helped themselves to the explosive. Within a short time, they were packing dynamite into the federation hall building.

"Every window in Butte rattled," John Sullivan noted, "but only a part of one wall fell. She was a well-built hall." Indeed, she was. It was only with the twenty-fifth blast, long after midnight, that the boys considered the job done. Except for a piece of one wall, the building was a mass of bricks and mortar. "That and a thousand headaches," said John Sullivan, "was about all that was left in the morning to remind Butte of the old union hall and the Western Federation."

Harry Orchard could hardly have missed the news from Butte, and perhaps reflected about what happens to those who take the sword, as reported by Matthew 26. Two days later he could read what Charlie Moyer himself said about it. "The wrecking crew of the I.W.W.," said the Western Federation's president, "is the force at work in Butte. They started six years ago to get me and failing that they determined to get the federation." (One can only wonder if in his diary Orchard made any comment other than "G D S, B G," or "Very G D S, BG.")

Staunch old Debs refused to concede, at least in public, that the dynamiters of the Butte hall were other than "employees of the Waddell-Mahon Detective Agency who were also members of the I.W.W." Debs spoke of Moyer, then whom, said he, "there is not a man in the labor movement who has gone through more that is calculated to try men's souls and break their hearts in the last ten years." One who has seen the record is likely to agree with Mr. Debs.

Little matter who blew up the old hall in Butte, Bill Haywood's Wobblies were becoming the violent sensation of the American labor scene,

25.

The Shadows Grow Longer

It was a dull week indeed, for nearly two decades after 1907, when the Industrial Workers of the World did not get into the headlines of American newspapers. They began their great era with a sawmill strike in Portland, Oregon, that gave notice of what was in store for the lumber industry of the Pacific Northwest. By the time the saws started whining again, a crew of Wobblies had turned up in Skowhegan, Maine, on the other side of the continent, to pull twenty-five hundred textile operatives away from the looms. They struck next in murky McKees Rocks, Pennsylvania, where they organized "fourteen different kinds of Bohunks" into a union and fought bloody battles with the state constabulary, whom they called Cossacks. The gun smoke had hardly cleared in Pennsylvania before five hundred Wobblies converged on Spokane to put on a free speech battle that is not forgotten forty-five years later.

Reading his *Spokesman-Review*, Harry Orchard learned that a new day was breaking, sure enough, and a female both young and beautiful was in the thick of the Spokane trouble. Elizabeth Gurley (the) Flynn was described as a fire-eating soapboxer whose highly charged glance and diction was enough to send cloddish men running to the nearest I.W.W. hall to get their little red cards and do battle for abstractions such as free speech and against concrete things such as the nightsticks of Spokane's burly tough cops. The daily press did not carry Bill Haywood's remark about the Flynn, but it is worth repeating. "She is one hell of a girl!" said Big Bill in admiration. (Haywood was right. A bit later I heard the Flynn speak on Portland's Skidroad. She was superb.)

Orchard must have been startled by the appearance of a woman leading a strike, as the Flynn presently did in Lawrence, Massachusetts; and startled also by the rapidity with which the I.W.W. organizers moved over so much of the United States. Haywood was quick to sense disaffected spots and to send his hellraisers to them by fast freight, to use harangue or "incident" to foment matters into a strike. His men knew how to turn a modest barroom fight into a street brawl and turn the brawl into a riot that called out the reserves. Wobbly speakers always promised not only better wages and working conditions but also a rousing Revolution. The Wobbly press, uncluttered with anything like factual reporting, was wild, bitter, sardonically humorous, and much louder than Hearst.

The Wobs went after members among new immigrants. They published papers in several languages. Their speakers addressed crowds in all the languages of Europe and the many dialects of Russia. They had fine speakers, too, men like Carlo Tresca, Joe Ettor, William Z. Foster, Sam Scarlett, and Vincent St. John, all competent to convert the dehorns, the scissorbills, the hobos, tramps, and bums, the finks and Hoosiers and home guards into Rebels. Even the Wobbly-paper boys gave the working stiff a running lecture along with every copy of the *Industrial Worker* and *Solidarity* ... Get your *Worker*, boys, get your double dose of industrial unionism hot off the griddle, learn the truth about the Federation of Fakers, get into the One Big Union, be a Man, five cents buy a complete education for any Mister Block, get your *Worker* now ...

By the time Charlie Moyer was trying vainly to stem the trouble in Butte, the Wobs were invading Utah, long a Western Federation stronghold, to stage a whopping big strike at Bingham Canyon. One of the organizers was Joe Hill (strom), writer of the lyrics in the *Little Red Song Book*, one of the I.W.W.'s favorite publications, who was soon arrested in Salt Lake City and charged with the murder of a local grocer. He was convicted, appealed the case, and lost. Whereupon the I.W.W. organized a campaign the like of which was not to be seen until the Sacco-Vanzetti case of later years. Protest meetings were held all over the country and in the Scandinavian nations. Foreign ambassadors, even President Woodrow Wilson were induced to appeal for clemency. The State of Utah, however, was unmoved, and Joe Hill went down before an official firing squad at the penitentiary on November 19,

1915.

The astute Wobblies arranged to hold the funeral in Chicago where several thousand people walked five miles behind the hearse. Joe Hill became the first and favorite though not the last Official Martyr. In every I.W.W. hall hung a portrait, draped in black, and there they hang still, in such halls as remain. In all copies of the *Little Red Song Book* has appeared "Joe Hill's Last Will," which for years was declaimed at Wobbly meetings:

> My will is easy to decide,
> For there is nothing to divide,
> My kin don't need to fuss and moan—
> "Moss does not cling to rolling stone …"

Neither moss nor cobwebs clung to the Wobblies in their great roaring saga of violence. On Sunday, November 5, 1916, a group of I.W.W. organizers chartered two steamboats in Seattle, packed them with some four hundred members, and set out for strikebound Everett, thirty miles north. The leading vessel, the *Verona*, was met at the dock by Sheriff McCrae, who ordered the captain not to attempt to land his passengers. There was a moment of silence, then the shooting. A few moments later seven men lay dead. Fifty-eight more were wounded. This event went into Wobbly history as the "Everett Massacre." Within four months the United States went to war with Germany, and the I.W.W. sent their best men into the tall pines and even bigger Douglas firs of the Northwest in an effort to tie up the lumber industry.

There were riots soon on the log drives of Montana, Idaho, and Washington. In Puget Sound and Columbia River camps, Wob organizers were beaten up by tough bulls-of-the-woods and sent packing. At the sawmills, they were beaten up, then thrown into log ponds. The dedicated Wobs were gluttons for punishment. It took courage to be one in 1917.

Big Bill Haywood was in his glory. His one good eye constantly swept the scene for new opportunities to harass both the Western Federation of Miners and the American Federation of Labor. A likely chance seemed to open on June 8, 1917. On that night Butte's greatest disaster of all time occurred in the Speculator mine. Fire broke out at the bottom of the shaft at the twenty-four-hundred-foot level, and one hundred sixty-three miners died. Like the good strategist he was, Haywood knew the tragedy would put Butte miners into the right mood to organize and bring the camp back into the union fold. For four years, or since the Western Federation debacle, it had been an open-shop town.

So, to Butte went Frank Little, a member of the I.W.W. executive committee and a man both rash and courageous. A few days later all operations on Anaconda Hill ceased. The miners had joined the I.W.W. by the hundreds. Little and a committee presented demands for improved safety measures. On the night of July 31 six masked men entered Little's room in the Finn Hotel. They beat him, then carried him away still struggling. Next morning, his body, shot through in a dozen spots, was hanging from the Milwaukee railroad trestle. "Wobbly. by Organizer Lynched in Butte," said the newspapers.

Down in Bisbee, Arizona, where the I.W.W. had organized a strike against the United Verde Copper Company, vigilantes rounded up more than eleven hundred strikers and herded them into a ball park. A day later they were put into cattle cars and moved into the New Mexico desert, and left without water or food. In Tulsa, Oklahoma, a mob raided the I.W.W. hall, threw the occupants into automobiles, and took them out of town for a beating and coats of hot tar and feathers. Up in northern Minnesota, iron miners on the Mesabi range flocked to the Wobbly banner, and what one member quaintly described as gun shooting started at Biwabik: two dead, four wounded.

THE REVOLUTION WAS COMING, NO doubt of it. Bill Haywood's crew was lighting the fires of the morning. Thousands of working stiffs were sure the Red Dawn would blaze up over the mountain any minute. The money palaces of Morgan and Rockefeller would be blown into rubble. The rich holes in the mountains from which Anaconda, Bunker Hill & Sullivan, Homes take, and a hundred more outfits filched their wealth would be taken over by the miners. *Stand fast, you Soldiers of Discontent!* The world shall be yours ...

LIKE HARRY ORCHARD, BILL HAYWOOD'S eye had seen the glory of the corning of the Lord, but his was a different Lord, an angry Lord, direct out of the Old Testament, filled with loathing for His own creature, Adam, who time out of mind had permitted himself to be hornswoggled and cheated by the con game of Dives and his hellish crew. Haywood was in his element. Ralph Chaplin, the I.W.W. poet and editor noted that Big Bill seemed younger than ever before. He took on new dimensions. His manner was more assured. His good eye, said Chaplin, reflected a conscious power as at his desk in Wobbly headquarters "he leaned forward massively to affix his bold signature to one letter after another."[13] This was his big moment. "He was a revolutionary tycoon whose dream was coming true." He was at last building "the structure of the new society within the shell of the old."

It must have occurred to convict Harry Orchard, working away in the prison shoe shop and reflecting on what he had read in the papers, that the technique of labor wars was changing fast. Assassination seemed to be no longer popular. Even the secret use of dynamite for destructive purposes was passing. Sabotage was beginning to live up to the definition given it by Thorstein Veblen—"a conscientious withdrawal of efficiency." When the Wobs could not win a more or less formal strike, they did not simply call it off; they "transferred the strike to the job," to loaf and bitch up the works generally.

In early September 1917, the United States took a hand in the various labor wars. Federal men staged the so-called Palmer Raids on I.W.W. halls in fifty-odd cities and arrested several hundred members and sympathizers, Haywood among them. One hundred sixty-six Wobblies were held for trial on charges of sedition. Other raids netted prominent Socialists and all manner of radicals. A little later Eugene Debs was arrested while making a speech in Canton, Ohio, and sent to the Federal Penitentiary in Atlanta, Georgia, where he was to remain almost four years, during which period he was again nominated for the presidency of the United States and was given nine hundred and ninety thousand votes.

Rose Pastor Stokes, a free-wheeling reformer interested in many causes, was convicted of writing a seditious letter. The Army draft was on, and federal men soon hauled speakers of the Russellites, a religious sect, off to jail for obstructing the Selective Service Law. Soon after their release, the Russellites adopted a new style for their denomination. They became Jehovah's Witnesses.

---

13 See his excellent *Wobbly*, University of Chicago Press, 1948.

On May 18, 1918, the press carried an item reporting the death in Denver of James McParlan. He was seventy-five years old. If Orchard made any comment on the detective's passing, it seems not to have been published. The diary entry nearest to the date of McParlan's death deals merely with Orchard's spiritual difficulties: "Lost my temper this morning, and Joe rebuked me. The dear Lord had mercy on me to repent and ask forgiveness."

Haywood, Ralph Chaplin, and many more of the Wobblies taken in the Palmer Raids were sent to Leavenworth prison. Haywood appealed and was released on thirty-thousand-dollar bail.

The war in Europe ended. But not the I.W.W. war. On November 11, 1919, in Centralia, Washington, during a parade of American Legion groups, several of the marchers broke ranks and ran to the I.W.W. hall. Shooting was simultaneous and from at least three quarters. When the little city had calmed, four legionnaires had been shot to death and one Wobbly lynched.

While out on bail Bill Haywood disappeared. He was soon reported to be in Russia, where he was made welcome as a hero from the jungles of Capitalism. Letters from Comrade Haywood to I.W.W. friends first indicated he was to have an important place in Soviet councils; yet Ralph Chaplin had a feeling that "Bill's letters were written with somebody looking down his neck." He seems to have been quickly relegated to an obscure position, and on May 18, 1928, after a party in the home of Eugene Lyons, he died, an embittered man, of a paralytic stroke. (In his diary Orchard recorded Haywood's death without comment.)

Steve Adams, too, died in bed, and alone in the little cabin where he lived at Latah, a hamlet in Spokane County, Washington. "Of natural causes," said the coroner's report. Though his occupation at the time was given as "common laborer," Adams had done a good deal of expert and legitimate powder work after his release by the courts of Idaho and Colorado. "Steve Adams," recalled one who had employed him on road construction work in northern Idaho, "had forgotten more than most people ever know about explosives and their use." Steve was pretty closemouthed about his past, yet he once showed a friend a long deep scar on his right shin. "I got it," he said, "the time I like to have killed Harry Orchard." This, he explained, was when right after his arrest he was put in the same cell with Orchard in the Idaho penitentiary. Orchard had just told Steve that he, Orchard, had "confessed everything," whereupon Steve leaped at his former partner-in-crime, floored him, and started to kick him to death. Only by rolling under a cell bunk did Harry escape. "I got them scars," Steve reminisced, "by trying to kick the son of a bitch some more under that steel bunk." The uproar attracted guards who came in and, according to Steve, "beat the hell out of me." Though there seems to have been no official notice taken of this affair, it is known Steve was removed from the cell and the two men were never again alone together.

In the United States Senate, the senior gentleman from Idaho, William E. Borah, continued to be heard, battering away at the Treaty of Versailles, fighting the League of Nations.

Quite suddenly Clarence Darrow came into the headlines. For decades he had appeared as counsel for honest radicals like Debs and outright goons like the McNamaras. Now, in 1924, he was to defend the teenagers, sons of reputedly wealthy families named Loeb and Leopold, who had already confessed to the senseless murder of fourteen-year-old Bobby Franks. It was one of the first so-called thrill murders. Aging and ill though he was, Darrow agreed to defend the young degenerates in what looked to be a hopeless case. The verdict of imprisonment for life was perhaps Darrow's greatest legal triumph. He never got the fee one hundred thousand dollars promised him. One of his biographers wrote that Darrow had to settle for thirty thousand.[14]

It is conceivable that Harry Orchard might have found himself sympathetic toward the defense of the two thrill killers; but Darrow's next client was something else. His name was John T. Scopes, a young science teacher of Dayton, Tennessee, who was arrested for violation of the state's Anti-Evolution Law. To Fundamentalists, Scopes was an imp of Hell who sought to be "a killer of religion." Darrow defended Scopes. The prosecution was in charge of William Jennings Bryan. In a trial that had more than a little circus to it, the young teacher was convicted. Fundamentalists were understandingly delighted, though the victory was hollow enough. The conviction was soon reversed by the Tennessee Supreme Court, and the Anti-Evolution Law was laughed into obscurity.

ONE BY ONE, AS HARRY Orchard read in his daily paper, the great

---

14 See Irving Stone, *Clarence Darrow for the Defense.*

figures of his active days were passing. Eugene Debs died in 1926 near Chicago and was buried in his hometown of Terre Haute, Indiana, where ten thousand hometown folks attended the funeral and where he was "loved and respected by everyone regardless of party." Debs probably stood alone as the most beloved figure in the American labor movement of his time.

The next to go was James Hawley, "one of the best friends I had on earth," Orchard wrote in his diary of the locally famous attorney, judge, and Governor of Idaho.

Orchard was keeping up with affairs. In September of 1932, he read about banks closing because of a depression, and it became clear that "the uncertainties and failures of these upset times" were to continue indefinitely. He was safe now from such things. "I am so thankful," he wrote in his journal, "to have a refuge in the blessed Lord and Savior, Jesus Christ."

At last, in 1938, Clarence Darrow passed. He had lived almost eighty-one years. Orchard was then a mere seventy-two, but he still had sixteen years ahead of him.

In 1940 Senator Borah died, aged seventy-five. Save for Harry Orchard, he was the last to go of the leading figures of the Western Federation trials. Orchard had outlived them all—or had he? No newspaper had yet reported the death of or anything else about Jack Simpkins.[15] And there was also the business of the unknown assassin of Harvey K. Brown. Yet it was stated, correctly enough, in the obituaries of Mr. Borah, that of all the chief characters of the great drama, only Harry Orchard survived. It was a kind of eminence.

---

15 Simpkins is a tantalizing wraith. In the early 1920s, I used to hear a rumor to the effect that under an assumed name he had lived for many years and at last died somewhere in the Puget Sound region of Washington, possibly in the city of Everett; but the rumor, if true, has resisted documentation.

26.

A Goth Survives Them All

The wardens came, and the wardens went. Orchard remained. Now and again he thought he should like a pardon, and at least once he had a formal pamphlet prepared of "Arguments Presented in Favor of a Commutation" of his life sentence.

It is a most interesting document. In it the Honorable James H. Hawley, who had prosecuted Haywood, Pettibone, and Steve Adams, credited Harry Orchard for the new respect for law and all-around peaceful atmosphere that had settled like a benign blanket over the mining regions of the West. This was "due to his exposure of the men who had turned the Western Federation of Miners into a criminal organization" bent on anarchy. "I say that Harry Orchard," cried Mr. Hawley, "did a service unparalleled in the history of our country." He went on to say in so many words that Orchard should be freed because it was through his instrumentality the Western Federation was purged of "that radical element" responsible for "the most hideous crimes imaginable."

Mr. Hawley intimated it was not Moyer but Haywood and Pettibone who directed Orchard's murderous activities, and pointed out that, as soon as the latter two had been cast out, the organization was directed in a wholly lawful manner. He cited the affair at Butte when the federation hall was dynamited by its enemies and stated that Moyer had "almost lost his life" while trying to settle the chaotic labor situation by law instead of violence.

Next, Mr. Hawley painted a serene picture of current conditions in the mining camps. That is, the hard-rock or quartz camps, which had nothing to do with the mining of coal. "Go where you will," he said, "the camps are now free of the domination of Haywood. They are as peaceful as the farming communities of the land. It is so in California, Colorado, Nevada, and Idaho. The Western Federation absolutely obeyed the laws, once it was rid of Haywood, who went where he belonged as head of the I.W.W. and he is now [1922] a fugitive from justice.

"It seems to me, gentlemen, that we of Idaho owe Orchard a debt, and so do other mining communities of this country. We owe him a debt of gratitude for obliterating these enemies of the mining sections …"

In the same document prepared for Orchard, Frank R. Gooding, Governor of Idaho at the time of the Steunenberg murder, spoke at some length. He let it be known at once he "had never been able to find" in his heart the least sympathy for Orchard. "If he died a thousand deaths," he declared, "he could never atone for his crimes." Yet, the greater crime was that perpetrated by the Western Federation officials, and it was Orchard who had brought them down. "If," said Mr. Gooding, "you are going to protect the society of this country, then you must recognize that without men confessing, without men becoming State's witnesses against criminals, you can't have much prosecution, or at least many convictions." It was the fear of God in men's hearts, said Mr. Gooding, "that somebody is going to go back on them, is going to confess the conspiracy." In most countries, and in many parts of the United States, he explained, such confessions preclude punishment of a man used as a witness by the government. He is given his freedom.

Mr. Gooding told the Board of Pardons that Detective William J. Burns, he who arrested the McNamara brothers for the Los Angeles *Times* explosion, stated that without the confession of Ortie McManigal, the State of California could not have successfully prosecuted this case; and that McManigal would not have confessed had it not been for the example of Harry Orchard's confession in a previous and unrelated case. The inference was clear—telling all and survive, and meanwhile do society a good turn. McManigal had done so. He was freed. Why not Orchard?

Mr. Gooding asked the Board of Pardons to recall that Harvey K. Brown had been assassinated in exactly the same manner as Steunenberg. And why? As if to say to the next jury, "We do not forget." It was pure intimidation. "It did not take long," Gooding remembered, "for the jury trying Pettibone to find that he was not guilty."

"Now, then," said Mr. Gooding in summing up, "unless you do something, unless you encourage men to turn State's evidence and become a witness for the State, you cannot have convictions, and the whole situation becomes dangerous."

So far as the Idaho Board of Pardons was concerned, the situation could remain as it was. They refused to grant Orchard's application for commutation of sentence.

THE WARDENS CAME, THE WARDENS went. Orchard saw in the papers that the Western Federation had changed its name, to become the International Union of Mine, Mill and Smelter Workers. Of more significance was the fact that the federation also changed its Preamble. Since 1907 the Preamble had been specifically based on the class struggle. The union's new objectives were merely better wages, shorter hours, and improved working conditions. Tame enough. Neither the new name nor the new Preamble could prevent the union from fading. Then, in 1926, President Charlie Moyer and his entire executive board were voted out of office. Headquarters were moved from Denver to Salt Lake City. The organization continued to grow more "respectable," and weaker.

The I.W.W. did not grow respectable, but, without Haywood to keep fire at their tails to battle capitalism, the boys grew bored and began fighting among themselves. In 1923, the order split into two groups, each claiming to be the one and only blown-in-the-bottle brand. In Chicago were two Wobbly headquarters offices. And in Portland, Seattle, San Francisco, and other cities was the shameful sight of two Wobbly halls, each with standard fixtures and icons like the draped and framed portrait of Martyr Joe Hill. Each was prepared to issue red cards (certificates of union membership) and to collect dues. Two weekly papers, the old *Worker* and the new *Unionist*, attacked each other with all the patent venom Wobbly editors had formerly devoted to other unions and the capitalist press. It was more than discouraging; working stiffs did not like to pay double dues, else be called scabs, or finks, or fakers. One after the other the halls were closed. The rift was finally healed, but the I.W.W. did not grow, either in respectability or in numbers. It simply faded.

Union labor went ahead, however, to become big business. Some of its big unions suffered from racketeers, who were assorted goons of a finesse and commercialism far beyond the understanding of simple primitives like Harry Orchard, the McNamaras, and others of an earlier period. But the majority of unions came, in time, to be operated in as businesslike a manner, and as ruthlessly, as any industrial corporation.

WITH FAILING EYESIGHT, ORCHARD CONTINUED to work over the manuscript about the man God made again. With the help of a collaborator it was finished in 1951 and published a year later. The book gave him considerable satisfaction. So, did the smaller book by Elder Frank Steunenberg. Less and less did he want to see visitors who were simply curiosity seekers. In 1953 he suffered a light paralytic stroke, though he seemed hardly to be aware of it and was never told. In that year Walter Mattila of the *Oregon Journal* was among the callers Orchard consented to see.

In the prison, Reporter Mattila heard shuffling footsteps, "like those of the faithful in a temple," and Orchard entered the warden's office. "He was beaming broadly and took his chair without fuss and spoke to the assistant warden with a friendliness that was amazing between inmate and keeper." The old prisoner's hearing, at eighty-seven, was failing, but he "was tanned a healthy glow, and his cheerfulness seemed natural." The visitor noted he was wearing a farmer's straw hat, which "he removed from his head and put back on with manly grace and rural charm." There was something of the old cheese maker of Ontario about him. "Throughout our brief talk," Mr. Mattila said, "the past seemed always to be only yesterday. This illusion doubtless sprung from his ready and full memory, plus the obvious fact that he managed without effort to overlook the actuality of being a prisoner."

Orchard lived another year, to die in the penitentiary hospital early on the morning of April 13, 1954. He was eighty-eight years old. He did not take his last ride alone. A big plane chartered by the Seventh-Day Adventist Church brought a delegation from Portland. Many other friends of the old man gathered from Boise and several Idaho communities. They gave him a handsome funeral, and with him they buried the last of an era.

HARRY ORCHARD WILL DO AS a symbol of the struggle between the opposing forces that dominated the primitive industrial frontier of the American West. It was a period of expanding enterprise explosive in its haste and its power. Men seemed not to have time to think overly much. They merely threatened one another briefly. Then they acted. It was a period of trial and error, and the action taken stood an even chance of being the wrong thing. The bolder empiricists tried dynamite. It turned out to be a fatal delusion.

Granted the bitterly opposing forces, into the middle of which Orchard unwittingly stumbled, he was not far wrong when he thought of himself as a creature of circumstances. Yet his ethical side was by then more than tarnished, so perhaps he was less a victim of circumstance than a willing creature of opportunity. One should bear in mind that he was no dedicated partisan. He was strictly a professional, a "most wicked man for hire to the highest bidder." As such he was truly a Gothic figure of some stature in an era when the classic enemy camps of Labor and Capital both harbored barbarians beyond number.

Acknowledgments

It was well over fifteen years ago, and all unwittingly, so it turned out, when I began interviewing people and making notes for this book. Unwittingly, because then I had no idea of writing a book. I was motivated by my casual interest in the already legendary figure of Harry Orchard and the fabled if fading Western Federation of Miners. The idea of the book originated much later in the lively mind of Howard Cady, a friend of long standing.

All of the people I interviewed so many years ago are important to the story. All are now dead. I talked with Edward Boyce, the Coeur d'Alenes miner who became president of the Western Federation; with Clarence Darrow; with Frank Therriault of St. Maries, Idaho, who had known Jack Simpkins and Steve Adams, and also the murdered claim jumpers of Marble Creek; and of course, with Harry Orchard himself. I had the good fortune, too, to talk with the late Mrs. Frank Steunenberg, widow of the late governor of Idaho.

There were to be many others who contributed something or other to the making of this book, and my thanks for help go to:

Charles N. Beebe, Dick D'Easum, Mr. and Mrs. Harry Dennison, Stanly A. Easton, Malcolm Glendenning, LeRoye Harris, Herbert H. Hewitt, Elizabeth Johnson, L. C. Johnson, Bruce Kelley, Priscilla Knuth, Charles H. Leavitt, Kelley Lowe, Preston MacMann, Walter Mattila, Judge Claude McCollough, P. C. Meridith, Louise Prichard, Nondes Schmehl, Harry Shellworth, Frank W. Steunenberg, James Stevens, and William Walsh.

If I could recall it, I would gladly add the name of the "Professor of Graphology," making a pitch in Seattle, to whom I gave a sample of the handwriting of Albert E. Horsley (Harry Orchard), along with one dollar and a request he perform graphology analysis. The professor of graphology did so and reported thus on the mind, spirit, nature, and talents of the professor of dynamite:

"Active, adaptable, creative, imaginative, observant, psychic, resourceful ... Aggressive, independent, jovial, noncommittal, strong-willed, and witty ... with the possible weaknesses of dislike for detail; impulsiveness, moodiness, too frank, too emotional ... but adapted to athletics, commercial art, dramatics, medicine, music, public speaking." Then the graphologist added a note of warning: "and his health should be guarded."

Surely the analysis was worth a dollar. I only regret that I did not show it to the subject himself.

The manuscript was prepared for the printer by Miss Esther L. Watson; and my daughters, Miss Sibyl M. Holbrook and Miss Bonnie S. Holbrook helped to prepare the Index.

Bibliography

Books, Documents, Pamphlets

Arguments, Presented in Favor of Commutation; at the Hearing Before the Pardon Board of the State of Idaho in the Matter of the Application of Harry Orchard, 1922.

Barrymore, Ethel. *Autobiography*. New York: 1955.

Benedict, C. Harry. *Red Metal, the Calumet and Hecla Story*. Ann Arbor, Mich.: 1952.

Bums, William J. *The Masked War*. New York: 1913.

Chaplin, Ralph. *The Centralia Conspiracy*. Chicago: 1924.

———. *Wobbly*. Chicago: 1948.

Cleland, Robert Glass. *A History of Phelps Dodge*. New York: 1952.

Coleman, J. Walter. *The Molly Maguire Riots*. Richmond, Va.: 1936.

Coleman, McAlister. *Eugene V. Debs*. New York: 1931. Congress (56th) 1st Session, *Senate Documents Nos. 24 and 25, relating to the Coeur d'Alenes Mining Troubles*. Washington: 1899.

Darrow, Clarence. *The Story of My Life*. New York: 1932.

Dictionary of American Biography, 21 Vols., New York.

Fargo, Lucile F. *Spokane Story*. New York: 1953.

Froom, L. E., and Harry Orchard. *The Man God Made Again*. Nashville: 1952.

Harrison, Charles Yale. *Clarence Darrow*. New York: 1931.

Haywood, William D. *Bill Haywood's Book*. New York: 1929.

Holbrook, Stewart H. *Holy Old Mackinaw*. New York: 1938.

———. *Murder Out Yonder*. New York: 1941.

Howard, Joseph Kinsey. *Montana, High, Wide and Handsome*. New Haven: 1943.

Jensen, Vernon H. *Heritage of Conflict*. Ithaca: 1950.

Koelsch, Charles F. *The Haywood Case*. Boise: 1946.

Langdon, Emma F. *The Cripple Creek Strike 1904*. Denver: 1904.

Lavender, David. *The Big Divide*. New York: 1946.

MacLane, John F. *A Sagebrush Lawyer*. New York: 1954.

Orchard, Harry. *The Confessions and Autobiography of Harry Orchard*. New York: 1907.

———, and L. E. Froom. *The Man God Made Again*. Nashville: 1952.

Quiett, Glenn Chesney. *Pay Dirt*. New York: 1936.

Rastall, Benjamin McKie. "The Labor History of the Cripple Creek District," *Bulletin of the University of Wisconsin*. No. 198 (Feb. 1908).

Siringo, Charles A. *A Cowboy Detective*. Chicago: 1913.

Sprague, Marshall. *Money Mountain*. Boston: 1953.

Steunenberg, Frank W. *Greater Love*. Mountain View, Calif.: 1952.

Stoll, William T. *Silver Strike*. Boston: 1932.

Stone, Irving. *Clarence Darrow*. New York: 1941.

Sullivan, Mark. *Our Times*. Vol. III. New York: 1930.

Thompson, Fred. *The I.W.W., Its First Fifty Years*. Chicago: 1955.

Tompkins, George R. *The Truth About Butte*. Butte: 1917.

Who Was Who in America. Chicago: 1942.

Wolle, Muriel Sibell. *The Bonanza Trail*. Bloomington, Ind.: 1953.

Works Progress Administration. *Copper Camp*. New York: 1943.

Newspapers

The Idaho Statesman and *The Capitol News*, Boise; *The Idaho Tribune*, Wallace; *The Spokesman-Review*, Spokane; *The Oregonian* and *The Evening Telegram*, Portland; *The San Francisco Call* (November,

1904, only); *The Industrial Worker* (Spokane, Seattle, Chicago); and a broken file of *The Miners Magazine* for 1902, Denver.

Index

A

Adams, Steve 93, 94, 95, 97, 99, 100, 101, 102, 103, 104, 105, 123, 124, 125, 135, 136, 137, 142, 145, 154, 162, 163, 189, 191, 192, 193, 194, 195, 213, 214, 215, 216, 217, 219, 220, 222, 223, 230, 242, 245
Aikman, Billy 85, 86, 99, 139
Ailshie, Judge James F. 193
Ajax mine 76
Altman, Colo. 57, 59, 60, 110
American Railway Union 152, 195
Ames, Iowa 167
Anaconda, Colo. 59, 60, 73, 240
Appeal to Reason 197
Arequa, Colo. 59
Aspen, Colo. 61

B

Baker, Ore. 180, 193, 194, 195, 214, 215, 216, 217, 218, 219
Barrymore, Ethel 199
Baston, Art 123, 154
Bates College 197
Beck, Melvin, blown up 86
Bell, Sherman M. 75, 110, 149, 154, 182, 198
Bingham Canyon, Utah 54, 238
Bliss, Ida. 171
Boise, Ida. 9, 48, 160, 176, 182, 191, 192, 193, 194, 195, 196, 197

Borah, William E. 9, 181, 182, 192, 199, 204, 206, 207, 208, 209, 211, 212, 213, 221, 222, 243, 244
Boulle, murdered claim-jumper 136, 163, 192
Bourne, Ore. 219
Bowers, Sheriff Frank 61, 62, 65
Boyce, Edward 36, 37, 50, 68, 117, 119
Boynton, W. S. 66
Bradley, Frederick W. 31, 124, 126, 127
Brewery Workers' union 152
Brewery Workers' union 153
Brighton, Ontario 19
British Columbia 20, 87
Bronco Busters Union 153
Brooks, Gen. E. J. 66, 67
Brown, Harvey K. 180, 214, 215, 217, 218, 221
Bull Hill, Battle of 64
Bunker Hill & Sullivan Mining and Concentrating Co. 29, 34, 70, 124
Burch, Albert 37
Burke, Ida. 18, 30, 54, 118, 200
Burns, William J. 234, 246
Butte, Mont. 18, 22, 60, 118, 235, 236, 240, 245

C

Calderwood, John 60, 62, 63, 65, 67

Caldwell, Ida. 12, 123, 154, 156, 159, 163, 165, 166, 167, 172, 180
Calumet, Mich. 235
Canon City, Colo. 112, 143, 144, 145
Carlin, Gen. William P. 34, 35
Carlton, Bert 107
Cassidy, Butch 124, 125
Cataldo, Ida. 35
Centralia, Wash. 242
Chandler, Phil blown up 106
Chaplin, Ralph 118, 241, 242
Cheyenne, Wyo. 105, 119, 120
Cheyne, Jim 44, 52
Cleland, William 222
Clement, C.U. 34
Cody, Wyo. 121, 122
Coeur d'Alene Executive Miners' Union 31
Colfax, Wash. 219
Collins, Arthur 68, 223
Colorado City, Colo. 73, 87
Colorado Fuel & Iron Company 138
Colorado & Midland railroad 60
Colorado Reduction & Refining Co. 73
Colorado Springs, Colo. 57, 59, 62, 63
Corcoran, Paul 38, 39, 52
Cousin Jacks 58
Cripple Creek, Colo. 18, 22, 56, 57, 58, 59, 60, 61, 68, 70, 73, 75, 110, 137

D

Darrow, Clarence 9, 124, 192, 194, 195, 197, 199, 204, 207, 211, 217, 243
Davis, John, shot 109
Davis, W. F. 42, 43, 44, 45, 70, 73, 75, 81, 86, 90, 97
Debs, Eugene V. 151, 152, 195, 197, 198, 234, 236, 241, 243, 244
De Leon, Daniel 152, 153, 154
Dennison, Pat 49, 50
Denver, Colo. 18, 31, 40, 48, 87, 88, 93
Denver & Rio Grande R.R. 157
Devy, Mike 38
Divide, Colo. 60, 65, 66
Duluth, Minn. 76
Duyn, Owen M. Van 192

E

Eagle Valley, Nev. 116
Easterly, Bill 169
Elkton, Colo. 59, 75
Elkton mine 76
Everett, Wash. 239, 244

F

Fairbanks, Charles Warren 162
Findlay mine 76
Florence & Cripple Creek R.R. 60, 64, 81, 99, 102
Flynn, Elizabeth Gurley 237
Frances, Steunenberg 175
Frisco mill 33, 40
Froman, George 180
Froom, L. E. 230

G

Gabbert, Justice William H. 138, 145, 146, 147, 154
Gaffney, Bill 85
Gem, Ida. 29, 30, 33, 163
Glenns Ferry, Ida. 48
Globeville, Colo. 119, 140, 141, 143
Glover, John M. 87
Goddard, Justice Luther M. 138, 140, 142, 148, 154, 160, 192

Index

Golden Cycle mine 74, 75, 76
Goldfield, Colo. 59, 75, 87, 110
Goldfield, Nev. 131, 135, 149, 155, 159, 169, 192
Gooding, Gov. Frank 168, 176, 178, 190, 194, 246, 247
Gorki, Maxim 199
Granger, Wyo. 124
Granite, Ore. 218
Gregory, Lyte, shot 95, 96, 191

H

Hagerman, J. J. 65
Hagerty, Thomas J. 152
Hamlin, Clarence 108
Hammersley, T. S. 219
Hancock, Mich. 235
Harriman, Job 233, 234
Hawley, James H. 52, 192, 196, 197, 204, 211, 222, 244, 245
Haywood, William D. 9, 69, 72, 88, 91, 92, 114–122, 150, 190
Hearne, Frank 138
Helena & Frisco Co. 29, 39
Heney, Deputy Tom 41, 42
Hercules mine 23, 29, 200, 205
Hibernians, Ancient Order of 183
High-grading, described 71
Hill, James J. 162
Hill, Joe 238, 239
Hinks, Reverend Edwin S. 231
H. McCormick, Charles, blown up 86
Hooten, G. R. 112
Horsley, Albert E.. *See* Orchard, Harry
Hutchinson, Joe 176

I

Idan-ha Hotel, Boise 199
Imogene Pass, Colo. 68

Independence, Colo. 59, 70, 71, 77, 98, 107, 110
Industrial Workers of the World 115, 151, 152, 153, 154, 237
Iola 190
Iowa 167

J

Jackling, Daniel C. 54
James B. 234
Jensen, Vernon H. 32, 112, 235
Johnson, Junius J. 63
Jones, Mother 151
Junius J. Johnson 66

K

Kansas 190
Keith, Charles 62
Kellogg, Ida. 23, 29
Kellogg, Noah 28
Kiner, George E. 76
Kirwin, James 203
Knights of Labor 116, 151, 152
Knoxville 167

L

La Monte, Robert Rives 152
Langdon, Emma 76
Lashmutt, Van De 34
Lavender, David 65
Lawrence, Mass. 238
Leadville, Colo. 22, 67, 119
Leon, Daniel De 152
Lewis, B. R. 220
Lillard, J. W. 221
Lillard, J.W. 195
Little, Frank 240
Los Angeles *Times* 246
Lunt, Judge Horace Gray 65

M

MacNeill, Charles 73, 124
Maki, Henry 88
Malich, Max 140, 141, 143
Marble Creek, Ida. 136, 137, 162, 163, 196
Mattila, Walter 248
Mayberry, Andy 123
McAlpin, James 23, 200
McCleary, P. L. 202
McDonald, Muckey 235
McGee, Roscoe, shot 109
McKeesport School of Mines 61
McKees Rocks, Pa. 237
McKinley, President William 48
McKinney, H. H. 81, 90, 94
McManigal, Ortie 234
McNamara, James B. 234
McNamara, John J. 234
McParlan, James A. 31, 182, 183, 184, 194, 234
Meeteetse, Wyo. 121
Meldrum, Bob 191
Meridith, Warden P. C. 10
Merriam, Gen. H. C. 48, 51, 52
Midland, Colo. 62
Milburn, Foster 95
Miller, Fred 164, 192
Miller & Rosenthal 164
Mine Owners Assn. of Colorado 124
Mine Owners Assn. of Idaho 27, 31, 34, 54
Minor, Nevada Jane 116
Minor, Tom 153
Minster, Ed 125, 154
Missoula, Mont. 50
Moffat, Dave 65
Molly Maguires, the 109, 183, 185, 192
Moseley, Sheriff 180, 181
Moyer, Charles H. 69, 73, 88, 91, 94, 97, 119, 150, 154, 192, 198, 203, 213, 223, 230, 234, 235, 238
Mullan, Ida. 29, 30, 33
Munsterberg, Dr. Hugo 205
Murphy, James 97, 107

N

Nampa, Ida. 159, 160, 163, 171
Nelson 20
Neville, Charlie 104, 119
Neville, Johnnie 70, 75, 77, 94, 95, 100, 103, 114, 126, 159
Neville, Johnny 121, 154
Northern Pacific R.R. 28, 29, 50
Northumberland County 17, 20
Northumberland County, Ontario 18
Nugent, John 192

O

O'Neill, John M. 151, 153
Ontario 17, 20
Ophir City, Utah 115
Orchard, Harry
 birth 17
 works in woods 18
 marries 18
 cheese maker 19
 deserts family 20
 in British Columbia 20
 goes to Coeur d'Alenes 22
 has milk route 22
 coal and wood business 23
 buys interest in mine 200
 loses business 23
 becomes mucker 22
 joins union 24
 the Bunker Hill & Sullivan affair 36
 on the lam 49
 arrives Cripple Creek 56

(Orchard, Harry, cont.)
high-grading 71
WFM calls strike 72
dynamites mine 86
meets Pettibone and Haywood 91
Independence depot job 97
shoots Lyte Gregory 97
goes to San Francisco 125
blows up Bradley 131
other jobs planned 137
Gov. Steunenberg discussed 155
in Caldwell 159
leaves Denver 157
in Portland 162
visits Coeur d'Alenes 163
he and Simpkins go to Caldwell 164
the Steunenberg bomb goes off 175
arrested 181
confesses 189
witness for state 193
is sentenced 224
in prison for life 226
death 248
O'Rourke, Ida. 23

P

Pacific Hotel, Caldwell 159, 160, 165
Parker, Sherman 84, 86, 97, 170
Parsons, Lucy 152
Paterson, N.J. 155
Peabody, Gov. J. H. 75, 86, 110, 123, 138, 139, 140, 142, 144, 154
Pendleton, Ore. 32
Pettibone, George A. 34, 40, 69, 92, 93, 95, 97, 104, 123, 135, 149, 223, 233
Pinchot, Gifford 199
Pinkerton, Allan 183

Pinkerton's National Detective Agency 31, 183
Pocatello, Ida. 219
Pomeroy, Jesse 228
Portland, Ore. 34, 156, 219, 237, 247
Pritchard, Andrew J. 28

R

Rastall, Benjamin McKie 65, 112
Rathdrum, Ida. 222
Richardson, E. F. 190, 192, 199, 200, 201, 202, 203, 204
Robertson, Sheriff Henry 107, 108
Robinson 164
Rockwell, Porter 116
Rocky Ford, Colo. 145
Rogers, J. J. 44
Roosevelt, Theodore 198
Root, Elihu 52
Rossland 87

S

Saginaw, Mich. 18, 20
Salt Lake City, Utah 51, 54, 145, 163
San Francisco, Calif. 18, 55, 126, 133, 135, 223, 247
Saratoga Hotel, Caldwell 165, 168, 170, 173, 177, 180
Schenck, W. H. 167
Schultz, Joe 74, 82, 84
Scott, D. C. 91, 92
Seattle, Wash. 161, 162, 163, 239, 247
Seventh-Day Adventists 10, 168, 229, 230, 248
Seward, F. E. 126, 202
Sherman, Charles O. 152, 153
Shoddy, Charles 170
Shoddy, Charlie 159, 169
Silver City, Ida. 117, 163, 166, 169

Silverton, Colo. 192
Simpkins, Jack 194, 196, 219, 220, 221, 222, 224, 244
Sinclair, Bartlett 48, 52
Sinclair, Upton 198, 203
Siringo, Charles 31, 184
Sister Joseph 31
Smith, Jack 43, 63
Smith, Major Allen 52
Smuggler-Union mine 68, 224
South Park, Colo. 84, 105
Speed, George 151
Spokane, Wash. 21, 48, 220, 233, 237
Sterling, K. C. 91
Steunenberg, Charles 180
Steunenberg, Frank 181, 182, 185, 186, 213, 224
Steunenberg, Gov. Frank 48, 52, 118, 154, 158, 160, 165, 167
Steunenberg, Julian 171, 175
Steunenberg, Mrs. Frank 10
Stevens, James 182
Steward, W. W. 229
Stratton, Winfield S. 59
Strikes
  Bisbee
    1917 240
  Butte
    1917 240
  Cripple Creek
    1894 60
    1903 72
  Idaho
    1892 31
    1899 37
  Michigan Copper Range
    1913 235
  Telluride
    1903 137
Strong mine 64, 65, 76
Strow, Lewis 24

Sullivan, Ida. 23
Sullivan, John, miner 235, 236
Sumpter, Ore. 216, 219
Sumpter Valley, Ore. 55, 216, 219
Swain, Captain, detective 215, 218, 221

T

Tekoa Junction, Wash. 32
Telluride, Colo. 18, 68, 87, 88, 137, 191, 192, 223
Thermopolis, Wyo 121
Thermopolis, Wyo. 122
Therriault, Frank 136
Thiele Detective agency 215
Thompson Falls, Mont. 50
Thompson mine 76
Tiger-Poorman mine and mill 22, 24, 36, 38, 47, 48
Tornado mine 76
Trautmann, William E. 152, 153
Tucker, Frank 218, 219
Turner, George Kibbe 204
Tyler, murdered claim-jumper 136, 137, 163, 192

U

Union Pacific R.R. 28, 41, 125, 162, 171, 176, 191, 214
United Metal Workers 152, 153
United Mine Workers 192, 195, 235

V

Vaughan, William J. 144, 145
Victor, Colo. 59, 60, 64, 70, 73, 75, 107, 108
virginia city 30
Virginia City, Nev. 30

W

Waite, Gov. Davis H. 62, 65, 66
Wallace, Ida. 21, 29, 34, 46, 48
Walla Walla College 175
Walla Walla, Wash. 48, 220
Walley, Merritt, blown up 147
Wardner, Ida. 23, 29, 30, 31, 48
Western Federation of Miners 56,
    58, 60, 63, 67, 68, 69, 72, 234,
    239, 245
Whitney, E.L., warden 182, 229
Wilson, Edgar 192, 212
Womack, Bob 59
Wood, Judge Fremont 197, 212,
    213, 224

Y

Young, Sheriff Jim 41, 42